W9-AQH-053

Until Brazil

Until Brazil

a novel

Bethe Lee Moulton

The **GLIDE** *Press*
Boca Raton, FL

Published by The Glide Press
2234 North Federal Highway, #438
Boca Raton, FL 33431
www.theglidepress.com

Until Brazil is a work of fiction. Names, characters, places, and incidents are the product of the author's imagination or are used fictitiously. Any resemblance to actual events, locales, or persons, living or dead, is coincidental.

The poem "Estatua Guanabara Mitológica" by Cristóvão Leite de Castro, appearing on page 161, is reprinted with the permission of Maria Ercília Leite de Castro, Presidente de Companhia Caminho Aéreo Pão de Açúcar—CCAPA. This poetic representation of Rio de Janeiro can be found inscribed near the statue Guanabara Mitológica by sculptor Remo Bernucci on the Pão de Açúcar (the Sugar Loaf) in Rio de Janeiro.

Designed by theBookDesigners
www.bookdesigners.com
Produced & Edited by Brookes Nohlgren
www.booksbybrookes.com

Publisher's Cataloging-in-Publication data

Moulton, Bethe Lee.
    Until Brazil : a novel / Bethe Lee Moulton.
    p. cm.
    ISBN 978-0-9836365-6-4
1. Brazil --Fiction. 2. Brazil --Description and travel --Fiction. 3. Women --Brazil --Fiction. 4. Women executives --Fiction. 5. International business enterprises --Fiction. 6. Women in the professions --United States --Fiction. I. Title.
PS2438 .U5 2011
[Fic]   2011930152

First Edition: November 2011
10 9 8 7 6 5 4 3 2 1

Printed in the United States of America

For Oscar—
without you there is no story

Resistance

"Brazil?" Sue blurted out. "Why on earth would they send *you* to Brazil? You don't speak a word of Spanish!"

"Brazilians speak Portuguese." My quick comeback was a defense against Sue's disapproval. I focused on the pie dough I was rolling out on her dark-green granite countertop. In truth, I had been just as ignorant a few days before.

"Well, whatever they speak, you don't." Thin, even apple slices plopped onto the cutting board where Sue wielded her German-made Henckels professional slicing knife. "Who else is going from the Boston office?" She wanted details.

"One of the Partners, Bob White, will direct the project."

"Bob White. Isn't his wife about to have their first child?" Her memory was too good.

"Yes, next month," I said, trying to sound nonplussed. "He'll come down after his baby is born."

The knife stopped its rhythmic beat and clattered onto the granite. Sue put her hands on her hips. "In other words, you're going alone. They're sending you alone to a country where they don't speak English...and you are supposed to develop

1

a corporate strategy." The crow's feet deepened in Sue's face. "You may have a Harvard MBA, Beth, but this is not smart. GCC is crazy and you are, too."

To avoid her bossy blue stare, I kept rolling the already thin crust. Sue might be right, but I didn't want to question my decision. Surely Harvey knew what he was doing.

A few days earlier, the smell of pipe tobacco had announced his presence at my office door. Despite being the highly respected founder of Global Consulting Center (GCC), Harvey Osborne had never traded faculty garb for the consultant's suit and tie. He crumpled into the armchair across from my desk, adding a few more wrinkles to his British tweed jacket. Its salt-and-pepper weave matched the bristly eyebrows that over-arched his thoughtful eyes. Still a business school professor at heart, Harvey often dropped by to expound on his client's management challenges.

I shifted my attention from number-strewn papers to the man who had recruited me a decade ago. I set down my gold Cross pen, the firm's gift on my recent tenth anniversary. I fluffed the paisley silk scarf that adorned my navy suit. I was ready for an academic discourse, but Harvey had a different agenda and wasted no time in laying it on the table.

"Samuel Cohen, head of GCC-Brazil, has made a proposal to a very large Brazilian company. The country's economy has been in turmoil, with inflation over two hundred percent per year. However, new economic measures are being taken to get things under control. Sam's client, a drug company named BomFarm, needs a strategy for the new scenario. They'll accept his proposal if the team includes consultants who understand how to make money in a stable economy. Bob White has just the expertise they need; he'll be the Partner-in-Charge. We'd like you to get things rolling and cover the project in the field until Bob can get down to Brazil."

Both pride and panic swept over me. I had never worked outside of the United States. My textbook knowledge of macro-economics was rusty and my experience with drugs was an occasional aspirin.

"Why me?" The question popped out and ambushed the cool confidence I should have shown.

Harvey got up and walked to the plaque on my wall. "That's why," he said, tapping the Insight Award that read: "Beth Ann Bartlett, Provider of Insights, Intellectual Depth, and Integrity for the Success of GCC's Clients."

"Those are the qualities we need on this job." Warmth rose in my cheeks as Harvey circled back to face me. "I want GCC to be a worldwide consulting force. Beth, with experience in Brazil, you'll be part of our international growth. You could be our first woman Partner."

Harvey beamed. I blushed. "Thanks for your confidence, but..."

"No *buts*, young lady," Harvey admonished with a shake of his index finger as he headed for the door. "This train is leaving the station. BomFarm wants to get started immediately. I knew I could count on you. I'll let Sam know you're on the team." Harvey was telling me, not asking me, to manage the project. Still, being railroaded left me flattered instead of furious. Brazil could be just the break I needed.

When I joined GCC in 1976, I was in demand as a junior consultant. One of three women in the firm, I had worked extra hard to outperform my male counterparts. My rapid rise from Associate to Senior Associate was based on my merits, not because I was a woman in a man's world.

Or so I thought, until my career stalled. After receiving the Insight Award two years ago, I hit a glass ceiling. My reputation as a great Project Manager became an obstacle. I felt pigeonholed as a project mechanic, without opportunities to be the trusted advisor to the top executives who hired GCC.

Now, Harvey was giving me a chance to prove myself; being in charge at the start of the project would establish my credibility without being in Bob's shadow. As if he had read my mind, Bob barged into my office, armed with his monogrammed leather briefcase. "So, I hear you're going to take on the machos," he quipped. "Just kidding," he said before I could counter. "Don't worry, you'll be fine. Just get the project off the ground and keep things running until I can take the reins. As soon as Junior shows up, I'll head down there. I'm off to Parker Medical; we'll talk more tomorrow." Full of self-importance, he was out the door, leaving a pile of doubt behind.

Like Harvey, Bob thought I should keep a finger in the dike until the Partner came to the rescue. Maybe this wasn't such a great opportunity after all. Harvey had said I was the right one for this job, but maybe I was the only Project Manager who was gullible enough to accept the assignment. Harvey had said that going to Brazil was a good career move, but maybe he just wanted to fill a staffing gap. Was this a trampoline or a trap? My doubts were irrelevant; failing to object meant the assignment was mine. It was a done deal.

George, my husband, was furious. "You've got to be kidding," was his first reaction. "Do you really want to work in a dictatorship? In a place where men beat women with impunity? A place where human rights are non-existent?"

"Hold on. Take it easy," I tried to appease him. George respected facts, so I cited the information I had dug up that afternoon. "Brazil is in transition. After being a military government for two decades, it is now a republic with a civilian president. In fact, my assignment is precisely to help an important company succeed in the resulting economic conditions." I tried to paint a positive picture of Brazil's inflation and turmoil of the mid-'80s.

George wasn't convinced. "South America has a lousy reputation. Why would you waste time in such a place? Just tell GCC you won't go."

To counter his protests, I couched Brazil as a step toward promotion. George understood ambition; honors at medical school had landed him a choice job at Massachusetts General Hospital. His aspirations extended to me. He had pushed me to apply to the Harvard Business School and was proud of my position with a prestigious firm. Whenever I asked about starting a family, George asserted that raising children would be a waste of education and talent. While I knew I could be a good mother, George would not be an enthusiastic father. After numerous attempts to change his mind, I had resigned myself to being childless. At first, success at work had been a balm for sadness, but with a stagnant career, a nagging void had grown. I needed more advancement to ease the pain.

"Look, George, my career is going nowhere. I need to do something to stand out from the pack. This could be my big chance."

"Isn't there another place you could prove yourself? Like Europe? GCC has offices in London and Paris."

"Right now, the opportunity is in Brazil. If I can make this work, all kinds of doors will open." Then I surprised myself. "Besides, I want to go. I know nothing about Brazil...I've never been outside of the United States!"

"Well, if you want to go, I can't stop you...but I think you'll regret this." George walked away. The conversation was over.

Our uneasy truce was preserved through deliberate silence, but George was mad and now Sue had joined his ranks. I could cope with my husband's anger, but not my sister's disapproval. She saw the tears of uncertainty well into my eyes. Baking a pie was no longer sufficient cover.

Sue wiped her hands on her apron and touched my sleeve. "I'm sorry if I was too harsh. I just think you're taking a huge professional risk. It seems like GCC is setting you up to fail; I don't want you to get hurt. And I don't like the idea of your being so far from home." Sue had grown protective during the past five years, since we had lost our father to a heart attack and our mother to cancer. As our family shrank, our sisterly bonds tightened.

I let the rolling pin rest and laid my hand over Sue's. I needed to talk. Turning to face her with forced composure, I admitted my fears for the first time. "Maybe I am a little crazy." I managed a weak smile. "Sometimes I ask myself, can I be credible in a country where I don't know the language or the culture? Harvey seems to think so." Sue knew I admired GCC's founder. "He's always been my champion and now he's giving me a unique opportunity." My lip started to tremble. I still questioned Harvey's motives, but didn't want Sue to worry.

"Take a deep breath," Sue insisted in her motherly way. So I did and regained control. "That's better." Sue pulled away but kept her eyes locked on my face. She could read me like a book.

"Sue, it's a little risky; for the project launch I'll be on my own in a foreign country, without the backup of a Partner. It's a real stretch for me and things could go wrong, but I have to give it a shot." I wanted to convince her (and myself) that I was doing the right thing. "I don't want to be left behind. Here's my chance to prove that I can be a strong international consultant. Yes, I'm a little scared, but I can do this."

Sue gave my arm a squeeze and turned back to the pie. With ease, she fitted the crust into the waiting Pyrex dish, layered the apples with cinnamon sugar and butter. I watched her crimp the two crusts together with precision and then add her trademark slits to vent the steam. The pie she slid into the oven would emerge fit for a photo in *Gourmet* magazine. Closing the oven door, she reached to set the timer and then turned all her attention to me. "Don't expect to accomplish anything in Brazil." She was firm. "Go to learn. Go for the adventure. Do the best you can, but don't be too tough on yourself if things don't work out."

"That's fine for you to say, Super Mom. Who taught me to be a perfectionist?" In thin-wale corduroys and a cable stitch navy cardigan from Talbots, Sue looked like the perfect wife and mother that she was. Being a homemaker, she changed diapers and dealt with temper tantrums while I plotted data and counseled executives. She planned birthday parties while I ran strategy workshops. We had made different choices and our lives had taken different shapes. Trading places once in a while would have been fun, but instead we lived vicariously through each other, with mutual affection and envy. Sue provided the comfort and traditions of a family homestead and I shared behind-the-scenes tales of a fast-paced corporate life.

A car pulling into the driveway brought our sisterly chat to a halt. Our husbands had returned from *Sea Spirit*, David's sailboat in Marblehead Harbor. Sue's children burst into the kitchen first.

"Did you have a good sail?" Sue asked.

"I steered all by myself," Mark boasted with an eight-year-old imitation of his father's stance.

"Good for you," Sue approved, relieving him of the windbreaker that was otherwise destined for the kitchen floor.

Not to be outdone, five-year-old Melody piped up, "I steered, too."

"Yeah, but Dad helped you. I steered all by myself," Mark bragged as he grabbed a cold Coke and headed for the television.

Melody, still in her puffy orange life jacket, bellied over to her mother. As Sue unsnapped the fasteners, Melody insisted, "I did too steer. All by myself." A kiss on Melody's forehead assured my niece that her mother believed her. Liberated from the bulky vest, she ran off to play with her stuffed animals.

Laden with boat gear, the men came next. David's balding forehead led the way; George was close behind with his abundant blond hair tousled by the wind. In khaki shorts and Lacoste polo shirts, they carried their summer tans with ease. Their Sperry Top-siders squeaked on the wooden floor as they deposited sails and duffle bags in the corner, ready for the next sail. They moved in unison without words. Their close friendship in college had evolved into family bonds. Marrying sisters had converted fraternity brothers into brothers-in-law.

Both men approached: David to give Sue a quick but genuine hug, George to peek in the oven. "That pie sure smells good. Sue, you know the way to a man's heart." George's warmth toward Sue was a notable contrast to the cold shoulder I had received since deciding to go to Brazil. I felt a twinge of jealousy that stemmed not from their mutual affection but from feeling inadequate as a wife.

Oblivious to my heavy heart, David added, "I'll drink to that," as he passed a can of Budweiser to George and then popped one open for himself.

Sue sensed my discomfort and diverted any further praise with a gentle press on David's arm. "Can you start the grill, honey? We're having swordfish."

"What are we celebrating?" David asked.

"Our last weekend together before summer ends…"

"And before Beth goes to the hinterlands." David finished her sentence and raised his Bud in a mock toast. So, George had told him about my upcoming trip. "Who knows, maybe she'll pick up a few tips to coach the kids' soccer teams."

I appreciated David's knowing that Brazil was a World Cup champion, but wanted to get out of the kitchen before moods could sour. "Shall I set the table?"

"Sure," Sue said, coming to my rescue. "The Williams-Sonoma picnic cloth and napkins are in the pantry." I escaped to fetch the blue-and-white gingham that gave Sue's table the perfect summer casual look.

I heard Sue shooing the men outside. "George, let's get that grill going." The men went out on the deck, armed with the bar-beque tools we had given David last Christmas. No one wanted to ruin the evening. The subject of Brazil did not come up again.

Early Monday morning in the office kitchen, Joe Dupree, a fellow Senior Associate, was stirring white powder into his mug. He'd left just enough coffee in the pot to sidestep brewing the next batch. Typical. I opened a new filter pack and poured a carafe of cold water into the coffee maker.

"Pretty soon, you'll be drinking Brazilian coffee." Word had spread about my assignment; Joe's voice held a mix of envy and sarcasm. "I hear they aren't too happy about a woman coming down to tell them what to do." Joe could be sexist, but he was a straight shooter who would not invent a rumor.

I wondered who "they" might be, but did not want to reveal my confusion to Joe. I fell back on a cliché: "Don't believe everything you hear."

"Good luck with the Latinos," was his smug farewell. He walked away, leaving me hostage to the slow drip of the black brew.

Back at my desk, I couldn't shrug off Joe's wisecracks. I had my doubts about being effective in another culture with a foreign language, but it had not dawned on me that being a woman might be a problem. *Am I too naïve?* I thought. *Where did Joe pick up this tidbit? If it is true, why does he know something I don't? Is the "Old Boys Club" still operating at GCC?*

Unable to concentrate, I went looking for Harvey to try to get some answers. Alone in his office, he looked up over his reading glasses as I closed the door. "I ran into Joe Dupree, who said, and I quote, 'They aren't too happy about a woman coming down to tell them what to do.'" Avoiding confrontation was my specialty and I gave Harvey an opening to take me off the project. "My passport and ticket are ready, but I'll back out if the Brazilians won't listen to a woman."

Harvey shook his head slowly. "Where's your spine, Ms. Bartlett? Don't belittle yourself. You're the right person for the job and I've told Sam as much." So, there *was* an issue. Harvey slid his glasses back to the bridge of his nose. His brevity made me more worried, not less.

I stepped closer to his desk. "Harvey, if you think I should bow out, just tell me." I didn't want to go where I wasn't wanted. I liked to make friends, not enemies. "Has something come up that I should know about?" What I really wanted to know, but didn't have the guts to ask, was why Joe knew more than I did.

With a paternal smile, Harvey placed his reading glasses on his desk. "Here's the deal. Sam talked to Bob on Friday. There are no women in the senior ranks of BomFarm and Sam is worried about their reaction to you. This is the biggest project he's ever sold and it is very important for the São Paulo office. Bob promised to explore options and talked to a couple of other Project Managers to see who else might be available. Joe was one of them. I wish Bob had consulted with me first, but the Partner-in-Charge does have the final say in project staffing.

"Early this morning, Bob and I held a conference call with Sam. I've convinced them that we've armed the best team possible. Don't worry; everyone is on board." Harvey got up and gave me a pat on my back. "Everything is under control, so get your bags packed. You might have cold feet now, but once you're in the ring, you'll knock 'em dead."

"I'll do my best," I promised, but wondered if my best would be good enough. Sam and Bob had accepted me reluctantly, maybe because no one else was free to replace me. Despite Harvey's fatherly assurances, I was starting with a handicap before the game had begun. GCC's founder had gone to bat for me and had won, but in doing so he must have set some lofty expectations. Stakes that were already high had just gotten higher.

To boost my confidence, I went shopping after work. I rarely shopped alone and was certainly not an impulse buyer. My wardrobe and hairstyle had been shaped by George's stamp of approval. My closet was full of conservative black, grey, navy, and white. Each item had been carefully selected, following the dictates of John Molloy's handbook, *Dress for Success.*

My intuition told me to buy something brighter for Brazil, something less structured. Although I had never ventured into the trendy shops on Newberry Street before, I found myself pushing open the door to a ladies' boutique. A pleasant chime summoned a perky salesgirl. "Looking for something special?" she asked with unexpected warmth.

"I'm going to Brazil on business. I need something that will travel well and can take me from a day in the office on through a dinner with clients."

"Wow. Brazil. Lucky you! I've got just the thing." Her enthusiasm buoyed me up as she led the way to a rack of soft jackets and skirts. "These came in yesterday and will be perfect." She eyed me for size, pulled several items in jewel colors, and ushered me to the dressing room, perfumed with the soothing scent of lavender.

Ruby, turquoise, and amethyst—each on its own hanger, all stylish and alluring. My hand reached straight for the purple skirt. Soft rayon slipped over my head and fell to my waist with a pleasing whoosh. A perfect fit. After a satisfying swirl, I donned the matching shell, then the sculptured jacket with raglan sleeves. My five-foot-six frame carried the long jacket well. The outfit was formal enough for clients, but feminine and flattering. Unclipping my business-like bun, I let my fine, mousy hair fall shoulder-length around my face.

With expert timing, the salesgirl arrived. "Does this look Brazilian?" I asked as she draped a silk scarf around my neck. With a light violet background, it was the perfect complement to the purple separates, while its hand-painted flowers in ruby and turquoise matched the pieces still waiting to be tried.

"I haven't a clue about Brazil, but you look terrific. Those are great garments; they are wrinkle resistant and won't show the dirt." With confidence, she urged me to try several tops, adorning each with a different scarf or necklace. "You'll look lovely for a week with these plum separates as your anchor and all these accessories to mix and match." She was a pro; the outfits were much more striking than the stand-alone pieces.

"Let me think for a few minutes," I requested.

"Of course, take your time," was the gracious reply. "Just let me know when you are ready for me to ring you up."

Alone, I admired my reflection before changing back into my black pencil skirt with its pinstriped blazer. The purple separates were a "yes," but which of the pretty blouses and accessories should I keep? Nothing was on sale. I had to choose; I couldn't buy all these clothes. As I tied back my hair, a nagging conscience kept asking, *How will George react?*

George tracked our income and expenses to the penny. As treasurer of his college fraternity, he had mastered precise bookkeeping. When we got married he applied his skill to our graduate student budget, and the habit still controlled our purse strings despite two healthy incomes. Having to detail my purchases tended to curb my spending. Choosing three blouses, two scarves, and a necklace was an unprecedented buying spree.

At the register I tried to be nonchalant, but had second thoughts as I signed the credit card slip. As the salesgirl wrapped each item in floral tissue paper, I asked, "If I need to return something, can I get a refund?"

"No problem, as long as the tags are still attached." She smiled and slid the pile of treasures into bags that matched the tissue. "You've made wonderful choices," she beamed and came from behind the counter to hand me the bags. "Enjoy your new clothes and have a great time in Brazil." Her bright confidence eased my buyer's remorse and I left the store with my bold apparel.

The rest of the week was a flurry of tasks to prepare for BomFarm and put my other project, Northern Airways, on auto-pilot for two weeks. With a lot of nagging, I cornered Bob for a two-hour work session. "Neither you nor I ever heard of this company; I'm just doing a favor to help the Brazil office. The way I see it, our job is to teach the people down there how to be consultants. I don't think any of them even has an MBA. So, use your project management skill to keep them in line. Remember, we need lots of data and rigorous analysis. Send me everything you can get your hands on."

Bob paused in his monologue and reached for the phone. "Hey, maybe I can send Roger down with you." Recruited from Bob's alma mater, Roger Doyle flaunted pinstripes and the "know-it-all" attitude I detested. Roger took shortcuts and glossed over mistakes. Recently, I had caught him manipulating some data to tell the story Bob wanted told. When I questioned him privately, Roger called me "more pious than the Pope." Resentfully, he revised his analysis and I didn't report him, but things were still uneasy between us.

"Isn't Roger your right-hand man on Parker Medical?" It was common knowledge that Roger was working overtime to meet the deadlines on Bob's most important client.

Bob pulled his hand back. "You're right. I can't afford to divert him now. Maybe in a few weeks." Relieved, I asked Bob when he expected to travel to Brazil. "I'll be there for the mid-point and the final report; that's when clients need me to push them to make decisions." Bob liked to leave the details to others; he tended to parachute into projects to get the spotlight. If BomFarm fit the pattern, I would do all the work and Bob would hog all the credit. This time had to be different. My resistant colleagues and my disapproving family made the risks clear. It was not so obvious whether I could reap the rewards.

My marriage was already paying a price. Short business trips were routine. George accepted my nights away, just as I accepted his being on call at the hospital. Work schedules put us in different beds on many nights, but Brazil would separate us for weeks at a time. That made George bitter. "We can't plan anything for the next three months. What am I supposed to do with our season tickets to the symphony? Why not stay down there for the whole project and save on airfares?!" His sarcasm hurt.

Nonetheless, George set his anger aside and traded shifts at the hospital so that we could be together my last night before departure. Hoping to replace rancor with romance, I had reserved a table at Maison Robert, Boston's finest French restaurant. I wanted to show George that I loved him despite our disagreements; dressing up was part of that show.

I pulled my new clothes from their hiding place and donned the ballerina-length skirt and sculptured jacket; a delicate scarf fell softly at my neck. My hair was free from its usual French twist; eye shadow and blush brightened my rarely adorned face. I felt pretty.

When George arrived home, I greeted him with a "Ta Da!" and a twirl. He raised his chest, tucked in his chin, and tensed his lips. "Where did you get *that?*"

Trying to ignore his reproach, I planted a ritual kiss on his mouth, after which I stepped back and took a pose. "This is my new outfit for Brazil. Isn't it great?"

"You are kidding, right?" He surveyed me thoroughly. "It's not business-like and it's not you."

"Sure it's me," I replied, struggling to stay upbeat. "I can't wear tailored business suits all the time. This is fun without being flirtatious."

"Fun? How about outrageous? What's gotten into you, Beth? You yourself said this is a high-stakes assignment. If you want them to take you seriously, you've got to dress the part."

His angry punch deflated my joy and raised self-doubt. Maybe George was right. Had I been carried away by the skillful salesgirl? "I suggest you return that costume and get something classy." Turning his back on me, he reached for the mail.

I felt bitter but wanted to please George. "I'm sorry," I said contritely. "I'll change into something else for dinner."

"Please do." George voiced the certainty of a man who knows he's right. "Don't take too long or we'll lose the reservation." I stomped toward the bedroom. "I like that black dress with the wide belt. Wear it with the pearls I gave you for our tenth anniversary," he directed as I shoved the bedroom door shut.

Determined not to cry, I took a deep breath. *It's just a dress,* I thought. Or was it?

The silk scarf kissed my neck as I pulled it aside. I folded the soft jacket and gored skirt tenderly into my suitcase, reserved for times when I wasn't with my husband. I was glad that I had already cut off the tags.

As I dug out my old standbys, my anger surprised me. Why couldn't George share my excitement? I tried to swallow my distress and think rationally. Surely he wanted me to succeed and didn't want a gaudy outfit to stand in the way. His rejection cut deep but maybe I was at fault. On top of Brazil, my shopping spree was salt in a wound. I hastened to repair the damage with a strand of pearls and a little black dress.

The following day, I arrived early at Logan Airport. Restless, I browsed the shops. My eye fell on the display of pretty blank books. Like many teenagers, I had kept a diary, but abandoned the practice as a college student. Suddenly I had the urge to write. Emotions were swirling inside and I wouldn't have Sue as a listening post. I looked wistfully at a small book with a single rosebud embossed on pale pink leather. Here was something feminine to accompany me in a foreign macho world. After some debate, I took it to the register. It was a small indulgence that I could justify to George.

As the small commuter jet took off for New York, the whirr of propellers blocked out the presence of my fellow passengers. Alone, I cracked open the pages and started my log.

Sunday Night—August 24
En route to São Paulo, BRAZIL

Dear Diary,

I'm off to Brazil. What will fill these pages?

The skeptics are many, but I mustn't be one of them.

I am on my own and determined to succeed.

How do I feel?

1) Excited about Brazil – I have no idea what to expect, but I'm tingling with anticipation.

2) Scared about the work – Am I in over my head? Is the resistance of the Brazilians justified?

3) Sad about George – His negativity hurts. He's been distant and cold; withholding affection has always been his way of censuring me. But why is he so mad? Being away is nothing new; is being gone for two weeks at a time the problem? Does he think Brazil is too far away? Too dangerous? Is he worried that I will fail professionally or make a fool of myself? Maybe he's just upset because I made this choice against his counsel. I tried to ask him to talk about it but he refused, as if having a dialogue would excuse my going.

4) Good about myself – for taking the plunge despite the naysayers. Sue says, "Don't expect to accomplish anything," but I've got to do something bold if I want to get promoted. No risk, no reward.

Beyond My Comfort Zone

I was the only woman in Varig's VIP lounge at JFK. BomFarm had sent a prepaid business class ticket that gave me the privilege of waiting in a dimly lit room with a self-service bar. I poured a strong gin and tonic and settled on a banquette near the door. Fellow passengers filled the easy chairs clustered around the room, but it felt awkward to join them.

In one alcove, dark-suited Japanese smoked. In another corner, beer-drinking Americans watched a Sunday football game. Scattered on the remaining couches were well-groomed, dark-haired men. Some wore tailored suits with monogrammed shirts; others, pressed jeans topped by cashmere sweaters—distinctly different from the wash-n-wear and flannel attire of New Englanders.

While taking stock of these travellers, I noticed someone was watching me. Straight out of *Esquire*, an elegant man in a perfectly fitted blazer and creased trousers leaned on the bar, swirling a glass of whiskey. He smoked with relaxed confidence and looked at me with unabashed amusement. Embarrassed, I looked away.

Business travel was an integral part of being a management consultant. Assignments in Chicago, Phoenix, St. Louis, New York, and Los Angeles had made me a road warrior, at ease in hotels, airports, and conference rooms. Travelling with colleagues usually served as a shield, but sometimes I was exposed as a businesswoman alone. I had mastered the art of the cold shoulder as a defense against interested strangers.

Some overtures came from clients and colleagues. A certain intimacy lurks beneath the business crust. An intense intellectual challenge can be alluring. The alcohol poured at business dinners lowers barriers. More than once, desire for approval had brought me to the brink of sexual liaisons. However, something always held me back. Perhaps it was the moral code, embedded in my relationship with George, a code that forbade affairs. Perhaps it was the fear of tarnishing my professional reputation; sleeping with a client or colleague could easily lead to rumors about "sleeping her way to the top."

The gentleman at the bar raised a red flag. Scrambling to get ready for Brazil, I had not thought about the temptation "Latin lovers" might pose far from family and friends. Ashamed, I squelched my own train of thought. George was loyal to me and I owed him the same fidelity.

To forget the sexy stranger, I pulled a manila folder from my briefcase. A meticulous work plan outlined who would do what for the next twelve weeks. Interviews, data collection, analysis, presentations. It was all there. With this document I would deliver the project on time, within budget, and meet Bob's expectations.

Next, I reviewed the presentation that would explain GCC's methodology to the BomFarm executives. Bob had given me the firm's boilerplate on the pharmacy industry and we had inserted "BomFarm" in a few places to "customize" it. "No need to change a good thing," Bob had crowed. I tucked the speech back in my bag.

I fished out an awkward binder that had arrived just in time from Brazil by DHL. Handwritten notes on ragged-edged pages were held in place by a spring-loaded metal clip. Although I wanted to give my Brazilian colleagues the benefit of the doubt, the amateurish folder engendered little confidence. My first phone interaction with Sam had been rough around the edges, just like this package.

After introducing myself, I had asked, "Could you pull together whatever you can—financial data, competitive data, market share information? I'll appreciate anything that will help me up the learning curve before I get there."

"We don't have much; we'll send what we can." Sam had been non-committal, so I was pleasantly surprised when a thick courier package arrived. But when I opened it, I was dumbstruck. The tables were in Portuguese! It was ludicrous; I figured this was a joke and had set the data aside in frustration.

Now, with time to kill, I used my English-Portuguese dictionary to pencil translations next to the strange words: *ano* (year), *despesas* (expenses), *lucros* (profit), *fábrica* (factory). It was slow going, but my struggle unveiled the information I had requested. I had been too quick to judge; it didn't look pretty, but the binder was a goldmine. Unfortunately, I lacked the tools to extract the treasure. Foreign language, foreign currency, and foreign accounting practices left me humbled.

My head started to ache so I stuffed the data and dictionary back into my bag. To ease the throbbing, I downed two aspirins. Drinking water and stretching were supposed to reduce the hazards of international flights. Having violated the no alcohol rule, I hoped extension and elongation would offset the gin. Unhindered by my shapeless sweatshirt and baggy jeans, I touched my toes and reached for the ceiling. As I finished, the club attendant announced that boarding was in progress, so I picked up my briefcase and headed for the gate.

On board at last, I discovered that my window seat had been a poor choice. On this red-eye, there would be nothing to see but a few stars and a wing light. Next time I would choose an aisle with access to the lavatory.

Spicy cologne announced the arrival of my seatmate. I hid my curiosity by staring out at the ramp activity. Reflected in the window was a suntanned face over an open collar. As he bantered with the stewardess, I strained to hear some Portuguese words. Sam had assured me that BomFarm's senior executives could speak English. Nonetheless, I had tried to learn a few phrases. High school Latin and French had not prepared me for the sonorous vowels and spongy consonants of *bom dia* and *obrigada*. Berlitz tapes had not prepared me for the jovial exchange between my first real Brazilians. I could not decipher a single word.

Soon we were airborne. I was a frequent flyer, but this time was different. Safety instructions came first in Portuguese, then English. Instead of calming burgundy and blue, I was surrounded by the green and yellow of Brazil's flag. The foil packet of butter said "*manteiga*" and the server with the beverage cart asked, "*Alguma coisa para beber?*"

"Would you like something to drink?" My seatmate's bass voice resonated beside me. I flashed an appreciative smile and asked for red wine. "Of course, Madame," came the stilted reply of the flight attendant, who would exercise her airline English for the rest of the meal service.

"Your first time in Brazil?" His handsome, chiseled face looked squarely at mine as he waited for an answer. His hazel eyes and warm smile made it impossible to be aloof. *We'll be companions for many hours,* I rationalized, *being cordial can do no harm.*

"Yes, I'm going for business," I said, in my professional voice.

A tiny shift in his jaw was the only hint of surprise. "Business in Brazil is at a turning point. Brazil itself is at a turning point. We are learning how to be a republic. Hopefully, the Plano Cruzado will stabilize inflation. Perhaps the price freezes are necessary to get things under control, but I would prefer a free market." He stopped suddenly before saying, "Goodness. Forgive my boring you with such a weighty subject; a pretty lady deserves more pleasant dinner conversation. Even if she is a business lady," he added with the slightest tease. "Let me start again. *Bem-vinda e boa sorte.* Welcome and good luck."

"*Obrigada,*" I replied, hoping I did not sound foolish.

"*Parabéns.* Congratulations for your Portuguese."

"'Thank you' is the only word I know," I confessed.

"Well, I'll teach you more while we dine." Soon we were laughing as I struggled to mimic him; the wine eased my inhibitions but I was still a hopeless case. As the meal was cleared, he said, "Don't worry. You'll be just fine, as long as you can order coffee—*dois cafezinhos,*" he voiced to the attendant, who was beside us with the after-dinner drinks. She set a tiny cup and two sugar packets on each of our tray tables. Following his example, I sweetened the strong coffee and took a sip. Being a gracious companion might keep me awake all night, but I didn't care. Upon draining his cup, he said, "Now you need one more phrase: *Onde é o banheiro?* That will get you to the bathroom in any restaurant. Ladies first." He rose from his seat and stepped aside, giving me access to the aisle.

"*Obrigada.*" It came out easily this time. I really was grateful; I had dreaded asking him to get up so that I could use the head. Upon my return, he stood chatting with another passenger, so I slipped into my seat. I unwrapped the eye mask and earphones that had been distributed in a zipper case, settled under the blanket, leaned my head against the window, and closed my eyes. To the sound of samba, I drifted off before my companion returned.

Groggy from fitful sleep, we ate breakfast in silence. As the plane descended through the cloud cover, I had my first sight of Brazil. Below my window, an endless expanse of terracotta and corrugated metal roofs lined dirt roads. The dominant orange and tan was broken by scraggly, sharp-edged foliage. On the distant horizon, gray concrete structures were barely distinct from low-lying clouds and fog. The uninviting vista made me somber until we touched down and unexpected applause filled the cabin. I glanced about in surprise. "It's a tradition," my seatmate explained. "Some cheer the captain; some thank God."

"I've never heard passengers clap for a safe landing; it's nice."

"You'll discover many nice things about Brazilians. We celebrate life." Once again, his rich voice charmed me. "Americans live to work; Brazilians work to live." Then he faced me squarely and said earnestly, "Have some fun during your stay; let Brazil rub off."

"That sounds like good advice." The plane had arrived at the gate. Even though my buttocks were sore and my bladder ached, I felt a tinge of regret.

Without waiting for the seat belt sign to be extinguished, he stood to retrieve belongings from the overhead bins. "This must be yours." He handed me the bulging canvas briefcase with amusement playing in his intriguing eyes.

"Yes, thanks." I acknowledged with chagrin. Being from a culture where a woman fends for herself, I favored practicality over good taste. I had never wished for a classy leather satchel until now.

Passing it to me, he read the monogram. "B.A.B. What does it stand for?"

"Beth Ann Bartlett." I hoped my jet-lagged eyes did not look as grainy as they felt.

"Beth Ann, it has been my pleasure." He pulled an engraved business card from his jacket. "If you need anything while you are in Brazil, call my office."

I puzzled over his name. *Joaquin Antonio Carlos de Ocampo. Advogado.*

"People call me Jaco. That's my nom de guerre."

I tried to recall my French. Name of War. What war? At least his nickname was short. "Jack was my father's name. It will be easy to remember."

"Except it's Jaco with an 'o' at the end. We Brazilians like to end words with a vowel. So it's Jaco, not Jack."

"Jaco," I tried again.

"*Perfeito*, Bethania."

Bethania. It was so musical and much prettier than down-to-earth, monosyllabic "Beth."

I blushed. "Thanks for the coaching...and for your card." I tucked it into my purse. "I'm sure I'll be fine. The consulting firm I work for is taking care of everything."

I sounded surer than I was. Sam had promised that someone would meet me at the airport to take me to the hotel. Unsure whether they would show up, I was happy to have Jaco's card.

The other passengers began to press toward the front of the plane. Jaco stepped into the aisle and waved me ahead, "After you." I smiled my thank you and took my first steps as a lady in Brazil.

The flow of passengers carried us down the modern jetway into the glass corridor that separated inbound from outbound. Jumbo jets sat at the end of each finger: Varig, Pan Am, Eastern, Aerolíneas Argentinas, Air Portugal, Iberia, Air France, and Lufthansa. Simultaneous arrivals disgorged grumpy passengers in a herd toward immigration.

As we entered the undisciplined chaos of the immigration hall, Jaco explained apologetically, "Brazilians have a separate line, so I must leave you here." He paused long enough to hold my eyes with his. "I hope to see you again sometime, Bethania. *Boa sorte. Tchau.*"

"*Tchau.* Goodbye and thanks again." As Jaco went off, I eyed the unorganized crowd and patted my purse where I had stashed his card.

I joined an uncordoned crunch of cranky people. Where were the "Order and Progress" professed on the Brazilian flag? Wanting to be assertive but not rude, I jockeyed toward the booths marked "*Polícia Federal.*"

An hour later, a uniformed man in a metallic cubicle opened my virgin passport to the Brazilian business visa, good for ninety days. Oblivious to the impatient hoard behind the yellow line, he leafed through the empty pages. Grudgingly, he stamped my passport and scribbled something illegible. After several more loud bangs of his stamp, he shoved the crisp booklet back through the small slot in the glass barrier. His wordless nod of disdain signaled that I had arrived.

Amid the fray at a screeching carousel, I spotted my soft Lands' End bag. Crushed between two jumbo Samsonites, it looked as helpless as I felt. I squeezed forward and hauled on the handles. A pair of stronger arms reached beyond mine and lifted my bag with ease. "*Aí está!*"

"*Obrigada,*" I stammered as the stranger placed the monogrammed Square Rigger onto a wobbly trolley.

"*De nada,*" the man replied casually and turned back to the loaded conveyor belt. I moved away and discreetly checked the bag's tag, just in case there was another traveller with canvas luggage and the initials "B.A.B."

I followed top-heavy carts trundling toward signs in Portuguese and English.

Saída – Exit
Alfândega – Customs
Nada a Declarar – Nothing to Declare

A stern guard ensured that passengers pushed a big button before exiting. A colored light chose victims for bag search. Three passengers in front of me got green. A red light and a harsh buzz routed me to one of ten inspection tables.

With a glance at my passport, the customs inspector motioned for me to open my suitcase. On top lay the purple outfit that had provoked George. Below my new clothes were the requisite blue suit, black pumps, and white blouses. Next came white underwear in a plastic grocery bag; a windup alarm clock; a small cosmetic bag filled with my toothbrush, Crest, dental floss, a plastic hairbrush, Oil of Olay, contact lens solution, and one tube of lipstick. At the bottom were tampons, sneakers, running shorts, a Harvard t-shirt, and a jump rope.

The inspector waved me on, turning to a more promising trolley with bulging suitcases. I zipped my bag, abandoned the cart, and followed the signs toward the exit. Around a sharp corner, eager faces pressed against a glass wall. At Boston's airport, greeters kept a dignified distance, concealing feelings beneath a cool veneer. Not so in São Paulo. Joy and anticipation penetrated the thick plate glass.

As I emerged through the doors, drums sounded over a noisy crowd. My heartbeat quickened to the rhythm. Greeters strained against the portable barriers that created a narrow funnel into the main terminal. Sprinkled among the impatient family members were uniformed drivers. Cardboard signs with corporate logos read "Shell," "Ford," "Saab-Scania," "Citibank."

"Someone will be there," Sam had promised.

I scanned for "GCC" or "Bartlett" as a trolley rammed my ankles. Dirty looks did nothing to deter the woman pushing from behind. Annoyed, I kept walking as if I knew where I was going. Finally, I heard my name.

"Beth. Beth Bartlett?"

To my right, I spied a business suit waving beyond a group of boisterous children. Clutching my bags with both hands left just my head free to nod in response. Waving arms gestured to keep moving ahead. Then the pressing horde swallowed the suited figure. I lurched forward without knowing who had greeted me or what he looked like.

Suddenly, a firm grip clasped my left arm; on my right side, a large hand grabbed my lumpy suitcase. The two men escorted me out of the melee. "We're the guys from GCC-Brazil. Welcome."

"I'm Sam Cohen," said a stooped man at my elbow, "and this is Marcelo Pereira." Marcelo towered over both of us. Like many GCC consultants, he was about thirty—but there the likeness ended. Marcelo sported a rumpled shirt and a bandit's black beard...hardly the smooth GCC stereotype. He nodded a silent hello.

Sam did all the talking; his flawless English had the neutrality of a radio announcer. His light linen suit was a far cry from the pinstripes of Boston. Forty-some years gave character to his impish face with a prominent nose, a crooked smile, and intense blue eyes.

A compact man with a potbelly that rolled with his gait joined us. "This is Vicente, our driver," Sam explained. With a toothless smile, Vicente nodded and took my suitcase. Unburdened, Marcelo insisted on carrying my briefcase. A picturesque foursome, we trooped toward the exit.

Sam spoke at my side. "It's a long drive to downtown; would you like to use the *toilette?* There's a Ladies Room right here."

"I would. Thank you for asking."

"Leave your bags with us. We'll be right here when you're ready," Sam assured me.

The international symbol for women was a welcome sight. I entered a cinderblock room with two narrow stalls. A woman dressed like a prison inmate handed me a single sheet of scratchy brown paper. I wasted no time in relieving the tension of touching down.

I refreshed my straggling French twist and dug for lipstick to brighten my tired face. Cheap metal reflected my jeans and sweatshirt, hardly the look of a strategic guru. Had I known that my colleagues would be at the airport, I would have worn business attire. In Boston, visiting consultants were met by an efficient, impersonal chauffeur.

For some reason, Sam and Marcelo had come to greet the Project Manager chosen against their wishes. If they were resentful, it didn't show. They seemed relaxed and without rancor. Was this Latin hospitality or a sign that they had nothing better to do? Were they here to impress me or to con me?

When Beth Bartlett headed toward the Ladies Room, the men lit up.

"So, where's the Chanel suit?" Marcelo challenged as he inhaled deeply.

Sam's silver, French-made Dupont lighter snapped shut with a pronounced click as he admitted, "OK, she's not wearing the pinstripes or ascot, but her hair is up."

Earlier, Marcelo had asked, "How will we know her?" and Sam had replied, "No problem. Just look for a Chanel suit, a paisley scarf, a leather briefcase, and a schoolmarm's bun. Your typical lesbian bitch...that's what's coming."

Both men were upset about a woman boss. Marcelo had heard Sam ask Harvey to reconsider. "You know, Harvey, I have nothing against women myself, but this is a Latin culture. She won't be credible...

"I'm sure she's an excellent professional, but women's lib hasn't made it to Brazil yet. BomFarm has a hundred directors; not one is a woman...

"I realize that GCC selects its Project Managers carefully, but this is not Boston. Brazilians speak Portuguese, not English. Does Beth speak Portuguese?"...Sam had signaled thumbs down.

"I see. How about Spanish?...You're not sure...

"What experience does she have working abroad?...

"So, this is her first international assignment." At this point Sam had thrown the BomFarm folder on the floor.

"Harvey, give me a break. I hope you're kidding...

"Well, make sure she has a visa or she won't be able to board the flight." Sam was boiling as he hung up.

"Son of a bitch! Harvey won't budge." Sam had kicked the papers on the floor. "Doesn't he realize that BomFarm is *the* opportunity for GCC-Brazil? And they're sending this witch who doesn't even have a passport! We'll just have to contain the damage until Bob White gets here."

Sam and Marcelo had made a pact. They would stick together to get through this. That included meeting the flight. "It is common courtesy," Sam had argued, "and will show her that we have the upper hand."

Marcelo had concurred with his new boss. Two months before, Sam had convinced him to become GCC's first Brazilian consultant. Marcelo's wife had asked, "Can you work for an Argentine? They can be pretty arrogant." Brazilians joked about their southern neighbors who took their egos very seriously.

"Sam's OK. He values my skills as an economist and is offering twice my present salary. Besides, the office is just starting up; I'm getting in on the ground floor. It's worth the risk."

The Argentine and the Brazilian made a good team. Sam sold the projects and Marcelo delivered them. The BomFarm executives liked them and wanted more work. Everything was great until headquarters had assigned a woman to manage their most important project.

"A woman who shows up in jeans can't be all bad." Marcelo crushed his cigarette underfoot and added, "She looks scared to me."

"She's scared? What about me?" Sam took the last drag on his Marlboro and watched Beth emerge purposefully from the Ladies Room. Under his breath he asked, "How will I convince BomFarm that *that* is a strategy expert?"

Reunited, we walked to the parking lot. Sam asked, "How was your flight?"

"Fine, thanks. Long, but fine." The squat figure stopped behind a scratched and dusty VW hatchback. A removable "Taxi" sign perched on the roof. A large metal cylinder occupied half the trunk.

"Good. Soft," squishing my bags around the tank, Marcelo voiced his first words. Sam looked on. Vicente closed the hatch with a satisfied grin. "*Jóia!*" Marcelo said to Vicente. I decided to look up this delightful word that seemed to mean "terrific" or "great." I had done at least one thing right—I'd packed light.

Sam held the back door open for me and cranked down the window. "Things will cool off once we get going."

I sank into a concave dip and was affronted by stale cigarette butts in the overflowing ashtray. Loose ash would fly once we started moving. I instinctively reached for the seat belt that was not there.

Marcelo sat up front with Vicente, and Sam settled in next to me. Before we left the parking lot, Sam and Marcelo lit up. No one asked, "Do you mind?" Acrid smells assaulted my nostrils. Smoke and smog stung my eyes. I felt vulnerable without being strapped in. Wind through the open windows plastered my hair to my brow, which was already damp with perspiration.

"Perhaps we should use this time productively," I suggested.

"Productively?" Marcelo echoed from the front seat. "What's that?"

"Well, you are productive when you use time well." I sounded like a first-grade teacher.

"Ah, *produtivo*." Marcelo looked back at Sam with a deadpan face. "New idea."

"Watch out for Marcelo," Sam warned. "Sometimes he doesn't know and doesn't let you know, but sometimes he knows and doesn't let you know."

"Then sometimes I'm going to be pretty confused." I tried to respond in kind to Sam's witty remark, but still wanted to know, "So, should we be *produtivo*?"

"We'll have plenty of time at the office, once you're rested." Sam saw no urgency to get to work right away. "Besides, the ride from the airport is tough. If you were alone, you might turn around and go home. Over there is a Brazilian prison." He pointed to watchtowers above concrete walls and barbed wire. I had seen a TV documentary on third-world prisons, but never thought I would be so close to one.

As we drove on, the sights and sounds of a roadside *favela* shocked me. The slum consisted of lopsided walls on a mud embankment. Some shacks were made of loosely mortared concrete block or bricks; others, of soggy cardboard. A woman in rags stood in a dark doorway, her pregnant belly bulging on her skinny frame. Toddlers crouched in grimy puddles, splashing murky water onto their bare bodies. A mangy dog skulked down a muddy path where rows of makeshift shelters stretched out of sight. Insects buzzed around a young boy hoisting a heavy bucket across a doorless threshold. A rock on the tin roof above threatened to roll onto his head.

Silent, I shifted in my seat, embarrassed by my morbid curiosity. Images from *National Geographic* were just a few feet away. A lifeless figure lay under a ragged blanket in the ninety-degree heat. A barefoot man led his mule-drawn cart loaded with cardboard.

My stomach was queasy with jet lag, fear, sadness, and guilt. The squalor outside my window made me realize the abundance I had left behind. These shacks were on the banks of the stagnant Rio Tietê. My elegant home overlooked the Charles River. Here, rough-hewn planks and rusty metal chairs were the neighborhood bar. Polished granite and overstuffed chairs set the stage for cocktails at home. Desperate figures searched the riverbank for food or metal scraps. My garbage disposal, oblivious to hunger, consumed leftovers after every meal.

The silence was awkward. "You were right," I said to Sam. "This is tough. I've never seen poverty like this; I guess I've been pretty sheltered."

"Welcome to the Third World. São Paulo is a city of extremes with millions of people, most of them very poor and a few very, very rich."

Vicente detoured from the highway at a construction barrier. He was intent on the road as we crawled single file with the other vehicles. Marcelo was alert, too. They exchanged a few tense words in Portuguese: *"Cuidado. Muito cuidado."*

"Vicente must be very careful. There are nails in the road," Sam explained. "Punctures bring some money into the *favela.*" A crude, hand-lettered sign with the word *"PNEUS"* was propped against a pile of retreads. Unlucky cars with flats were on the shoulder.

Passengers waited behind locked doors while teenage boys changed the damaged tires. Their mud-splattered shirts were like travel posters: "Paris." "I ♥ New York." "Toronto." Teens who would never leave Brazil wore the cast-off memories of the wealthy.

As we crept on, I wiped sweaty palms on my jeans. I glanced sideways at Sam in his summer linen and fine leather shoes. Should we run into trouble, I would place my trust in Vicente's stocky frame and Marcelo's tough-looking face.

Unscathed, we drove on past Quonset hut factories that hunkered behind barbed wire. Beyond a maze of utility lines, bland concrete apartments rose skyward; laundry hung dark and limp on decaying balconies. A colorful three-story shopping mall, topped by McDonald's golden arches, broke the bleak panorama.

After an hour, the city engulfed us. Brown skin, dark hair, and feet in flip-flops filled the cracked, uneven sidewalks. Expressionless eyes stared down from bus windows. Trolley passengers clung to poles to avoid falling with the next lurch.

Larger-than-life bodies on provocative billboards pushed underwear, while larger-than-life faces on political banners promised *Saúde. Educação. Progresso.* Was *health* an impossible dream for babies slung on the breasts of begging mothers? Could *education* reach the twenty percent who were illiterate? What did *progress* mean for the ragged souls living under each overpass?

Slowly, the surroundings began to change. Scary tenements with shattered windows gave way to dense office buildings. Modern apartments sprouted up next to the highway; university buildings hinted at scholarship. Vicente shifted gears up a hill, passed a small city park, and finally turned onto Avenida Paulista.

"This is São Paulo's Park Avenue," Sam explained. "Many multinationals and large Brazilian companies are headquartered here."

"There's *Gazeta Mercantil*, our *Wall Street Journal*," Marcelo said, pointing proudly.

Modern glass and steel dwarfed sporadic mansions, crumbling and overgrown. Once the place of colonial grandeur, they now housed bats, rats, and the hopes of speculators.

A few turns later, Vicente stopped in an elegant entry. A uniformed doorman sprang forward to unload my canvas bag onto a shiny brass cart. "This way," a bellman motioned me into the atrium lobby of the Maksoud Plaza. Sam reached the check-in counter first and soon had a room key in hand.

"*Mil duzentos e dois*," Sam told the bellboy, who then disappeared with my bag. "You're in Room 1202." Sam steered me toward glass elevators. We floated up through an oasis of marble, hanging plants, and fountains—a surreal contrast to the world outside.

In my room, Sam checked the bathroom and the closet. "Do you need more towels? More hangers?"

The dozen hangers were more than enough for my simple wardrobe. "Everything looks just fine." In fact, it seemed very luxurious, as if I were a VIP.

"If you need something, call the front desk; they speak English. The maids speak only Portuguese." A buzz interrupted. "Your bag. Good." Sam bantered with the bellboy, tipped him, and thanked him. "*Obrigado*."

"*Brigado você*," the boy replied easily. "Have a nice stay," he said to me with much effort as he backed into the hall.

"Now that your bag is here, I'll leave you to rest. Call home. Order room service. I'll pick you up at 2:30 to take you to the office." His hand was on the doorknob.

"Thanks for making my first hours in Brazil a little easier. I'll be in the lobby at 2:30."

"See you then." The door latched with a substantial click. I snuck to the peephole and watched Sam's rumpled suit retreat. His gruff courtesy had been touching, yet a bit invasive. I turned the deadbolt and secured the chain.

Alone at last in a quiet, elegant place. Crisp sheets and soft towels beckoned. I would not resist. Closing the heavy blackout drapes, I shut out the modern offices and the urban bustle. But I could not forget the sight of the polluted Rio Tietê, sprawling *favelas*, or hungry children. The ride from Guarulhos had stripped me of the blinders that had protected my world. Here, I was definitely outside my comfort zone.

Before crawling into bed, I wanted to hear a familiar voice. I found a crisp card with phone dialing instructions in the drawer of the night table. The international rates were in the stratosphere; my calls home would be few and perfunctory.

My first call to George reached an answering service at the hospital. Even though I didn't expect to find him, I was disappointed. Because it was his workplace, I said nothing intimate, just, "Hi, George. I made it safely to Brazil. It was a long trip but I'm fine. I'll call you at home tonight."

I didn't bother to record the hotel's phone number. Before my leaving Boston he had said, "I won't try to call you; you call me. Phone bills should be paid by GCC." George's being tight-fisted was nothing new. We rarely spoke by phone while I travelled on business; when we did, it was my responsibility to initiate the call. "Besides, I don't want to deal with operators who don't speak English." Feeling powerless in a foreign language was one more reason my husband would not be trying to reach me.

In contrast, I knew that Sue would be anxiously waiting for my call.

"Hello?" a young voice answered the first ring.

"Hi, Mark. It's Aunt Beth. I need to talk to your mother."

"OK." Then a shout, "Mom! Aunt Beth!" For once, I appreciated his blunt manners. I didn't want eight-year-old chit-chat to drive up the phone bill. Sue picked up, a little breathless.

"Finally, it's you. Are you safe? How was the trip?"

"My plane was late, but the trip was fine. So far it's weird, like a dream. The poverty and pollution are unreal. My hotel is first class but getting here we drove through a UNICEF documentary."

"*We*? Who's *we*?" Sue didn't miss a thing.

"Two GCC consultants met me at the airport."

"That was nice."

"More than nice. The drive to downtown took over an hour and we passed some pretty rough territory. I would have been scared to death in a taxi by myself." Telling Sue about my arrival made me realize how much the personal welcome meant.

"So what are they like, the Brazilians?"

I wished my sister could see Marcelo and Sam. "One is burly and bearded and the other is a cross between Woody Allen and Walter Matthau."

Sue laughed, "So they're not the proverbial Latin lovers?" As teenagers, Sue and I had pasted photos of handsome movie stars in our scrapbooks. Mine were tall, blue-eyed, and blond, like George, but Sue's were usually dark-eyed and swarthy. Her comment evoked those carefree days and made me smile.

"I won't tell David you said that." Knowing that Sue's fantasies did not diminish her devotion to her husband, I could tease her. "My colleagues don't have that profile, but you should have seen the guy I sat next to on the plane! Good looking, fascinating hazel eyes, and a real gentleman." I didn't refer to Jaco's card. Before Sue could probe, I changed the subject, "By the way, I left a message for George at work. Can you tell him I'm fine? Calls from this hotel cost a fortune."

"Sure, I'll let him know you're safe…but I won't mention all the men you've met in the first few hours." Sue was a little envious; we both laughed.

"We'd better sign off before we break the piggy bank."

"OK. I'm taking the kids to the beach. Our last picnic before school starts. They're in their bathing suits, ready to go. Wish you could come."

"Me, too. Have fun and say 'Hi' to everyone for me. Bye."

"Bye." I could just see them piling into the minivan. The kids would fight over the front seat. Sue would negotiate, "Mark rides in front going and Melody coming back." Rusty, the golden retriever, would jump in, his tail banging against the cooler and beach toys. Theirs was a carefree world, circumscribed by good fortune, but circumscribed nonetheless.

Jogo de Cintura

Promptly at 2:30, Sam met me in the Maksoud's lobby and we walked three blocks to GCC-Brazil. "Tell me something about the office. It's new, isn't it?"

"Yes, about six months ago I convinced GCC to open in São Paulo. Right now we're like a branch of Argentina, but I'll change that. Brazil is four times the size of Argentina." Ignorant about South American markets, I just kept listening. "So far I've recruited Marcelo, two analysts, and Jenny, the girl who cleans. It's a low-budget operation."

On the sixth floor of a modest building, a metal plaque marked the door: "Global Consulting Center – São Paulo, Brazil." The one-room office housed four tables laden with papers. At one sat Marcelo, wearing a yellow headset and oblivious to our arrival. He stared into the dim screen of the only computer in sight. "That's our IBM clone. It runs with five-inch floppy disks and a lot of prayer," Sam remarked. A pin-feed printer spat out analyses onto paper already dingy from polluted air. "Marcelo's lost in his Walkman and his analysis. We won't disturb him yet."

I eyed the papers weighted down with filthy ashtrays. "Someone's been hard at work," I observed.

"Our part-time analysts. They're at business school. You'll meet them tonight at dinner.

"We'll work in here." We passed a flimsy divider and crossed into the windowed side of the room, which featured an empty table surrounded by metal folding chairs. A lone uncluttered desk hugged the corner. On it was the office telephone, a leather-bound book, a single folder marked "BomFarm," and a black wand from a child's magic kit.

"We've ordered a desk for you. Meanwhile, you can use the conference table. Want some coffee? It's do-it-yourself." Sam led me to the "kitchen"—a bar-sized refrigerator next to the tiny lavatory. We rescued some chipped mugs from the bathroom sink, washed them, and prepared instant coffee.

In the Boston office, the aroma of gourmet coffee welcomed visitors to a first-class firm of successful professionals. A pretty receptionist ushered guests to the designer conference table and padded armchairs. There, weighty recommendations were revealed with slides and reports from the latest laser printer. I would soon discover whether those accouterments were essential to good consulting.

Coffee in hand, we coaxed Marcelo out of his headphones and sat down on three sides of the big table. From my briefcase, I pulled my neatly drawn Gantt charts and project calendar. To kick off a new project, I always distributed the work plan and reviewed roles and deadlines.

My teammates were expectant, but this time, my hands hesitated, keeping hold of the crisp papers. I recalled my phone call with Sue. "Before we start, I want to thank you for waiting for me at the airport. Meeting me was beyond the call of duty."

Marcelo scratched his beard quizzically. Sam waited for my pause, then said, "It was no trouble; it was a pleasure." His masculine voice unleashed the fears that had been brewing.

"Well, it really meant a lot. I am somewhat intimidated." My admission came out of nowhere in a wavering voice. "I don't know the language. I don't know the culture. I've never worked in a foreign country." As the men exchanged questioning looks, the truth tumbled out. "I need your help." Sam said something to Marcelo in Portuguese. I cleared my throat in search of a more professional tenor. "This project is high stakes."

"That's for sure," Sam interjected. "We're hoping BomFarm will be a mainstay of GCC in São Paulo for years to come."

"So, we agree," I pushed on. "The stakes are high for all of us, but we have a common interest. We can be successful if we work together." Who was I trying to convince? Myself or my colleagues? "We must combine what I know about strategy with what you know about BomFarm and Brazil. As a team, we can win; otherwise, we'll fail." Marcelo turned his questioning look from me to Sam.

"Beth, let me translate for Marcelo." To confess my doubts was bad enough; to have them repeated in a foreign language was worse! When Sam finished, Marcelo looked surprised and Sam amused.

Marcelo asked in stilted English, "For sure you are American? No?"

"For sure. Of course." Now I turned a confused face to Sam.

"Marcelo is teasing you," Sam explained. "Most people from the States think they know it all. We expected you to have all the answers...even if they were the wrong ones."

I didn't understand their sense of humor, but I tried to banter back. "You were right about one thing. I'm as American as apple pie, and I'm not very worldly. I must learn a lot, very fast, if we are going to help BomFarm. You guys will have to teach me what I need to know."

"We won't let you down," Sam assured me.

"Count me," Marcelo added. I smiled but didn't make fun of his awkward promise. His English was better than my Portuguese.

"I think this is the beginning of a beautiful friendship." Sam's quote from *Casablanca* was a good way to transition.

"So, what are we waiting for?" I asked. "Let's get to work." I laid out objectives, questions to be answered, data to be gathered, key milestones, and review dates. Looks exchanged between Sam and Marcelo conveyed conciliatory tolerance. Without comment, Sam pushed the papers aside.

"Let us hear your presentation for tomorrow. That will determine whether we have a project or not." His calling the shots caught me off balance, but I started to rehearse, as he requested.

Sam interrupted my monologue midstream. "Only some of the executives understand English. The presentation must be bilingual. I will translate as you present." Sam had already bridged the language gap between Marcelo and me. He would use the same approach with BomFarm. "Speak naturally, but use short sentences."

I started again, trying to simplify my explanation. I felt lumbering and stilted. Sam stopped me again. "Be careful. Speak in short sentences, but don't be condescending. Just because someone doesn't speak English, doesn't mean they are stupid." Marcelo was obviously a case in point. "Remember, part of the group will understand you perfectly. A few could give this lecture themselves. So watch it." I tried again. "That's better. Now, another thing. Don't define everything. Leave some room for them to shape the project."

"But," I protested, "they hired us to provide methodology. Why would they want to define how to do things?"

"Trust me. Leave room for their ideas and contributions. Otherwise, you will be rejected. Remember, you are dealing with Latin egos."

We studied the work plan, identifying what was essential and where we could be flexible. "They aren't likely to make many suggestions," Sam predicted. "It's just important to show that you have *jogo de cintura.*"

"That I have what?" I asked, puzzled.

Marcelo jumped to his feet and started to whistle. He wove back and forth, shifting left and right, bobbing his head, doing fancy footwork. "That's *jogo de cintura,*" Sam cracked up. "*Cintura* means 'waist' and *jogo* means 'game.' It's the skill of a soccer player to control the ball and set his opponent off balance. Brazilians prize this quality on and off the soccer field."

Marcelo pulled me up from my chair, put his hands around my waist, and continued his spontaneous dance. What had become of the taciturn man in the car? His dour expression was gone, replaced by rhythmic sounds and a big grin. Letting go, he raised his arms above his head and moved his hips seductively to his own beat. I stepped away from my partner and felt my nipples pressing against my silk blouse. I turned my eyes away from Marcelo's undulating torso to find Sam swaying in his chair and clapping. With flushed cheeks I plopped back in my chair, a hopeless case of stiff inhibition.

Laughing, I confessed, "I knew I had a lot to learn, but I guess it's far more than I realized." I warmed to the idea of these two men as my teachers, but I kept that to myself and redirected our attention to BomFarm.

The provocative dancer transformed back into a serious economist. Using Portuguese and broken English, Marcelo explained the government's new economic plan and its impact on BomFarm. With Sam's help, Marcelo defined concepts that were foreign to me: "indexation," "devaluation," "official dollar," "tourist dollar," and "monetary controls."

I pulled out the thick binder they had sent me. "We searched for the information you wanted," Sam explained, "but data that's easy to find in the U.S. simply does not exist here. Most companies, like BomFarm, are family-owned. It's not so transparent."

Another challenge, I thought. *Could we develop a good strategy without reliable data?*

"Well, we'll have to work with what we have," I replied philosophically, realizing Marcelo would interpret information that I could not verify.

The last topic on our agenda was a review of the key players—their names, positions, and biases. Power and politics mirrored my other clients with one big exception—at BomFarm, I would meet the owners, face-to-face. In lieu of abstract institutional investors, we would be accountable to real people. Flesh-and-blood shareholders put consulting in a new light.

My project plan and presentation were covered with notes. From afar, I had plotted a straight line from start to finish, with clear boundaries among the team members. I had assumed everyone would do things my way. Obviously, I was wrong.

Success in Brazil would require a strong dose of trust and flexibility. My confession, unplanned and unscripted, had set the stage for teamwork. Sam was coaching and translating. Marcelo had opened up in an unexpected outpouring of pure fun and intellectual acumen. His sinuous dance was a sexy reminder of a new survival skill, *jogo de cintura*. But could a stiff New Englander learn to maneuver and sway her hips? I was not so sure.

And could my stomach learn to wait for dinner at 9:00? To welcome me, Sam had reserved a table at a São Paulo steakhouse within walking distance. A little before nine, we entered a dimly lit bar, where spotlights shown on an enormous agate. As I admired it, a mixture of melodic greetings floated my way. *"Boa noite." "Oi, Marcelo, como vai?" "Tudo bem com você?"*

Sam pulled me into a circle formed by himself, Marcelo, and three new faces. "Beth, meet the rest of the team. This is

Luciana. When she finishes her MBA in March, she'll join us full-time." I did not expect to find a woman working for GCC-Brazil, especially one in a low-cut blouse and tight pants.

She put her right cheek to mine, then her left. I soon discovered that this intimate greeting was equivalent to a handshake.

"*Bem-vinda*. Welcome. I've looked forward to meeting you." Luciana had the looks of a model and the poise of a diplomat's daughter.

"Thank you." I questioned her analytical ability but realized I was being sexist and deferred any judgment. "I look forward to working together."

Sam nudged me on to a young man with wire-rim glasses and a mustache. "This is Ed Yamato. He dug up the competitive data you asked for. He also keeps the computer alive."

Ed was more formal and shook my hand with a respectful bow of his head. "My pleasure."

"Mine, too. Thanks for the good work," I acknowledged his role in compiling the binder of background information. Ed nodded back in silence.

"This is Antonio," Sam introduced a man whose dark suit and dark hair were impeccably cut. French cuffs and monograms embellished his white shirt. "Antonio is from the Buenos Aires office; he's here to sell a new project to IBM-Brazil."

Antonio greeted me with a single cheek-to-cheek. "In Argentina, one is enough," he explained. "We are more refined than these Brazilians. Right, Sam?" He tossed his head toward Marcelo, Luciana, and Ed, who bantered back. I didn't understand the words, but recognized playful rivalry.

"Tonight, in Beth's honor, we'll set aside national pride," Sam told the group. "Grasping the differences between a Brazilian and an Argentine isn't a priority for this week."

"But next week…a quiz on the subject," Marcelo warned with a twinkle in his eye.

For me, South America had been one big bucket. The lively exchange made it clear that countries had different customs, languages, and styles of which their citizens were proud. Far from homogeneous, this continent enjoyed a diversity of which I had been ignorant. On the verge of asking for clarification, I was stopped by the bustle of a newcomer. Unruly curls poured over her shoulders and her woodsy perfume poured over me as she enveloped me in a hearty *abraço*. She squeezed my arms and touched my cheeks *three* times.

"*Aqui*! *Finalmente*! Welcome. I'm Sandra, Marcelo's... *esposa*," she pointed to her wedding ring. Then she proceeded to greet the others, knowing when to shake hands and when to touch cheeks once, twice, or thrice. What stymied me was second nature to Sandra.

"*Vamos*? Shall we eat?" Sam proposed before we could settle into bar chairs. I was famished and agreed without hesitation.

"*Vêm*. Come sit with me," Sandra insisted as the maître d' steered us to a heavy square table, set for eight.

An army of waiters in white jackets sprang into action. As one skinny young man held my chair, another attempted to take my pocketbook. "Don't worry," Sandra said, noticing my reluctance. "He'll put your bag on a chair with mine." She offered her bag to the young man; I set aside my paranoia and followed suit. A huge napkin, embroidered with the restaurant's logo, was spread carefully over our purses to protect them from spills.

We had barely settled into high-backed, leather chairs when I heard, "*Alguma coisa para beber?*" From Jaco's airplane tutorial, I knew the man with pen and paper was asking for the beverage order.

"Try a *caipirinha*," Luciana suggested, "our national drink." Experimenting with alcoholic concoctions had been a fun pastime with George until we transitioned to wine tasting. Feeling adventuresome, I ordered a *caipirinha*.

Next, the head waiter handed out enormous leather-bound menus. The first section listed carpaccio, *palmitos*, *muçarela de bufalo*, *casquinha de siri*—all unknown to me. Patiently, Sandra explained that the first was thinly sliced raw beef; next, hearts of palm; third was a large white ball of mozzarella cheese; and, finally, a spicy crab paste served in an open shell.

In my Boston apartment, *The Living Heart Diet* guided our daily intake of fiber, vegetables, and fish. George insisted on low-salt, low-fat, and low-calorie alternatives. I steamed or grilled, never fried our food. George would have shied away from raw meat and high cholesterol, but I asked for carpaccio.

For the main course, beef was the specialty. Entering the dining room, we had passed a gleaming grill laden with steaks, sausages, and sweetbreads. Huge knives were part of each place setting. Pictures of prize cattle hung on the walls. It was imperative to order meat. But which cut? The menu descriptions did not include Porterhouse or New York Strip.

Fatigue was setting in and I didn't want to think. "Sam, would you order for me? Just not too much." The table was spread with nibbles to accompany our drinks—cheese bread, olives, cream spreads. Despite my good intentions to stick to celery and carrot sticks, everyone insisted that I try each taste. I would be full before the main course arrived.

"Leave it to me," he offered. "How about a fillet mignon? How do you like it cooked?"

"Medium rare," I replied.

As Sam dealt with the waiter, I turned my attention to my tablemates. Goodwill and good humor compensated for different languages—Portuguese, Spanish, and English. When I asked Marcelo where his parents had come from, he dropped his utensils, made the sign of a bow and arrow, and tapped his hand to his mouth. The table broke into laughter. No translation needed. But to this day, I don't know if he was telling the truth, having fun, or a little of both.

With my second *caipirinha*, the first course arrived. Everyone insisted that I taste their dish and, as the guest of honor, I broke all my dietary rules. The ultimate violation was *quindim*, a dessert of egg yolks that Antonio called "heart attack on a plate." The send-off was *cafezinho* in a tiny cup with no resemblance to decaf.

Back in Room 1202, I collapsed into bed. I was woozy and the world was rosy. This morning, smog and smoke and squalor had repulsed me. This afternoon, I had been challenged to lead and challenged to listen. Tonight, people of different nationalities had welcomed me with camaraderie and culinary adventures. As we left the restaurant, some said goodbye with kisses on the cheeks and some with handshakes. After *caipirinhas* and wine, I did not worry about protocol. Instead, I relaxed and mimicked the diversity of my hosts. Perhaps I already had a little *jogo de cintura*.

Showtime

Early the next morning, wearing my blue suit, I watched a battered Volkswagen pull up to the hotel entrance. Sam crawled out and waved me over. The front passenger seat was gone, leaving the backseat unobstructed. Even so, my entry with bulging briefcase and high heels was far from graceful. Sam wedged in beside me. The driver tugged the door shut with a frayed rope, and we were off.

A collector's item in the States, the "original" Beetle was still ubiquitous in São Paulo. Maneuverable and inexpensive, these taxis could transport passengers and luggage across town for less than five dollars. Mark and Melody would have giggled to see Aunt Beth squeezed into the back of a *Fusca* en route to BomFarm headquarters.

After exchanging a few words with Sam, the driver inserted an unmarked cassette into the dash. Samba filled the cramped quarters as we jostled across the rough pavement and eased into a jumble of traffic. Avenida Paulista was bumper-to-bumper. The *taxista* skillfully inched between belching buses and other taxis. Fumes from diesel and natural gas engines poured through the open windows. My contacts burned in the palpable, humid air. Trying to be unobtrusive, I popped the lenses into my unwashed hands and stored them carefully in their plastic case.

"Something wrong?" Sam asked.

"Just my contacts. Your client will have to meet me with glasses," I bemoaned as I hooked the wire-rimmed frames around my ears.

"Don't worry. Glasses make you look intelligent and that's what BomFarm's paying for."

The tight quarters forced my thighs next to Sam's. Perspiration formed above my upper lip. Each bump in the pavement punctuated a closeness that made me uncomfortable. I needed Sam's company for my first drive across town to BomFarm headquarters, but I vowed to become more independent. I studied a card of numbers posted on the window. "How does this work?" I asked.

"That's the fare card," Sam explained. "Adjusting the meters to keep pace with rapid inflation is expensive. So the card translates the meter reading into the current fare."

"That seems easy enough. Could you help me change dollars to *cruzeiros* for taxi fares? Is there an exchange house near BomFarm?"

"You won't need *cruzeiros*. If you have to go somewhere alone, I'll arrange for Vicente or another driver. But usually you'll be with Marcelo or me."

"That's very kind, but I ought to be able to manage" was my halfhearted protest. The circuitous route did not boost my confidence about getting around São Paulo on my own. Maybe independence could wait.

The taxi veered off the main avenue, forcing me to push Sam against his window. "Sorry," I stammered.

"No problem." Sam was unfazed.

High walls and iron gates loomed on both sides. Big trees arched above; it was the only green I had seen outside of the Maksoud atrium. On the shady sidewalks, stray dogs sniffed for food scraps beneath wire garbage baskets perched on posts at the curbside. At the corner, a metal cabin, barely larger than a phone booth, sheltered a guard with a gun slung on his hip.

"This is Cidade Jardim, a residential enclave in the middle of the city. Politicians and wealthy families live here." Behind a wrought-iron gate I could glimpse second-story verandas on colonial style mansions. All was hidden behind Bermuda shutters, closed tight. German shepherds paced in the cobblestone driveways. No children were at play.

After numerous twists and turns, our taxi bolted onto the Marginal without the benefit of green directional signs or a cloverleaf ramp. I wondered which was worse, the slow crawl through city streets or speeding along a highway where the painted lanes were merely decoration.

A flatbed truck with wooden slats rumbled beside us. Scrolls and flowers decorated the sides. "*Jesus Vive*" and "*Confia em Cristo*" announced religious convictions. Across the median, another truck bore primary colors and a woman's name. These trucks did more than haul goods; they sang out and brightened the world.

In contrast, bland Fords and Volkswagens surrounded us. Missing were the plethora of luxury brands, sports cars, and expensive options. Sam explained, "Government policies encourage local production and discourage imports. Merely owning a car is a status symbol." He saw my business brain working and added, "In fact, cars increase in value in this inflationary economy."

"Wow, that's a switch. In the States, the first drive off the dealer's lot drops thousands off the value of a new car."

"I know. I learned that the hard way when I lived in Texas."

"In Texas?" I was surprised. "Is that where you mastered English?"

"No, my accent comes from Humphrey Bogart and my vocabulary comes from Daniel Webster." Before I could probe, Sam announced, "We're here."

As we stopped at a modern glass building, I glanced at my watch. The seemingly endless ride had taken just forty-five minutes; we were in plenty of time for our appointments. Sam clambered out and offered me a helping hand. I unfolded my tense body and snagged a stocking as I stepped from the Beetle. Squashed next to Sam with my briefcase on my lap, I had wrinkled my suit. Stepping into the office building, I felt a run crawl up my leg. I was a mess and my day had not begun.

Sam strode with purpose to the reception desk. His suit was wrinkled, too, but that didn't deter him. First impressions would be crucial today, but they would have to come not from bandbox looks but from a healthy dose of self-confidence and whatever trust we had built in twenty-four hours. Although I was frazzled, I was determined to prove to Sam that I was an asset to the project.

The initial hours at BomFarm were not so different from the first hours with any client. The executive floor was atop a skyscraper with panoramic views. Pretty secretaries guarded each man's territory. Our first activity was a series of meetings with key executives.

Isaac Goldstein, the bald "godfather" of our project, welcomed us into his book-lined office. His diploma from Harvard Business School declared him a Baker Scholar. The *McKinsey Quarterly* sat prominently atop his many papers, and spiral-bound reports showed his penchant for consultants.

On a blackboard that filled one wall, Isaac rapidly sketched BomFarm's organization chart. Having grown through acquisitions, BomFarm was a portfolio of regional divisions with centralized administrative functions. I scribbled madly to keep up with Isaac's rapid-fire explanations. Staying ahead of him would be no small feat.

As he talked, Isaac looked at Sam with complicity. I began to perceive an unspoken understanding between them. As Head of Strategy, Isaac was sure about a new direction for BomFarm, but he could not tell the CEO what to do. By hiring GCC, Isaac had found an elegant out. As Sam's coach, Isaac could influence the new strategy. But would the tacit partnership extend to me?

Isaac tested my ability to think on my feet. He pulled Michael Porter's *Competitive Strategy* from the shelf and placed it like a gauntlet on the desk between us. "Will you use his approach?"

GCC's training included Porter's analytical tools. "We'll definitely review the pressures that are changing the industry. However, we'll adapt the analysis to recognize the difficulty of getting reliable data on Brazilian companies." Marcelo had alerted me to this pitfall. "Bad data can lead to bad decisions, so we must move with caution, validating as we go."

Isaac looked toward Sam with a satisfied smile. "Have Marcelo come see me. We have a lot of information in-house." I thanked Isaac but knew that relying exclusively on data from the client could be dangerous. Hopefully Marcelo knew some neutral sources.

As we left Isaac, he said, "Good luck with Kipper. His bark is worse than his bite." Isaac chuckled as he shook my hand. "Again, welcome to Brazil. It is a pleasure to have you here." I had passed the first test. Isaac would be an ally—if I continued to meet his intellectual standards.

Next, we met the Chief Economist, educated at the London School of Economics. "Dr. Kipper, let me introduce Beth Bartlett, the Project Manager for the strategy project." Sam was formal and subdued.

"How do you do?" Kipper extended a hand from an imposing, bear-like body. We shook and he motioned us to take a seat. Above a walrus mustache, inquisitive eyes peered out through bifocals; the economist asked brusquely, "So, what *does* a Project Manager do?" Kipper's blinking made me squirm.

Instead of questioning methodology, Kipper was asking why I was here. How should I respond to a voice that harbored skepticism, not curiosity?

My eyes fell on the two posters of symphony concerts that hung behind his desk. "It's like being a conductor," I began. "I'll coordinate the efforts of everyone who contributes to the strategy and I'll keep things moving at the right pace."

"You make it sound like a nice job." Kipper was deadpan. I wasn't sure if the analogy worked, but I risked extending it.

"Well, the final result will reflect the efforts of all the musicians. In fact, I understand that you are a virtuoso in economics. We'll need to test our recommendations against the reality of this economy. I look forward to your contributions."

"In economics there are no guarantees, but I'll be glad to react to your ideas." Kipper lifted his phone and spoke for a moment to his secretary in Portuguese.

When he hung up, Sam added, "We plan to appoint a Strategy Steering Group, a small team of senior executives to review our work at key points. We hope you will be a member."

"On principle I have no objections, but I don't want to waste a lot of time in meetings." Kipper would reserve the right to opt out. "I cannot attend on Fridays. I work in Rio on Fridays."

Sam was quick to accommodate. "Doctor, we'll schedule so that we don't miss your valuable participation...or maybe we'll have to join you in Rio." Kipper did not react to Sam's jest, but instead turned to his secretary, who entered and handed him a brochure. He glanced at it and then extended it across the desk.

"If you like music," he said, "you must hear a concert at the Teatro Cultura Artística. Here is the program for this season."

"Thank you. That sounds lovely. But I fear BomFarm may keep me busy twenty-four hours a day."

"Only if the Project Manager is a taskmaster, or should I say taskmistress?" With a twitch of his mustache, he savored his own remark and then asked his secretary to escort us to our next appointment.

We were ushered into a huge corner office and straight toward the piercing blue eyes of Dr. Heinrich Mueller. Ramrod straight, he extended his hand without a flicker of a smile.

Sam introduced me as I took the rigid hand. "Dr. Mueller, this is Ms. Beth Bartlett from GCC-Boston. She will be directing our strategy project."

Mueller's "good morning" sounded like *"gutten morgen."* Germanic to the core, he controlled every muscle in his face and everything going on at BomFarm.

Mustering my confidence, I held his blue eyes with mine. "Thank you for choosing GCC for this important project. I am pleased to meet you and look forward to working with your executives."

"This company has high standards and GCC has promised us a first-class team. Welcome." His words had a steel edge; this was the man who had insisted that GCC add international consultants to the project. Sam shifted beside me.

"Ms. Bartlett has met Isaac Goldstein and Dr. Kipper. Both meetings went well."

Mueller nodded. "You will have everyone's full commitment." No doubt his executives had clear instructions to cooperate. Mueller's centralized authority was channeled through an unambiguous chain of command. I wondered if the CEO realized the degree to which this project would force him to share his power.

"Sir, what do you expect from this project?" It was a classic inquiry to understand client perspectives and likely demands.

"BomFarm is one of Brazil's most professional companies. We must adapt to changing conditions, but we must hold true to our historical values—the safety of our products and the trust of our customers." His unyielding spine inched even taller. "No plan that cuts corners or contradicts those values will leave my desk."

"I can assure you," I leaned forward slightly, "cutting corners is not a strategic option. Cutting costs, on the other hand, may be essential. We'll know better in a few weeks." Mueller stiffened slightly at my rebuttal, so I added, "As for product safety and customer trust, the strategy can reinforce those historical strengths." I jotted a note on my yellow pad. Too often company values were words in the minds of management instead of real attributes perceived by the market, but I didn't mention that to Mueller.

"Would you like a preview of this afternoon's presentation?" Sam redirected the agenda. I wanted to know more about the CEO's view, but Sam had deliberately put Mueller back in the driver's seat.

"Just the highlights," he replied, downplaying his approval of Sam's suggestion.

I wanted to dash through the presentation; after all, this was standard GCC material and I wasn't going to change it. Sam kept signaling for me to pause; each time, I held my breath and eyed Dr. Mueller's clean-cut head.

"Do you have any questions or concerns?"

"No questions," Mueller responded. I went on.

"Is our approach clear?" Sam inquired.

A simple nod from Mueller. "So far, yes."

"Do you have any suggestions?"

"Not at this time."

At the review's end, Mueller was thoughtful, "This is very professional but it is all new for this company. The men may not understand very well." Sam explained our plan for sequential translation. Mueller's face relaxed.

Let's leave while we're ahead, I thought and was ready to say thank you and goodbye. But Sam asked patiently, "Any other thoughts?"

Mueller was pensive. Sam waited.

"My executives have never had access to this type of information. It might confuse them." He paused, and then added, "I want to discuss your findings before you present them, as we did today. This is the right way to do things."

It was a courteous order, but an order nonetheless. One that made me uncomfortable. No client should filter GCC's work, not even the CEO. I opened my mouth to object, but Sam spoke first. "We'll be happy to do that, sir."

"Fine." Mueller was satisfied. "I'll see you at quarter to four; this is the first item on today's agenda." He dismissed us with a handshake, just slightly less rigid than the first.

We descended in the elevator in silence, but as we emerged on the ground floor, I confronted Sam. "You should not have agreed to his request," I insisted. "GCC makes impartial recommendations."

"Look, Bartlett, we are months away from making recommendations. Right now our priority is raising Mueller's comfort level with us, or perhaps I should say with *you.*" Sam kept going. "Remember, Mueller has never done anything like this. The only ones who tell him what to do are his shareholders. Embarking on this project is a giant step; we've got to ease him into it.

"Let's go get a sandwich." Sam led the way onto the sidewalk; broken pavement threw off suffocating heat. After picking our way along crumbled cement for a couple of blocks, Sam nudged me toward a glass door. "In here." The small mall offered cool air and a modest food court. "This isn't fancy, but it will be quick." We stopped at a self-service counter; the white Formica top was scarred but clean. Sam ordered two sandwiches while I claimed a spot at a rickety wooden table with equally rickety chairs.

Balancing our sandwiches and drinks on a flimsy cardboard tray, Sam arrived without mishap. He placed two Cokes between us and passed me a goopy tuna sandwich atop a napkin. "Sorry. We'll compensate at dinner tonight."

"No apology needed," I assured him. "Last night's feast will keep me going for a week. I'll order room service tonight. Don't feel you need to host me all the time."

"We'll see. Dinner is a long way off." Sam took a bite of his sandwich.

"Yes, and we have a major hurdle to cross before then," I added, thinking about the three senior executives I had just met. One brilliant and ambitious. One cultured and skeptical. One proud and reluctant to change. It would take all three to endorse a new strategy, but just one could derail it. "Did the morning change our game plan for this afternoon?" I asked Sam. "Will Isaac raise more methodology questions?"

"Unlikely." Sam was confident. "Isaac wants us to succeed. If he asks a question in the boardroom, chances are he already knows the answer. He uses that technique to look smart and request clarification for the others."

Sam's knowledge of his client impressed me and I wanted to give him some credit. "You were right about the sequential translation. Mueller liked that."

"He did. Just remember, crisp but not condescending. Short sentences will improve my translation."

"Speaking of languages, can I ask you something?"

"Depends."

"Where are you from? Brazil? Argentina? Texas?"

"Ah. Americans always ask that at parties. 'Where are you from?'" Sam bit into his sandwich, pausing for dramatic effect.

After a sip of Coke, he sang, "*No Soy de Aquí, Ni Soy de Allá.*" I had no idea what he was talking about. "I'm not from here; I'm not from there. It's the title of a song by Facundo Cabral." I did not recognize the name.

"But you must be from *somewhere*," I insisted, picturing the Bartlett family tree going back sixteen generations.

"Why?" Like a child's artless query, it made me think.

"I prefer the windshield to the rearview mirror. Life is out in front, not back where I've already been. I like to keep moving; roots are for trees."

I was proud of my family ties and disagreed with Sam. Yet, I sensed his bravado might be covering an unhappy past and wanted to avoid a sensitive subject. I back-pedaled. "I didn't mean to pry, but you can't blame me for being curious."

Sam glanced at his watch. "I'll make it short. I'm an Argentine with Russian blood, Jewish genes, and an American passport."

"Living in Brazil," I added to his litany.

"Living in Brazil," he echoed, and then rose from the table. "If I want to keep living here, we'd better get going."

I was dying to know more but we needed to return to the safe terrain of business. "Yes, I'd like to rehearse the presentation once more before the meeting."

"Your interpreter is ready. Let's go," he urged, stepping away from the debris on the table.

"Shouldn't we put this trash somewhere?" I got up and piled our dirty paper napkins onto the cardboard tray.

"Leave it. That's a job for someone who needs it." As we left, a boney brown figure in a limp uniform and flip-flops cleared the table.

At 3:45 sharp, Dr. Mueller stationed himself at my side at the boardroom entrance. No one entered without a formal introduction. If Mueller was displeased with a skirted consultant, he did not show it.

Isaac, the first to arrive, assured his boss that we had already met. He shook my hand professionally before choosing a chair beside Sam. With heads bent close together, they spoke in inaudible tones.

Next, a man arrived with a military bearing. A manicured hand extended from a crisp French cuff clasped with a ruby link. His sharply chiseled face did not reveal his reaction to me nor much else. Sergio was the head of the São Paulo division, the largest of six regions.

Next, Kipper's bulky frame filled the entrance. He gave me a knowing smile and said to Dr. Mueller, "I had the pleasure of meeting the young lady from Boston this morning. I am curious to hear what she will teach us this afternoon." Our morning meeting had not diffused all of his skepticism. I feared his veto could block our efforts as easily as his body blocked the boardroom door.

Behind Kipper came a man with protruding eyebrows that were like dark clouds over the canyons of his face. Trusted counselor of the shareholders, the lawyer rarely spoke. What would he relay about the lady consultant from the States?

Next, a high-strung man carrying a pile of papers under his arm gave my hand a perfunctory shake. Introduced as the Chief Financial Officer, Alvaro flaunted a Rolex that measured his impatience. Without wasting time on pleasantries, he sat down and started studying computer printouts. I doubted whether he would look up during my presentation.

The Head of Production and the Head of Technology arrived next. Their rumpled brown suits and unobtrusive entrance suggested that they fell outside the inner circle. They sat together and, I was sure, voted together.

Last to arrive was a dapper man in a fine Italian suit, Hermes tie, and highly polished shoes. He greeted Dr. Mueller with deference, and then bowed and raised my outstretched hand to his lips. "Miss Bartlett, it is an honor to meet you. Hélio da Silva, at your service." The whole room was attentive to his theatrical entrance. "The young lady from the Varig lounge has shown up again." The man from *Esquire* had reappeared as BomFarm's Head of Human Resources. Red-faced, I stood speechless as he basked in the limelight.

Dr. Mueller did not permit Hélio's smug drama to last. He called the meeting to order and introduced me in Portuguese. Beside me, Sam scribbled a few words so I could catch the gist—"disciplined," "important," and "full cooperation."

In some ways, the windowless room felt familiar. The large oval table and rolling armchairs would do justice to any boardroom in the States. The screen and projector were up-to-date models that were commonplace in American companies. There were pitchers of water with glasses, ready to refresh parched presenters. The set was familiar, but the characters were foreboding. In lieu of bland faces, conservative ties, and look-alike suits, I saw ethnic features, strong personalities, and European fashions. The men waited—expectant, doubtful, impatient, skeptical, curious, and amused—for me to begin. If I failed to deliver a strong performance, they could easily become *Twelve Angry Men*.

After the Executive Committee meeting, Isaac nabbed Kipper in the corridor. "What did you think of Ms. Bartlett's presentation?"

Last week, Kipper had complained, "This strategy project better not be a waste of time and money. GCC promised a Senior Partner; now they're sending a young woman instead!"

To shield his pet project, Isaac had defended the unknown consultant. "GCC claims she is one of their best Project Managers, and her resume looks solid. Among other things, she's a Harvard MBA."

But Kipper cut in, "That's no guarantee. I'd be more impressed if she were from Chicago or MIT." Kipper valued rigorous analytical training over case studies. Furthermore, he didn't like consultants; he preferred to work with people he knew and trusted.

"I bet she lives in a bubble, convinced of her own superiority and ignorant about anything outside the United States," Kipper had predicted a few days ago.

But now after hearing the American, Kipper wanted to be fair. "The methodology was pragmatic and she explained it clearly. Expecting everything to work according to her plan is a bit naïve. Obviously, she hasn't lived in a country where debating politics and reliving soccer games take priority over business. Still, it was a good presentation and she treated us like schoolchildren only once."

"That was awkward," Isaac agreed. "She did start to lecture us, but Sam got things back on track with a more palatable translation."

"Sam is quick," Kipper conceded. "And I like Marcelo. He's a good economist."

"And our guys trust them," Isaac reminded Kipper.

"That's true," Kipper had to admit. "No doubt the men can help us. The question is whether this unsophisticated American can add value. Miss Bartlett is smart and means well. I just have the impression that she has a lot to learn."

Sam and I were jubilant driving back to the office. We had launched the project without letting each other down. Sam's humor had broken the ice and brought life to my dry presentation. Everyone was intrigued, if not on board.

At the office, we pulled Marcelo away from the computer and went to celebrate over *caipirinhas*. My stomach was growling. No longer shy with my GCC colleagues, I gobbled up peanuts and fried mozzarella.

By telling Marcelo all the details, we relived our roller-coaster day. "I really used your lessons on economics and *jogo de cintura*," I said, grinning.

"Another lesson?" Marcelo offered, rising out of his chair.

"No. No." I didn't want to create a scene in the bar, though secretly I wanted to dance with him again. Instead, I focused on our next steps. Sam and I would interview executives while Marcelo worked on the numbers with Luciana and Ed. "Isaac is really keen on a competitive analysis. Can we develop a model to understand how the competitors make money?" I asked Marcelo.

"Of course he can. Marcelo's a whiz." Sam was in a good mood.

"If we don't have numbers, we'll make them up," Marcelo bragged. Sam shot him a look of warning, but the cat was out of the bag.

"I hope you're not serious." I didn't want to be gullible if they were joking, but I suspected there was truth in Marcelo's remark. Bob White's words echoed like an alarm bell: "This BomFarm contract is a real plum. Make sure the Brazilians don't mess it up. São Paulo is a new office. These guys haven't had training yet; they're not going to be up to standard. Try to instill some discipline down there." As the Partner-in-Charge, Bob would demand quality work. And, even more important, men like Isaac and Kipper would know if we invented data.

"You *are* joking, aren't you?" I asked hopefully.

"Just joking," Marcelo insisted. "Don't worry."

When Sam hastened to assure me that Marcelo was kidding, I smiled. But my radar would be working.

The next day, Isaac invited me to dine at his home. "Bring Sam along to translate," he joked. "Let me tell him how to get here." I passed the phone to Sam and admired the ease with which he switched to Portuguese.

Unfortunately, Sam's sense of direction did not match his skill with languages. We got hopelessly lost trying to find Isaac's home in Morumbi, the hilly suburb where mansions lay ensconced behind fortress-like walls. After serpentine curves and false turns down unlit streets, Vicente finally found the number we were seeking beside a heavy, barred door.

In response to the doorbell, a speakeasy window slid open. Sam exchanged words with a muffled voice. A bolt slid back. The iron door creaked open. An armed guard guided us up steep steps to the massive main doors, where we were handed off to a woman in a crisp maid's uniform. She guided us through the slated entry hall to oversized couches under high ceilings. As we sank into the plush seats, a male servant approached, bearing a tray of cool drinks and hors d'oeuvres.

I tried to sit up straight on the deep, cushy sofa, wondering if my boarding school days had prepared me well enough for the evening. Abbot Academy provided more than a first-rate education. The academy turned adolescent girls into proper young ladies by insisting on chapel every morning, six-eyelet tie shoes, and dressing for dinner. By the end of four years, I knew how to "lower left and raise right," serve lemon meringue pie, and participate in intelligent conversation.

"This is a bit intimidating," I whispered to Sam, lest my voice carry in the cavernous room. "I'm glad you're here."

"I'm glad he's here, too," echoed Isaac's jovial voice. He came around the corner in a batik shirt hung loosely over casual trousers. We jumped up to greet him. "Next time, no business suits," he chastised Sam and me. "Consider yourselves at home. Myra will join us in a moment."

"Meanwhile, I'll show you around. Bete, Sam, right this way." All my life I had corrected anyone who called me "Betty" instead of "Beth." By adding a vowel to my name, Isaac made it Brazilian; even though it sounded strange, I didn't object. For him, I was now Bete instead of Ms. Bartlett.

With obvious pride, he stopped in front of the paintings and sculptures, lit with perfectly placed spots. Art history classes had introduced me to Michelangelo and Monet. Trips to Boston's Museum of Fine Arts had deepened my love of Renoir, Homer, and Copley. Isaac pointed to works by Portinari, Cavalcanti, and Amaral—all Brazilian artists who were new to me. "And for my Argentine friend, here we have Botero and Berni."

"You could start your own museum of Latin American art," Sam said with admiration that stopped short of being obsequious. Isaac smiled proudly.

I also wanted to sound impressed but not awestruck. "What a beautiful collection." In fact, I could not imagine owning so many valuable originals. "I am totally ignorant about Latin American art, but this is a lovely way to be introduced."

"Go to the Art Museum on Avenida Paulista, just a few blocks from your hotel." Isaac turned to Sam. "You must take her; she mustn't miss it."

Before we could promise to go, a rich alto voice announced Myra's entrance. "Oh, and you must go to the Biennial Exhibition. We'll take you some weekend." Her African caftan conveyed a relaxed mood with a hint of formality. Her necklace and earrings hung prominently; the dramatic coral and shells were not beachcomber's fare.

Her expansive figure and flowing garb enveloped me in the ritual of kisses to the cheeks that I now knew were *beijos*. Next, she swept us out to the patio where city lights stretched to the horizon, lost in an eerie yellow haze. At our feet lay a kidney-shaped pool, its underwater lights glinting off elaborate mosaics. Padded lounge chairs promised repose. Our voices provoked the watchdogs behind the garden wall. A sharp bark announced, "Stran-gers. Stran-gers." Soon a volley of replies pierced the night air.

The barking evoked memories of Sue's golden retriever chasing the children's bikes or pestering the squirrels in the tall backyard pines. Rusty was a playful pet, not a guard dog to be feared. I felt a tinge of sorrow for Myra and Isaac, who needed walls and security systems to protect their home. It seemed unnatural to live behind a barricade. Perhaps the cost of owning original art was too high; perhaps Sue was the rich one, possessing painted treasures on construction paper that no one would try to steal.

My musing stopped as Myra ushered us back inside. Large wooden panels had been slid open to reveal a grand table covered with linens of white lace, formally set with crystal, china, and silver. Isaac gestured to the chair, held out by the male servant. "You sit here, Bete, across from Sam." Isaac and Myra took their places at each end of the table, which could have seated ten or more.

As the guest of honor, I was served first. The maid with the starched apron approached with an elegant platter. With silver tongs, I carefully transported a slippery scallop shell onto my plate. I managed to land it, without dropping its seafood filling onto the Oriental carpet below. My Abbot training paid off.

As the meal progressed, Myra and Isaac explained each delicacy and its wine complement. Conversation ranged from museums to ancestors. Isaac was a second generation Brazilian, his grandfather having emigrated from Russia. Myra had uncles in Brazil, Israel, New York, and Los Angeles. They were both world travellers and were shocked at my parochial life.

"So, this is your first time abroad?" queried Myra.

"Except for Canada, which hardly counts," I confessed.

"How are you adjusting?"

"Oh, just fine. I am enjoying so many new things: sights, people, food. By the way, everything was just delicious. Thank you."

The maid was handing me strong coffee in a demitasse cup when Isaac asked, "Have you had a bowel movement since you arrived?" My demitasse stopped in midair. Had I heard correctly or was I tipsy? Nonplussed, I looked across at Sam, hoping he would come to my rescue. "You know," Isaac went on, "it is very important to have regular movements when you are travelling. Strange food and water can make serious trouble for your body."

I envisioned the parade of food moving through my digestive tract: seafood appetizer, cream of leek soup, steak au poivre, soft cheese with jam, and mousse of maracujá. All awash in fine wine, all proceeding to one destination.

My coffee cup jangled against its saucer. "I guess I have iron intestines," was the best I could muster.

"You're very lucky, then," Isaac said straight-faced. "I have terrible constipation when I travel."

"Where are you going on your next vacation?" Sam asked Myra. Smiling at him across the expansive table was my thanks for steering the conversation to safer ground. Soon thereafter we bid our hosts farewell at the massive front doors. The guard accompanied us out through the security gate and waited while we tumbled into our waiting car.

As Vicente pulled away, Sam mimicked Isaac perfectly, "Bete, have you had a bowel movement?" We burst into uncontrolled laughter.

"I nearly died. Some things Abbot didn't teach me."

"Who's Abbot?" Sam asked. His ingenuous question made me realize he felt like an old friend, despite our few days together.

"Abbot's not a *who*, it's a *what*," was my silly response. "Abbot Academy was my boarding school."

"You went to boarding school?!" he chortled as if I were from another planet.

"What's so funny?" My attempt at being indignant turned into more giggles. "Abbot couldn't teach me to answer Isaac's question because Abbot taught me that you never discuss bodily functions at the dinner table."

"Welcome to the real world, Beth Bartlett." It was too dark to see his face, but I sensed a playful gleam in his eye.

Early Saturday Morning—August 30
Maksoud Plaza Hotel

Dear Diary,

I survived the first week! I am exhausted but happy. I've lived and breathed nothing but BomFarm and I'm ready for a break. Today we're going to the beach.

The launch was successful. I've overcome tremendous odds, thanks to the GCC-Brazil team. They've worked as hard as I have.

Working in two languages is fascinating. Sam translates back and forth, giving me time to frame my next question. His distinctive, broadcaster's voice makes me sound smarter than I am. I already understand quite a lot of Portuguese. Many words are almost English (cliente, produto, hotel); in others, "ção" replaces "tion" (comunicação, educação). On top of that, the Latin I learned from Mrs. Dee is helping me to conquer: Veni, vidi, vici.

Brazil is a paradox—a land of haves and have-nots, without much in between. Many people have chocolaty skin; others have the features of parents or grandparents from Russia, Italy, Germany, Poland, Japan. No one looks dull here, except me!

To my surprise, I've been accepted by Sam. He's been a team player and a wonderful host. He's made working in a foreign culture fun instead of fearful.

Cuidado (Caution)

"You don't know Brazil until you know her beaches. We're going to Guarujá tomorrow and you must come."

Sandra's invitation for an outing was a double-edged sword. On one hand, I wanted to escape the concrete jungle; on the other, driving to and from the coast would consume several hours on top of the time spent at our destination. Besides, I was not a beach person. Around Boston, muddy tidal flats edge icy waters. Fine sand is scarce. The rugged shores and the Protestant work ethic discourage unproductive sunbathing.

"Thank you for including me, but probably I should stay here and prepare for next week," was my initial response.

"Beth, work can wait," Marcelo buttressed his wife. "Don't be a prisoner. Live a little." I started to weaken.

Sandra reached out to another ally. "Sam, come with us. If we go as a foursome, no one will be left behind working and no one will feel guilty. Please."

When Sam joined their ranks, I caved in and agreed to go.

On Saturday morning, I dug my running shorts, t-shirt, and sneakers out of my suitcase. Like the jump rope, they had lain untouched since my arrival. So much for good intentions to exercise. These could serve as beach garb, but my bathing suit, baseball cap, and nautical duffel bag were back in Boston.

I ventured downstairs to the hotel's gift shop. Full of Brazilian crafts, carved agate, and framed butterflies from the Amazon rain forest, the store had a small rack of beachwear. I thumbed through the bikinis, each one smaller than the last.

"What size?" A salesgirl offered her help.

"Medium," I replied tentatively. "One with more fabric." I splayed my hands over my chest.

She pulled out two hangers and offered them confidently, "Try these." In one hand were strings of neon orange; in the other were pocket-size triangles of flamingo pink. She accompanied me to a fitting room no bigger than a phone booth and pulled the curtain shut.

Neon orange, no way! I thought and set the tangle of strips aside. Reluctantly, I pulled off my shirt and tied the pink halter around my neck. It covered my small breasts and protruding nipples, just. Next I stripped to my underpants and tugged on the bikini bottom. It looked like decorative trim over my conservative briefs. I rolled down the top of my panties and studied my reflection. My summer tan lines had faded and a lot of white skin was being exposed for the first time. Thanks to rigorous exercise and eating habits back in Boston, my small waist and flat stomach looked pretty good. The shock was on my backside. The triangle covering my tailbone left my toned buttocks on display. I was proud of my fit body, but had never shown it off in such skimpy garb. *I'll just keep my shorts on*, I decided.

As if reading my mind, the salesgirl spoke from beyond the curtain. "Here's the perfect *kanga*, if you want a coverup." Into the fitting room she passed a sarong with pink hibiscus blossoms. Knotted above my breast, the translucent fabric provided modesty and intrigue. Feeling much better, I opened the curtain and posed for her approval. In a twinkling, she completed my outfit with a broad-brimmed sunhat, colorful beach sandals, and a tote bag adorned with a tropical toucan. "You'll be the prettiest girl on the beach," she assured the classy woman in the mirror. *She's a good salesman,* I thought, *but my pale skin is no match for the* brasileiras' *coffee-colored curves.*

Feeling a little self-conscious, I stayed in my getup, signed the accusing charge slip, and hurried to dump my old clothes in my room. Ready just in time, I headed back downstairs to meet my friends. A battered Parati, a Volkswagen hatchback, was parked in the opulent hotel entrance. The beat of samba spilled from open windows as Marcelo and Sam smoked on the sidewalk. Seeing me, Marcelo whistled and Sandra waved, unperturbed by her husband's harmless flirting. The men snuffed out their cigarettes; we piled into the VW and sputtered away from the formal luxury of the Maksoud.

Everyone from São Paulo was headed for the coast. We crawled, bumper-to-bumper, past roadside stands selling *coco* and *palmitos.* Straws poking out of whole coconuts promised relief for the thirsty. Long stalks contained hearts of palm, a delicacy that was criticized by environmentalists back home, but for which I was developing an expensive taste.

We crept behind huge painted eyes on the bus ahead of us. The three-foot-wide expression was fuzzy beneath grime left by belching exhaust. As the bus inched forward, black smoke poured in our open windows, stinging my eyes. I dug into my bag for my contact case. Once again, those bothersome lenses were coming out. Before long, I would forsake contacts entirely.

Sharing the backseat with Sandra was refreshing after a week with businessmen. She didn't seem to mind the ubiquitous blend of pollution and cigarette smoke. As miles passed, the breeze snatched her thick curls from her headband. The more unkempt, the prettier she looked.

"Anybody hungry?" she asked, unwrapping homemade coffeecake. She passed huge slices to Sam and me and then fed chunks to Marcelo from behind, grinning at him in the rear-view mirror. Both were oblivious to the crumbs. She had so much warmth and joie de vivre that it was hard to believe that she had a master's in biochemistry. In my vocabulary, "serious" and "studious" had been synonyms. No more.

Finally, I smelled the salt air. In New England, "coastline" meant slippery kelp hissing in the tide's ebb and flow, transient pools filled with hermit crabs, starfish, and mussels. Guarujá was about to transform my concept of coastline!

We pulled into a sandy parking lot. On a Hawaiian vacation, "beach" had meant footprints in pristine sand, classy cabanas, and drinks served in a fancy glass. Guarujá was about to transform my concept of beach!

As we tumbled out of the car, a barricade of vendors' stands blocked any view of the ocean. Marcelo secured four rusty beach chairs, two tattered umbrellas, and a lean young man to plant them in the sand, anywhere we chose.

Choosing a spot was easier said than done. After squeezing through a small crack between two vendors' carts, we emerged onto the hot sand, already dense with parasols, bodies, and beach towels. We wove through a patchwork of pudgy pale tourists and browns of every hue. We dodged energetic paddleball players and skirted sleeping sunbathers. Without trash barrels asking beachgoers to "Pitch In," our path was strewn with bottle caps, plastic cups, and lotion bottles. At sunset, municipal workers would collect the debris and earn enough to feed their children.

Eventually, our umbrellas and chairs were installed where we could watch the parade along the water's edge. Flesh and curves and laughter flowed past. *Bum bums* swayed rhythmically as the girls strolled by. Their bikinis revealed even more than mine. "That's 'dental floss,'" Marcelo explained smugly in perfect English. Round and sensuous, the buttocks were sexy, even to my woman's eye. The men were just as provocative in skimpy suits that covered, but did not hide, their private parts. Sexuality charged the midday air.

The food offerings were just as sensual. Homemade food and drinks were hawked by a stream of vendors. Beachgoers did not need to tote Playmate coolers or bags of Lay's potato chips.

A black woman moved barefoot among the beachgoers, her stained apron pressing against her dark legs. On her head she balanced a package wrapped in white paper. Soon we were feasting on her fried mozzarella sticks and cheesy *pão de queijo*.

Other vendors offered trays of sandwiches, bowls of watermelon, and strings of coconut. Singsong cries mingled with the splash of waves and children's laughter.

"*Água…suco…coco*."

"*Espiga de milho*."

"*Sorvete…Baunilha, Chocolate, Morango*."

As they passed, Sam asked me, "Would you like a cold drink? How about corn on the cob? Ice cream—vanilla, chocolate, or strawberry?" A young man approached, weighed down by battered Styrofoam coolers on each shoulder.

"*Caipirinha…Caipirinha*."

Sam waved him over. "*Quatro. Bem mexidos*."

With a big grin, the barman slung the coolers to the ground. He pulled out four plastic cups, ready with sugar and sliced *limão*, the lemon-lime hybrid that gives Brazil's national drink its distinctive flavor. With a wooden pestle, he mashed the sugar and fruit until Sam nodded approval. Then he poured a clear liquid from an unlabeled bottle.

"That's *cachaça*, the cane sugar alcohol that makes Brazilians so good natured." He passed *caipirinhas* to Sandra and Marcelo.

"It also works on Argentines," Marcelo countered, "and maybe gringas." We held the sticky cups high in a toast, before leaning back in our beach chairs.

Sipping the heady drink, I forgot the diesel fumes and the tiresome traffic. I forgot to question whether the food was safe. I was no longer shocked by the skimpy bikinis. I did not wonder if the children were wearing sunblock. I watched with pleasure as the young men showed off with soccer balls and volleyballs. I let the beach sounds lull me into an unproductive trance. And when my glass was empty, I pushed it into the sand beside my chair, without hunting for a trash barrel.

After a snooze, guilt drove me to ask, "Does anyone want to take a walk?"

Marcelo, lost inside the rhythms of his Walkman, could not hear me. Sandra, mid-chapter in a good book, declined. Sam pushed up and brushed the sand from his bathing suit. "Sure."

Stretched before us was a hubbub of splashing children, paddleball games, Frisbees, and vendors—a far cry from Madison Avenue's photos of unspoiled sand. We threaded our way among sandcastles and bodies lounging at the waterline.

"It's more crowded than the city," I observed.

"Guarujá is the beach closest to São Paulo. In the northeast, the shore is isolated with spectacular sand dunes. More your style."

"My style?"

"Graceful and natural."

Feeling anything but natural in my bikini and sarong, I downplayed his compliment. "I guess I am pretty natural, compared to the women in Brazil. 'Rustic' might be a better word. The cosmetic industry would go bankrupt if it had to depend on me. As for graceful, well...I would have been pretty awkward without all your help this week. Your doubts about me were justified."

"Doubts? What doubts?" Sam played dumb.

"The GCC grapevine is pretty good. I know you opposed my coming to Brazil. Now I understand why."

"OK, the truth. I was *very* worried. The wrong person from Boston would have derailed this project. But, you've been a hit with BomFarm. Something clicks. They trust you."

"Take some credit yourself. It's been a team effort. You warm them up so that I can ask the tough questions."

"You *do* ask tough questions, but you're not threatening. They have really opened up." Sam caught a Frisbee that was headed straight for my head and sent it back to the teenager who launched it. "*Cuidado!*"

"Which means?" I asked.

"Be careful." Then, he picked up where he left off. "Yesterday, I was talking with Isaac. He said, 'We don't understand it. She's a woman. She's a Yankee. She's a consultant. She had everything going against her, but she has won us over.'"

"There were so many strikes against me?"

"Oh, yes. No one expected this to work."

"Isaac must be relieved."

"Isaac and a lot of other people, including me." Sam grinned.

"Well it's working because *we* are doing something right. I would have flopped without you. Thanks for your coaching."

"Don't sell yourself short. On Friday, Hélio asked me, 'Where's Santa Bethania?'"

"Me, a saint? Why?"

"Because you hear all their confessions. Hélio claims no one hides anything from you."

My cheeks burned. "Well, I'm no saint. I'm just a novelty that has taken everyone by surprise." *Including myself,* I thought.

We walked without speaking for a while. With Sam at my side, I felt calm. "You know, I was really afraid of coming to

Brazil. That may surprise you but it's true. You've erased that fear and let me focus on getting the job done. Thank you, Sam."

"It's been my pleasure. I'm learning a lot and having fun."

"Next week won't be so heavy. I'll be more independent. You'll have more time to yourself."

"To do what?"

"To do chores or just relax at home."

"You haven't seen home." He sounded gloomy. "My apartment is pretty bare. When I got divorced, I left a decorator's showcase full of expensive knickknacks and imported wallpaper where I couldn't put my feet on my own coffee table. So when I moved to São Paulo, I stuck to the basics—a bed, a table, and a TV. No locks on the door. Nothing to own and nothing to own me."

I recalled his singing, *"No Soy de Aquí, Ni Soy de Allá."* Within his bravado, I detected loneliness. Wondering what the consultant's façade concealed, I was torn between safe ground and curiosity. I settled on caution, the new word I had just learned: *"Cuidado."*

"I think we've gone far enough." Sam accepted my verdict and we started back. I looked for a safer subject. "How do you like living in São Paulo?"

"São Paulo is great for business, but not a great place to live. Right now, it suits me fine. It's helping me begin again." Slowing his pace, Sam began his story of restlessness and new beginnings. His adoring mother had weaned her fatherless son on the movies. "Zorro was my favorite. I love scoundrels with redeeming virtues." He dropped out of high school and pursued adventures that took him from Bolivia to Texas.

Upon returning to Argentina, Sam married a model and had two children. "I was rich one day and poor the next. My wife couldn't stand the roller coaster and left with the kids; they're in Buenos Aires.

"A good friend threw me a rope and gave me a job at GCC. Before long I escaped Buenos Aires with the mandate to open the GCC office in Brazil. How do I like living in São Paulo? I like it. I am unknown and anonymous, free to recreate myself."

The floodgates were open and I was not sure how to close them, except by retreating into the world of business. "Well, I don't know about reincarnation, but your work this week was first rate."

"Thanks." Sam seemed pleased. "Maybe it's a step in the right direction."

Fortunately, we were approaching Marcelo and Sandra, who had started folding the beach chairs. Rescued from intimacy, I waved to our friends and Sam called out to Marcelo, "Looks like you guys are packing up. We got here just in time."

"It's time to head back," Marcelo confirmed. Lazily, we gathered our bags and began the trek to the car. While the men returned the chairs, couples ambled nearby with arms wrapped around backs and waists. Watching them, Sandra remarked, "You went a long way. Sam never walks. You're a good influence," she teased.

"No, I'm just a good listener," I murmured self-consciously. Sandra glanced at Sam with fondness, then smiled and did not press for more.

Driving home, everyone was quiet and sleepy. Sam dozed beside me in the hot car. A source of strength all week, this man had a vulnerable side. A window had opened in the professional wall between us...and neither of us had slammed it shut.

I had listened. Nothing more. I had simply been Santa Bethania. I was drowsy and tempted to put my head on Sam's shoulder. Instead, I kept my distance from this complex man with his complex life. I leaned against the hard metal of the Parati and closed my eyes. Adrenaline drained away, leaving me limp for the first time since boarding the plane, eons ago.

Edgy Encounters

Sunday brought a little downtime and a chance to be alone. Perched on the edge of the bed, I dialed George early and found him home. After some pro forma questions about his week, I asked cheerily, "Are you racing today?" George crewed on David's sailboat. On weekends, they exchanged their high-powered jobs for high-powered boats.

"We are; it's a Chowder Race." Compared to highly competitive class racing, a Chowder Race was fun. The name came from the soup. Different types of boats were assigned handicaps, allowing a mix of large and small, modern and classic boats. After the race, all the sailors socialized over bowls of clam chowder at the sponsoring yacht club.

George and I had met during a Chowder Race. David and Sue were engaged to be married. I was to be the maid of honor; George was to be best man. "You've got to meet him before the wedding," Sue had insisted. Convinced that George and I would make a perfect couple, she tried to fix me up with David's best friend. Always too busy, I resisted for several months. Finally, to get my sister off my back, I agreed to crew on David's sailboat one Sunday fifteen years ago. In the cramped cockpit, George and I bumped into each other; our hands touched while hauling in the sheets. Afterwards, on the porch of the Eastern Yacht Club, George had raised his glass, "To a great race. May there be many more." It was a favorite memory. We started dating and quickly fell into a comfortable foursome with Sue and David. Everyone expected us to get married and there was no reason to disappoint them. George was successful, supportive, and a good companion. Sue had chosen well.

Although George seemed very far away, talking about the Chowder Race helped to repair the frayed bond between us. "Well, have a good race; I hope *Sea Spirit* wins."

"Our chances would be better if you were here; we are short one crew member. We need you." Although he hadn't said so, I decided he missed me. Perhaps it was time to share something about Brazil.

"I feel like I'm on another planet. Things are so different here."

"How's the project going?"

"Way better than I expected. Everyone here is working super hard and it's paying off. The kickoff was a big challenge but it went really well."

"It better be worth the sacrifice." Bitterness was still there.

"So far, it's a fantastic experience. I have so much to tell you when I come home next weekend." I was looking forward to my first interlude back in Boston; I hoped George would share my enthusiasm for Brazil when he saw its positive effect on me. "The week will fly by; I'll be back in no time." To preempt any more objections, I rushed on. "So, I'll see you next Sunday. In the meantime, win the race and eat some chowder for me."

"We'll do our best; I need to get going."

I tried for a soft landing. "I'm glad I finally reached you. It's not the same talking to your answering machine. Your voice sounds good."

"Yours, too. Be careful down there."

"I will…and I'll be home soon."

Goodbyes were said and a receiver fell into a faraway cradle. For the first time, I admitted that feeling shortchanged had become the norm in my marriage. I pondered the conversation with my husband. Like our sex, our phone calls were mechanical and infrequent. Discharged with respect, both satisfied obligation but left me unfulfilled. Articulating that reality, if only to myself, made me uncomfortable. Surely I was being unfair.

I held the phone on my lap and wondered what had triggered my discontent. I pictured George and David boarding the launch, laughing with friends. Their fair hair and preppy looks were beginning to mellow, but they had the confident strides of men not quite forty. One a doctor, the other a fund manager, their easy smiles and shiny BMWs spoke of success. Life was good and "mid-life crisis" was not yet in their vocabulary. However, the past week made me see the idyllic scene with fresh eyes. I saw WASPs with a limited view of the world and how to live in it.

Last week, when joking around in the office, Marcelo had called me a "WASP." At first, I had been upset. Now, I could smile at his shorthand for my very different background. Being White, Anglo-Saxon, and Protestant vested me with values and assumptions that were deep roots, hidden from the flower. Being transplanted had exposed the whole.

Even so, calling my family members "WASPs" and being annoyed with George felt like betrayal. To shake my discomfort, I set the phone on the nightstand and picked up the papers waiting for my review. Marcelo and Ed had compiled financials about BomFarm and the competitors. Luciana's neat penmanship filled the margins with English translation. Figuring out whether and how these companies were making money kept me busy all morning. Distracted by my growling stomach, I searched the room service menu for a salad. Shocked by the prices, I was converting *cruzeiros* to dollars in my head when the phone rang.

"Hello, Beth Ann? Beth Ann Bartlett?"

"Yesss," I hesitated, pretending I didn't recognize the deep voice.

"Jaco here. May I invite you to lunch?"

"To lunch," I said stupidly before composing myself. "What a surprise. Where are you?"

"In the lobby. I hoped I would find you here." Goosebumps covered my arms. "If you don't have other plans, I hope you'll join me."

I closed the room service menu. The clock radio read past noon and I was still in my pajamas. "I would enjoy that, but I need to get dressed. I've been lazy this morning," I fibbed.

"I'm glad of that; lazy is good. It's early for a Sunday, but I hoped to preempt another invitation. What if we meet downstairs at 1:00? The Maksoud buffet is excellent; there might even be some Brazilian specialties you haven't tried yet."

"That sounds like fun. I'll see you in a half hour." Leaving work strewn across the bed, I raced to the shower. Soon, I was descending in the glass bubble with a bird's-eye view of the lobby bar. Trying to appear nonchalant, I glanced down and spotted Jaco waiting.

When I rounded the elevator bank, he was approaching. I extended my hand. He pulled me into the realm of his spicy cologne. "By now, you know our custom," he teased, "so I will greet you properly." One clean shaven jaw touched my flushed cheek, then the other. Stepping back, he looked me over with admiring eyes. "Brazil seems to agree with you."

"My first days have been great," I said, glowing and dying of curiosity. "How did you know I was here?"

"A lucky guess. Usually, Americans stay at the Sheraton, but you weren't there so I checked here." I was flattered that he had hunted me down. "Let's get some lunch." He steered me toward the atrium restaurant. As the hostess seated us at a table for two near the bubbling indoor fountain, she discreetly removed the card that read "Reserved."

After guiding me through the bountiful buffet, Jaco asked about my impressions of Brazil. Without inhibition, I poured out the week's events. Jaco listened and laughed at my bafflements and discoveries. It was fun to be so spontaneous. Time flew.

"Would you like a coffee?" he asked.

"*Um cafezinho? Sim, por favor*," was my cocky reply. Jaco raised his eyebrows in mock surprise. "My Portuguese vocabulary is still pretty limited...mostly about food. That's the fault of my first teacher." My open palm acknowledged him. His strong hand encircled mine and lingered for just a moment before he raised it to catch the waiter's attention. With his thumb and index fingers, he indicated a demitasse cup, then signaled two...all without a word. His speaking with only his hands seemed worldly and sophisticated.

As we sipped the strong brew, guilt set in. Apart from robbing time from work, the long lunch with Jaco had stirred up complex feelings. Brunching with him in the sunlit atrium on a Sunday afternoon had been more romantic than any Saturday night tête-à-tête with George. This glamorous man had sought me out and was lavishing attention as if I were desirable. While he behaved like a gentleman and listened with interest to my stories, his eyes caressed me from across the table. He wasn't just sexy; he made *me* feel sexy in an intoxicating way. Playing hooky with Jaco felt naughty; my common sense said, *Start your retreat.* "Thank you for this delightful break, but I must get back to work. I have a lot to prepare for tomorrow."

His steady gaze revealed neither rancor nor disapproval. "Thank you for joining me on a moment's notice." He signaled for the check. "I've been wondering how the lady consultant survived her first week in our macho culture. Obviously, there was no need for worry." Like an old friend, he engendered my trust; apparently I was the only one who was lustful. The waiter set the bill beside him.

"Won't you let me charge this to my room?" I reached for the bill in its leather case. His hand covered mine and stayed there. His warm skin against mine quickened my pulse.

"Bethania, by now you must know that a lady doesn't pay in Brazil. You insult me by asking." His lighthearted scolding left me helpless.

I conceded easily but sincerely, "I'd just like to thank you for being so kind." A little sheepish, I slid my hand back into my lap. He inserted his credit card into the folder without checking the bill.

"Thank me by seeing me again. Call me before you go back to the States next weekend." Another business card came out of his jacket. "Now you have no excuse," he teased.

We strolled back through the lobby. I paused, but this time I didn't extend my hand in farewell. As he kissed me on each check, he chuckled, "I knew you were a quick study."

"*Tchau*, Jaco." I headed for the elevators with deliberate, measured steps.

"*Tchau*, gringa. Remember to call me." His bass voice reverberated in the marble lobby. Heads turned. I paused, smiled goodbye, and kept walking, hoping no one noticed my shaky knees.

Sunday Night—August 31
Maksoud Plaza

Dear Diary,

This book was to be a travel log, but tonight, I'm like a teenager who scribbles her secrets. Saying that is silly because I only went to brunch, but what a brunch!

I was alone, recharging my batteries when Jaco found me! I was suspicious at first, but figured meeting in the hotel atrium was harmless. There was no need for concern; he was a gracious host. What fun to share my week with him!

Shedding the posture of a sexless consultant, I felt like a woman. Jaco's calling me "Bethania" was an emotional embrace. Am I playing with fire? Is this unfair to George?

Speaking of George, I finally talked to him today. It went OK. When I go home, I wonder if I can describe this amazing experience without provoking his criticism! Oh, well, I'll cross that bridge when I come to it.

Tomorrow I must brief Bob White. Leaving him out of the loop too long will just make it harder to engage him later.

Sam. Now there's a mystery. Tough on the outside, but with a soft heart. Although he resisted my coming, he's backed me from day one. No, that's not right. He's been at my side from day one. There's a difference.

On Monday morning, a dark figure with suspicious, furtive eyes was hunched in one corner of the office. Seeing my alarm, Sam explained, "Paulinho is our new office boy. 'Boys' are a business necessity in São Paulo. They are the human substitute for reliable mail and updated technology."

Marcelo confirmed that Brazil's *reserva do mercado de informática* limited imports of computers and technology equipment. While intended to stimulate domestic production, the policy slowed modernization of many processes. Thus, countless young men ran errands, stood in lengthy lines at banks, and waited in offices for their next chore.

"But why Paulinho?" I couldn't fathom why this pathetic person was sitting in a first-rate consulting firm.

Unabashed, Sam confessed that Jenny, the wiry young woman who cleaned the office, had insisted that "GCC needs a boy and my brother just needs a chance." Sam liked Jenny; she was outgoing, determined, and occasionally industrious. Sam had hired Paulinho without an interview or a background check.

Paulinho's first tasks were washing the dirty mugs and making coffee. "*Açúcar, bastante.*" Paulinho spooned lots of sugar and a little instant coffee into a big mug for Sam.

"*Para mim, forte e sem açúcar,*" Marcelo wanted his coffee strong and without sugar. Paulinho heaped black granules into a cup and filled it halfway with water.

"*Para mim, chá.*" Ed requested. A cup with a teabag appeared.

"*Café com adoçante por favor.*" Coffee with artificial sweetener arrived shortly for Luciana.

I had been avoiding Paulinho, but no longer had any excuse. "*Café puro por favor,*" I said awkwardly. Tentatively, he approached with black coffee.

When our cups were empty, he washed them and cleaned the bathroom sink. He sealed the coffee and sugar tightly to discourage the ants and cockroaches that had had free rein before his arrival.

Next, Paulinho sat down and waited. A few hours later he prepared another round of coffee. By late afternoon, he'd mastered the quirks of five demanding consultants.

At 4:00, I fidgeted with my fourth coffee of the day. Mary, Bob White's secretary, had assured me he would call at 3:30, but Bob was predictably late. My work papers lay in a semicircle on the conference table; I was ready for any question. Bob's rudeness made me mad and had drained my enthusiasm. When the phone finally rang at 4:30, I was terse. "GCC-Brazil. Beth Bartlett speaking."

"Hey, Beth. How ya doin'? How goes it in the jungle?" Bob's snide opening increased my aggravation.

"I'm glad you finally called. I was beginning to wonder if you'd forgotten about me."

"Oh, no, Mary's been bugging me for the past hour; I just couldn't get people out of my office. Now you have my full attention."

"How much time do you have, Bob?"

"I've got another appointment at 5:00, but I can push it to 5:15." I would be lucky to keep his attention for thirty minutes.

"Then we have no time to waste. If you read the courier package, you know more or less where we stand."

"I've got your stuff right here." The unmistakable sounds of ripping open an envelope and shuffling papers fueled my frustration. Reviewing the material now would consume precious minutes that might prevent discussing issues.

I was tempted to lash out, but feared this might be my only chance to get much-needed input from the project's Senior Partner. I decided to let it go. "I'll summarize where we stand; then we need to discuss two issues: the numbers and the shareholders."

"Go ahead."

"Bottom line: We had a great launch with lots of senior management support. Last week, we interviewed about twenty-five executives, outlined the data we need and how to analyze it. You have copies of the interview notes and our analytical plan." I jumped to my first concern. "Getting data is going to be a challenge. There is very little public information. Many companies are privately held; data about their performance is not available."

"That sounds like a smokescreen to me. I bet the data is out there and people are too lazy to get it."

"You're misjudging the situation. Marcelo, the economist on the team, is well-connected to government sources. Isaac, the strategy head, is giving us everything BomFarm has, but he has confirmed that there is very little reliable data about other companies. We're brainstorming about ways to approximate, using assumptions and cross-checking with the numbers we do have."

"I should have sent Roger Doyle with you." Bob's response angered me. Another consultant would not help, least of all Bob's protégé.

"Believe me, Roger will be helpless here. Getting information requires contacts and cultural affinity." I knew Roger would alienate everyone, but I dared not be so blunt. "Marcelo will get whatever data there is. I just want to set your expectations. We'll have to rely on judgment, intuition, and others factors, not just the numbers."

"Beth, don't go soft on me. I warned you about needing rigor down there."

"Rigor is not the only way to serve BomFarm. Brazil is not the United States."

"Look, Beth." Bob was getting annoyed. "I've developed strategies for Fortune 500 companies with operations around the globe, without relaxing GCC's standards. This project will be no exception."

"I'm not lowering the bar, Bob; I'm just suggesting that the game may be different. Think of it this way. American football is played in very few countries; to most of the world 'football' is a completely different sport." Brazilians took great pride in the speed, skill, and stamina of their *futebolistas* (soccer players) when compared to American football players. After just one week, I could see that business dealings had some parallels. However, fearful of antagonizing Bob, I dropped the analogy and pursued a more neutral tactic: "BomFarm is a large national company, not an international company. BomFarm is headquartered in São Paulo, not in New York or London. This is a different culture and a different context. When you come down, you'll see firsthand."

"By then, it will be too late. The diagnosis will be done. I'll see if Roger can join you next week."

"Bob, you'll waste time and money. At least read what I sent and think about it first. Please."

"I'm sure Roger's the answer. Besides, he needs international exposure. Listen, I've got to go rehearse the Parker Medical team. I'll let you know what I work out with Roger. Talk to you soon." He hung up.

Cut short, I was furious. Bob was Partner-in-Charge in name only; he hadn't committed his time or intellect to the challenges I was facing. Bob cared more about Parker Medical and Roger Doyle.

"That's the last time we prepare a briefing package for Bob White!" I exploded as I banged the receiver down. Sam and Marcelo emerged from behind the office partition; they had heard my end of the conversation.

"*Calma, Bete, calma,*" Marcelo said, motioning to take it easy.

"Bob wasn't too helpful," Sam presumed smugly.

"Not at all!" I fumed about his threat to send Roger Doyle. "Any new player, even the right one, will upset the applecart. But Bob's the Partner-in-Charge; he has final say," I whined.

"Why don't you call Harvey?" Sam asked simply.

"I can't end-run Bob," was my immediate response.

"Why not? Harvey gave you this assignment and wants you to succeed. If Roger will derail things, speak up."

"But I hate to make waves. What if I antagonize Bob?"

"Beth, you know what's going on; Bob doesn't. Believe in yourself. Be willing to take a tough stand. After all, which is worse—antagonizing Bob or antagonizing BomFarm?" If Sam were me, he would be calling Harvey already.

"Let me think by myself." The two men disappeared back behind the partition. With my elbows planted on the table, I massaged the tight knot in my right shoulder. Maybe Roger really could help. I had quickly learned to decipher Brazilian financial information; so could he.

I replayed the past week—my camaraderie with Sam and Marcelo, my warm reception by BomFarm. Would Roger really destroy the trust we were building or was I just reluctant to share the spotlight? Was I being intellectually honest or simply fearful that the magic would end? In conflict with myself, I fought off the tears that were blurring my vision. *I must do the right thing for BomFarm*, I thought. *If only I knew what the right thing is.*

Unable to stay holed up, Sam snuck over to his desk, picked up his magician's wand, and came quietly to my side. "Do you want me to dial Harvey's number?"

"What if Bob is right? What if we do need Roger Doyle?" My face was scrunching up and my nose got hot.

Sam put his hand on my shoulder. "Listen to your gut. Trust your instincts. You've met Isaac and Kipper and the others. How do you think they will react to a green MBA lording it over them?" Silence while his words sank in.

"Of course I don't want Doyle, but going behind Bob's back is dangerous," I sniffed.

"Listen. Bob hasn't dedicated time or energy to make this project a success. You have. As Project Manager, you have the right—in fact, the obligation—to gain support from the most senior level of the firm. If Bob is too busy to provide it, then you need to get it from someone else." He was making a strong case. "Just tell Harvey that you need a second opinion about the best way to ensure a bulletproof case in a country without a lot of public data."

"That sounds like a good angle. I would be asking for his advice without criticizing Bob."

"Yes, but don't be afraid to take a strong position. You have a unique vantage point because you are the one who knows the client. Doesn't the GCC vision say, 'The Client Comes First'?" I was still hesitant.

"Let's role-play," Sam cajoled. "I'll be Harvey." A playful twinkle accompanied his waving the wand; at any moment he would say "abracadabra" and my worries would vanish.

Harvey gloated as he hung up the phone. *I knew she could do it! I just had to throw her into the pool to get her to swim.* He buttoned his London Fog and cocked his beret at an angle. Before heading home, he set out to find Bob.

"Sorry to interrupt," Harvey had poked his head into the conference room where the Parker Medical team was rehearsing. "Bob, can I see you for a minute?"

"Keep going," Bob told the consultant at the projector. "I'll be right back." Hiding his annoyance, he asked, "What's up?" once the two men were alone.

"I got a call from Brazil, from Beth."

"I just spoke to her myself. The launch went well." He'd show Harvey he was on top of things. "She's concerned about the numbers, though, and I've got a solution. I'll send Roger Doyle down to buttress the team."

"That's what I want to discuss. Beth says qualitative and cultural factors are as important as the numbers in this case. She's probably right." Bob crossed his arms and kept quiet. "Trust is key. They've accepted Beth but the situation is delicate. Sending Roger looks like we're second-guessing Beth and the local team."

"We are second-guessing them. Obviously, the Brazil office is weak when it comes to analytical skills," Bob huffed.

"I don't know if they're weak or strong, but they do oper-ate in a different environment. Beth seems impressed with this Marcelo Pereira." Bob looked doubtful. "It's premature to send Doyle down there. Let the Brazilians collect and analyze the data. Beth promised to send their work up for your review. Roger can work with you behind the scenes."

Bob's face tightened. The Partner-in-Charge should call the shots, but Harvey had made a project decision without consulting him. On the other hand, Bob wasn't too keen about BomFarm in the first place. He was doing Brazil a favor. The project wouldn't affect his bonus or his partnership position, so it wasn't worth a fight. Besides, he needed Roger around for Parker Medical, not off in some God-forsaken place.

"I'll accept the decision you made, but I still have my reserva-tions. Just remember this conversation a few weeks from now, when they get into trouble and we end up sending Roger to the rescue."

"That shouldn't be necessary. When Beth comes back next week, she'll bring all the data. You'll have a chance to make nec-essary course corrections," Harvey assured him. "I'll let you get back to your rehearsal."

"Harvey, next time, talk to me before you interfere with one of my projects."

"Request acknowledged." Harvey touched his beret and started to shuffle toward the door. Bob thought Harvey looked like Columbo, but doubted whether he had an investigator's nose for problems. Time would tell. Bob turned back to the conference room, where he had plenty to worry about with Parker Medical.

On the sidewalk below, Harvey fingered the bowl in his pocket to be sure he'd remembered his Briar pipe. He rarely over-ruled the firm's Partners, but this time he had his reasons. The São Paulo office had been approved on a trial basis. The BomFarm project would determine whether to invest more or pull out of the turbulent, unpredictable market.

He cared less about the success or failure in Brazil than about promoting a woman to Partner. GCC had pioneered the hiring of women MBAs, but none of them had achieved senior status. Now, several other consulting firms with female Partners had gained a competitive edge in recruiting the best junior talent. *We can't afford to fall behind,* Harvey thought. *Beth is my best candidate, and Brazil is the perfect place to test whether she has what it takes.*

She had revealed an impressive command of a complex client situation. "BomFarm has a strong skeleton, a good reputation, and professional executives, but its muscles are weak. It lacks clear direction and the vigor to be a top-flight competitor. Numbers will show the way, but analysis won't unlock BomFarm's potential." Beth had expressed her convictions instead of just asking for advice.

He'd never heard such confidence in her voice. Managing alone in Brazil was forcing her to stretch. Harvey put the pipe in his mouth and chewed on the stem. Time would tell whether GCC stayed in Brazil; in the meantime, he had bought some more time for Beth to demonstrate her leadership and solidify relationships at the top of BomFarm. Antagonizing Bob was a small price to pay for grooming the next Partner.

Desafinado (Off-Key)

Traffic was gridlocked en route to the Bomforte Foundation. Vicente closed the windows and locked the doors. I sat alone in the backseat as we worked our way through the intersections on a now familiar thoroughfare.

We neared one spot that I thought of as the "family corner." Nothing more than a barren, dusty patch with one stunted tree; a place where mothers nursed their babies while the older children begged. Here, a few days ago, I had seen my first street child, just inches away. Compassion and denial mixed in my heart as nameless kids peered into the sealed windows of our locked car.

Now, a youngster looking for a sympathetic face pressed his nose against the window. I had seen this boy before. Sam called him Gorginho. His black, six-year-old eyes sparkled, defying his poverty. This child would never know Harvard or Yale, but could have run circles around many who would. Dirt and rags could not hide his bright mind. He invented ways to earn coins: juggling dirty tennis balls one day, dribbling a battered soccer ball the next. His devilish smile pierced the glass, making him irresistible.

Pretending to read the newspaper, I avoided his eyes. Vicente shooed the child away. The driver behind us passed a pack of gum through a cautious crack.

The traffic light turned green and we moved a bit closer to my interview with BomFarm's majority shareholder. "You should go alone," Sam had insisted. "His English is excellent and he'll be more candid if I'm not there." Although I owned shares in GCC's pension plan, I certainly did not consider myself a shareholder and could hardly imagine owning a whole company. As Vicente stopped in front of an iron barricade, I missed Sam.

After finding the unobtrusive call box, I announced myself. A guard unbolted a small gate, accompanied me to the elevator, and punched a secret code that shipped me to the designated floor. I was released into a stark hallway, with a lonely desk, a phone receiver, and the cold eye of a security camera. Letters in bas-relief told me I was in the premises of *Fundação Bomforte*. White walls were broken only by unmarked doors leading to nameless places. I felt like Alice after falling down the rabbit's hole and was startled when a door opened.

"*Bom dia, Senhora Bartlett.*" A stylish young woman in high heels and a tight skirt led me into a sterile room where white leather couches blended into white walls. "*Café?*" came the predictable question.

"*Sim, obrigada.*" At least the coffee would not be white.

The door clicked shut, leaving me in a windowless room bigger than the GCC-Brazil office. More unmarked doors. No telephone. No clock. A huge marble coffee table held the only concession to visitor comfort—a heavy stone ashtray.

Next to it was an elegant brochure describing the Bomforte Foundation. I glanced through it, hoping to be more informed before meeting my first Bomforte. The Bomforte family owned a coffee plantation, a sugar refinery, a bank, an insurance company, BomFarm, and a goldmine. This portfolio generated wealth, some of which flowed to the Bomforte Foundation. The glossy bilingual pages portrayed educational, cultural, and artistic works, none of which adorned this room.

A doorknob turned. Quickly, I prepared to rise, replacing the brochure with one hand and gripping my briefcase with the other. False alarm. It was just a maid in cap and starched uniform with coffee. She poured from a silver pot into a two-inch cup on a tiny saucer with a miniature spoon. "*Açúcar ou adoçante?*" she asked.

"*Puro*," I said, a little too brusquely. The maid hesitated, surprised at my refusing sugar or sweetener. "*Obrigada*," I added to assure her that she had understood me. Bowing slightly, she disappeared, taking the tray that would have broken the room's monotony.

I sipped and waited.

Time passed.

I sipped again, draining the tiny cup. Drinking a Brazilian *cafezinho* does not take long.

No sound penetrated the walls. Quiet and sterile, the chamber became ominous. Through which door had I entered? Disoriented, I was tempted to seek an escape route. I shivered, unsure whether my goosebumps were from the cold air blowing from the vents or from my apprehension.

The power of the Bomforte family pressed upon me through the whiteness of these walls. I felt small and insignificant. I scolded myself for being cowed. There was no interrogation or torture waiting beyond these doors. In fact, I was the one who would pose the questions, assuming of course that Mr. Bomforte would not cancel my appointment.

The forty-five-minute wait felt much longer, but finally a door opened. The sexy woman summoned me and I followed her tapping heels down a gleaming hall to a corner office.

Comb marks grooved the jet-black hair of the tan, fortyish man standing behind the massive desk with a polished ebony surface. Its expanse distanced him from visitors, but did not block the fresh smell of a recent shower.

I extended my hand assertively. "Beth Ann Bartlett." Introducing myself was unnecessary, but the formality was a semblance of cordiality and control.

"Marcos Bomforte." A tepid handshake was adorned with a monogrammed cuff and a gold watch. The expensive timepiece had nothing to do with being on time.

"Coffee?"

"No thanks, I had some while I was waiting." My pointed remark elicited no apology.

He motioned to a seat across from his own backlit, leather chair. The nearby sofa and easy chairs were reserved for friendlier moments.

"So, how do you find the company?" he asked pointedly.

"BomFarm deserves its fine reputation." A positive opening. "The management team is professional and capable. Everyone has been most cordial and welcoming."

"Mueller expects his executives to cooperate; it sounds like everyone is toeing the line. I'm not convinced about consultants; we've been pretty successful without them. But I respect Mueller, so I approved his request. Why do you think he called you in?" Without mincing words, Bomforte was already on the offensive; I scrambled to assert myself by dealing with his objections.

"Being skeptical about consultants makes sense. Good managers of good companies can produce solid results without outsiders...when business conditions are familiar. However, new operating conditions bring new rules of the game; profit dynamics can change overnight. Brazil's recent economic measures will threaten many companies. Your executives are smart, but they realize that they don't have all the answers. As I see it, Mueller wants to complement BomFarm's expertise with GCC's experience in stable markets. Together, we can define how to make money under changing conditions."

"I'm all for making money, but profits are second to the Bomforte values: integrity and ethical dealings. We've been ethical for the past fifty years and we'll be ethical for the next fifty. Our customers can count on all our companies through Brazil's ups and downs...most especially on BomFarm, where people's health is at stake."

Should I remind Mr. Bomforte that people could only count on a company that was still in business? That felt too aggressive, so I tried another approach. "A company can be ethical while being competitive. In fact, the best competitors serve their customers better than anyone else. Our recommendations will build on BomFarm's traditional strengths; product safety and customer trust must be part of a winning formula."

"It sounds like you've been talking to Mueller." There was a glimmer of satisfaction before Bomforte went back on the attack. "Just remember, this is not an American corporation. I dislike impersonal corporations obsessed with today's earnings. Remember, a family owns this company. My children will inherit what I leave behind."

Three teenagers—one boy and two girls—beamed from a portrait on his credenza. Inheritors of the Bomforte riches and reputation. Should I ask about them? Marcos had made me wait and had come out swinging. My time was running out; I decided to forego the pleasantries.

"At GCC, we recognize that myopia and short-term pressures drive too many companies. BomFarm exhibits a healthy balance between family values and professional management; as Project Manager, I will strive to respect that balance." Now... on to *my* questions. "Let me turn your question around. Why do *you* think your executives asked for GCC's help?'"

"You're here because Isaac is a good salesman. Goldstein likes consultants, new ideas, and challenging debates. Sometimes, he overdoes it, but maybe the intellectual stimulation is beneficial. Expensive but beneficial. Hopefully we'll get some return on our investment." Still confrontational.

I pushed back. "Your expectations are quite low. I am confident that we will exceed them. By strengthening BomFarm, we will repay our fees many times over." I pressed on, "To achieve that, we'll need to capture the opportunities and neutralize the threats facing BomFarm. What do *you* see as the opportunities and threats?" I still hoped for some substance to guide our efforts.

"I'm paying you to tell me just that. Come back with your findings and then we'll exchange ideas." Bomforte pushed his chair back, signaling the interview's end.

"I look forward to that conversation." I was disappointed at his unwillingness to share his perspectives, but was determined to end on a positive note. I eyed the credenza and added, "Seeing your beautiful children, I understand why you want them to inherit something of which you are proud."

With a glance at the photograph, Marcos Bomforte let a fleeting smile soften his stony face. My tactic had worked, so I asked, "How old are they?"

"Paula is a sophomore in college, Marcio a freshman, and Luiza is still in high school. Unfortunately, there's not a business major in sight." As Marcos turned, his eyes softened for the first time. Then, he shrugged, as if to reshoulder his cool demeanor. "My secretary will show you out."

The clicking heels led back through the antechamber. The marble coffee table was clear. The brochure was in its designated spot. No trace remained of my long wait. The white room was a shield. Perhaps just crossing the barrier had been an accomplishment, but I felt like a failure. Meeting a flesh-and-blood shareholder was humbling.

With relief, I spotted Vicente and his taxi at the curb. After the sterile offices, the smells and sounds of São Paulo consoled me. Driving back to the office, I watched for Gorginho. Maybe I was inspired by the Foundation's brochure; maybe I was struck by the counterpoint of street kid and shareholder; maybe I was learning to be a citizen of São Paulo. I pulled a ragged bill from my wallet.

As usual, the family corner was bottlenecked. As usual, we inched up to the traffic signal. But, something was different. The park was empty. No mothers nursed beneath the trees. No kids begged at the car windows. Anxious, I asked Vicente about the children, "*As crianças?*"

He hesitated before replying, "*A polícia.*"

Once, I had seen a TV documentary about police raids on the slums in Rio. The report had disturbed me then; my stomach churned now.

"*Por que motivo?*" I wanted to know the reason.

"*Não sei. Não sei.*" Vicente's voice caught and he shook his head sadly. Unable to explain, the stocky driver who was my protector seemed small and powerless. I fingered the limp bill and stuffed it angrily into my pocket. The light turned green; we passed the intersection; more traffic squeezed into our space. Yet, the corner was empty.

Wednesday Night—September 3
Maksoud Plaza

Dear Diary,

I'm down and overwhelmed.

Gorginho is gone, maybe rounded up. This morning, I refused to look into his eyes. I feel guilty and depressed about his disappearance.

I blew it with Bomforte. Being on the defensive, I missed an opportunity. Besides, I was afraid to cross the business line. Asking him about his children from the start might have changed the tone of the conversation. Why can't I think like a Brazilian?

I feel vulnerable about the numbers. If Marcelo makes up data, will I know it?

Sam is making me nervous. I appreciate his support, coaching, and company, but he's ever present. What is driving him?

As the week flew past, Paulinho's duties expanded to include making photocopies. GCC policy required that we copy everything sent to a client and that we leave no papers in the hands of strangers. In Boston, this was easy; a speedy in-house Xerox machine spat out reams of paper. Not so in Brazil.

Down the block was an antiquated copier, capable of producing one fuzzy page at a time. Paulinho yo-yoed between the office and the corner where the sluggish out-of-date machine churned out page after page. The lead time for translation and copying robbed us of opportunities to rewrite, making it essential to get it right the first time.

In addition to his weekly pay, Paulinho received luncheon tickets. Each coupon could be exchanged for a basic meal at snack bars and restaurants. On some days, Paulinho ate rice and beans; on others, he traded the tickets for cash on the black market. With cash in his pocket, Paulinho walked with a slight swagger.

Soon, Paulinho was delivering documents to BomFarm and joking with the other office boys waiting in line at the bank. As nourishment replaced starvation, muscle broadened his shoulders and a spark lit his dark eyes. A strut replaced his shuffle. Jenny was right. Paulinho just needed a chance. Sam had given him one.

On Friday morning, Marcelo arrived late but jubilant. "I got them," he announced, holding up an envelope triumphantly. "Four tickets, sixth row, center."

"Great work." Sam slapped him on the back. "Beth, we're going to send you off right. We're going to the Jobim concert tonight."

"Who's Jobim?" I blurted out a simple question; Marcelo's eyes widened at my ignorance.

"Antonio Carlos Jobim, the great Brazilian musician!" Marcelo crowed like a carnival barker. I knew Mozart, Bach, and Beethoven, but not Jobim. My musical world was dominated by the key of C and four-four time.

Bethe Lee Moulton

"Jobim is the father of bossa nova," Sam explained. "Surely you know 'Girl from Ipanema.'" I did. "Jobim has played in Carnegie Hall." *Well then, he must be worthwhile,* I thought.

For me, a concert meant Boston's Symphony Orchestra—musicians in seats assigned by Haydn, playing scores of dead composers, under the baton of a man in tails and with his back to the subscribers. The well-heeled audience listened politely, hushing anyone who dared to clap between movements.

With a piano at center stage, the São Paulo concert hall looked normal enough. But when the stage lights went up, it was transformed. Marcelo and Sandra joined the standing ovation that greeted a lumpy man in a rumpled suit. Unpretentious and warm, his smile bathed the waiting audience; his artistry flowed off the stage to embrace his listeners.

Without pretense, he took his place at the keyboard. He caressed the keys and a samba rhythm woke the soul of the instrument. Next his growly voice crooned the unique sounds of Portuguese lyrics.

After the opening solos, three sirens entered stage right. The tropical color of flowing gowns swayed with the rhythm of bossa nova. Harmony washed over me, putting me inside the music and the music inside me.

Some songs were romantic; some were nostalgic; some were wistful. Even the song titles were musical: *"Desafinado"* ("Off-Key") and *"Samba de Uma Nota Só"* ("One-Note Samba"). Here were classics that were not classical. It was a journey to new places, riding a wave of emotion born of music.

Like opera sung in a foreign language, these mysterious poems were beautiful but veiled. I relished being immersed in an artistic realm where my intellect took a backseat to my emotions.

The last song, *"Águas de Março,"* opened with unexpected plops. Then, the incessant rhythm built to a crescendo, a pulsing stream of harmony. Sung in English and Portuguese, "Waters of

March" celebrated the small and big of life with equal weight and joyful reverence. Like every tropical shower, *"Águas de Março"* stopped as quickly as it started, with a few playful drops.

The crowd thundered to its feet, begging for more. My hands stung with applause. And, yes, raindrops moistened my cheeks. Never again would I have to ask, "Who's Jobim?"

Back to Massachusetts

"I'll take you to the airport," Sam insisted.

"I'll be fine with Vicente," I countered but didn't convince him.

After checking in, we lingered over coffee. "Stay here. I'll be right back," Sam said, vanishing into a shop. He returned with a grin and a package. "A little bit of Brazil to take home."

I opened the package; it was a cassette tape of Jobim. My nose prickled. "Thank you, Sam. This music will remind me of these remarkable days. I am leaving with a sense of a job well done, or maybe I should say 'well begun.' Anyway, I can't thank you enough."

"No, I thank you. I've learned a lot; you're intelligent, professional, and you really know how to manage a project. Hurry back. I want more."

"Don't worry. I'll be back. The project is barely off the ground. There will be bumps in the road, but teamwork will get us through the tough times. Keep things on track while I'm gone, OK?"

"Yes, ma'am," Sam gave a mock salute and we headed toward passport control. I joined a long line of outbound passengers. Sam watched from afar until an officer stamped my passport; my exit was official. I waved once and walked down the concourse, resisting the temptation to look back.

Being a Saturday night, business class was sparsely populated; the empty seat next to mine meant the luxury of time alone. Once I was airborne, a gin and tonic unleashed my fatigue. For two weeks, a city of contrasts had saturated my senses, intellect, and emotions. The sharp stench of smog, the sunken face of poverty, the sweet taste of papaya, the off-beat rhythm of samba, the warm intimacy of *abraços* were all now part of me. Bold personalities and unexpected behavior had tested me...and I had passed, or at least I thought so. I reclined my seat back, closed my eyes, and let tears of relief and exhaustion roll down my cheeks.

I didn't expect to see George at Logan Airport; like most business travellers, I came and went without fanfare. But there he was. The unexpected show of affection raised my hopes for a positive homecoming.

On our balcony, I inhaled the crispness of a beautiful fall Sunday. Crews were practicing on the Charles. I heard the clap of coxswains marking the stroke and watched the eight oars sweep in unison. The nutty aroma of gourmet beans drifted from my spotless kitchen as George ground fresh coffee. Phone in hand, I sank into the padded deck chair.

Sue answered on the first ring. "Good morning, sis."

My run-of-the-mill hello was met with an enthusiastic welcome. "Hooray. You're home. I'm so glad. I can't wait to see you. Can you guys come for dinner? I've got a tuna casserole in the fridge." Given the cascade, you would think I'd been away for two years instead of two weeks.

"Sue, I'm dying to see you, too, but we'll take a rain check. I've been flying all night and," I smiled up as George handed me a mug of coffee, "my hubby and I have some catching up to do." George looked pleased as he plopped into the chair next to mine.

"It sounds like you've got your priorities straight. I'm envious of you two lovebirds. I promised the kids we'd go pick apples this afternoon, so I'll be thinking of you when I'm climbing up some ladder." It was classic Sue, relishing the season and being a perfect mom.

"Pick some for me. I promise we'll come get them next weekend."

"OK. That gives you a whole week to make up for lost time," she razzed, no doubt imagining George and me frolicking in bed without a care in the world. Probably Sue thought my marriage was like her own, mellowing into "happily ever after." Cheerily, she added, "Thanks for letting me know you got home safely. I won't keep you from George."

"It's good to be back. Say 'Hi' to David and the kids. See you next weekend."

"I thought you'd want to see Sue today," George said as I hung up.

"Marblehead can wait. Right now, I want to be with you." I was nervous but determined to find my way back to married life. Jogging by the river would help me shift gears. Having a good run, side by side, followed by a shower, would set the stage if George was in the mood for sex, something usually reserved for weekend nights. Having sex with George sooner rather than later would help patch up our rift and ease my transition back to Boston. So, although my eyelids were heavy and I was limp, I forced myself to ask, "Want to go for a run?"

"Sure. The weather's perfect," George agreed.

"I'll be lucky to do three miles; I haven't worn sneakers since I left," I confessed.

"Another strike against Brazil." George was religious about his daily workout and expected me to be the same. "It's time to get back in the groove," he teased as we headed to the bedroom to change. I stripped off my travel clothes and donned my running shorts. Already in his trunks, George eyed me in the bureau mirror. He liked athletic women. "Let me see if you still measure up," he pulled me to him, my bare breasts pressing against his chest. His masculine hands massaged my back as he pulled me close. "That run will have to wait."

He stripped off my shorts and then his own. He pushed me onto the bed and entered me with an urgent hunger, driven by the need to possess. While I had hoped to ease into intimacy, George needed to dominate and own the moment. Without any foreplay, this coupling felt territorial and savage compared to the mechanical sex of recent months. This was raw fornication; George was staking a claim.

His groans stopped, he withdrew and flopped on his back next to me; his eyes were closed after his release. To deny the sense of desolation I felt, I resisted the urge to roll over; instead, I draped one arm across his chest and begged sleep to suppress the disappointment in my heart.

When I woke from my nap a few hours later, George was in good spirits. He'd been for a run and was dressing for his shift at Mass General. "Why don't you come over at dinnertime and we'll grab a bite to eat in the cafeteria," he proposed. "Sunday nights are unpredictable; the ER might be empty or it could be packed. I'll call you later to confirm whether I'm free."

"Sure. I'd like to join you. There's a lot to share." Talking over a plastic tray in the bustling hospital would be easy. Conveying my adventure in a public place would keep it superficial and factual. "Meanwhile, I'll settle in."

With a perfunctory goodbye kiss, George was out the door and I was alone in our spotless, quiet apartment. Despite my intentions to immerse myself in Boston life, Brazil kept intruding.

When I unpacked, the smell of stale tobacco filled the neutral air of our bedroom. I quickly stuffed the clothes into a plastic bag before the odor could permeate the room. The cleaners would freshen up the rumpled purple dress, but chemicals would not erase the memory of Jaco's admiring looks.

The simple task of opening the mail evoked comparisons. A flood of solicitations had come. On top of the pile, George had left an itemized list of last year's tax-deductible gifts. A scrawled note read, "Same as before." The March of Dimes. The Red Cross. Habitat for Humanity. The United Way. Save the Children Federation. Following instructions, I wrote five checks; I licked five stamps. Instead of seeing letterhead and return envelopes, I saw Gorginho begging on a street corner. Faceless charity felt different this time. Watching Sam transform Paulinho's life had changed my perspective on doing good.

I pulled my passport from my bulging briefcase; I would store the blue booklet out of sight until my next trip. My hand fell on the cassette that Sam had given me. Happy that George was elsewhere, I dug it out, ripped off the cellophane wrapper, and popped the tape into our stereo system. Bossa nova flowed over the Oriental rug and leather furniture. Syncopation and spongy Portuguese reached out to console me, but not even Jobim could fill the uninvited void.

With a samba beat still in my head, I preceded George down the hospital cafeteria line that evening. On a single tray, he combined my food with his and made sure that my Caesar salad with dressing on the side, my strawberry Jell-O, and tap water did not push the total cost over the daily meal allowance for medical staff. Seated near the cashier, George exchanged nods with many uniformed medical staff. All kept moving. No one stopped to shake his hand, let alone give him a hug.

Interrupted by frequent paging over the intercom, I started to relate the sights and sounds of São Paulo. George seemed more annoyed than interested. Trying a different tack, I used neutral business jargon to describe BomFarm, but glossing over the uniqueness of Mueller, Isaac, and Kipper felt like betrayal. So I steered the conversation toward George's research. He brightened and explained a promising breakthrough in precise radiation treatment for localized tumors.

With his eye on the wall clock, George stacked our empty dishes on the tray. "Time to go," he announced. "I'm due back in the ER at 7:00." We walked to the clean-up station, where George separated silverware and dishes into the appropriate buckets before depositing the tray to be ferried to the kitchen. "You'll be asleep by the time I get home, so see you in the morning," he said above the clatter of dishes.

"I am heading for bed early," I agreed. "I'm still feeling the all-nighter from Brazil. By tomorrow, I'll be good as new," I assured him as we walked into the corridor, where staff and visitors hurried past. A kiss on the lips would be too risqué, so he gave me a goodnight peck on the cheek and headed for the Emergency Room. It was a confident Dr. George Pickering who navigated past a stretcher and two wheelchairs, before he disappeared around a sharp corner. From his stride, I was pretty sure he was glad that I had come; perhaps it had reinforced his sense of control over a well-ordered life.

On Monday, Joan Lloyd, GCC's receptionist, welcomed me. She was pleasant, efficient, and gave visitors a good first impression. I had always liked Joan, but that morning she seemed plastic with her predictable smile and perfect hair.

En route to my private office, I passed potted plants and locking vertical files. Some of my colleagues were at work in their private offices with plush leather chairs, up-to-date computers, and multi-line phones. I wondered if these well-equipped, isolated consultants were more or less productive than the Brazilians sharing one computer in a bare-bones office.

My office looked immense. I draped my overcoat on a brass hook. My bulging briefcase slouched on the teak credenza. São Paulo's dingy pages would look even dirtier when I stacked them on the polished desk. I would miss the constant interruptions as Marcelo showed me new data or Luciana translated a phrase. No one would be sharing my space and Paulinho would not be bringing coffee in a chipped mug. So I headed to the kitchenette with its two carafes, one for regular and one for decaf.

A cluster of staff enacted Monday's ritual...catching up on weekend doings while waiting for the coffee to brew. As I entered, everyone turned to me.

"Hey, Beth, welcome back," Peter said, leaning against the wall, twirling his cup by its handle. Brad grunted a greeting with his nose in the *Wall Street Journal*. Mary bustled at the counter, setting donuts on a platter. Their aloofness was perfectly normal, but I suddenly missed the *abraços*, the warm embraces, that had started my recent days.

"What's Brazil like?"

"How's your Portuguese?"

"Is BomFarm a good client?"

"How's it going?"

Such simple questions. Such complex answers. No one really cared. They were just waiting to pour their first cup, which

Peter and Brad did without offering "Ladies first." Superficial responses were all they expected. "Brazil and BomFarm are really interesting. So far, it's going well, thanks to the team down there."

I was in mid-pour of my own beverage when the paging system announced, "Phone call for Beth Bartlett on Line 3." I was the only Beth in the office, but protocol called for full names.

"Well, guys, I guess duty calls." Mug in hand, I retreated to my office trying to keep from splashing coffee on the spotless carpet. Line 3 was blinking. Probably Bob looking for an update. I lifted the receiver, "Good morning. Beth Bartlett speaking."

"Good morning, Beth Bartlett. This is Samuel Cohen." His radio announcer's voice flowed into my ear. "Are you OK?"

"Yes, of course, I'm just fine. Is something wrong?"

"Yes, something is wrong. You're late for work. I've been calling for the past hour."

"I just got here. Remember, it's two hours earlier here. What's up? Is there a problem at BomFarm?" Surely the project couldn't be in trouble so soon.

"BomFarm is fine. But you're too far away." I fidgeted in my chair, still wondering why he had called.

"How was your trip? Smooth, I hope." He was in no hurry to tell me.

"The trip was fine. Better this time. I had an empty seat next to me and slept most of the way."

"Everything is OK with George? And with your sister?"

"George is happy to have me home. I haven't seen Sue yet; yesterday she went apple picking with the kids."

"What's apple picking? Can't she buy apples in the supermarket?"

"Of course she can," I laughed, "but apples taste better when you pick them yourself. It's an autumn ritual."

"It's a funny way to spend a Sunday. Well, I'm glad you didn't go. I don't want you to fall off any ladders."

Although my office was private, the office phone lines were not; I hoped no one was listening to this unorthodox banter. I redirected the conversation, "So how's the project going?"

"Everything's fine. Marcelo and I are going to BomFarm in a few minutes to review their market research."

"So there's no problem," I was relieved but a little annoyed.

"*Nenhum problema.* I just wanted to know if you were OK."

"Well, thanks for the call. Say 'Hi' to everyone in the office. Maybe we should talk later this week. Thursday perhaps...by then you might have some news to report." Hoping to justify the call, I added, "And remember to send me any new data, so that I can review it up here with Bob."

"Right, boss," Sam mimicked my businesslike tone. "You know, you talk different when you're up there."

"It must be the phone line," I joked. To some extent it was true. In the Boston office, everyone stuck to business, including me.

"Have a good first day back in Boston. *Até logo.*" Sam's final "until later" meant he might call again soon.

"Talk to you Thursday." *And not before,* I wanted to add but refrained. "*Tchau,* Sam."

"*Tchau,* Bartlett." Sam was like a mother hen, watching after her chick. He meant well, but I was annoyed. I had been in the Boston office for less than one hour and already felt a tug from another continent.

In addition to BomFarm, I was Project Manager for Northern Airways. During my absence, GCC teammates had completed research and analysis that was stacked high on my desk. Hoping this client would help me reconnect to Boston colleagues, I dug in.

Steeping myself in airline statistics did the trick; by Tuesday I had hit my stride in Boston. On Wednesday, I briefed Bob and Roger on BomFarm and they provided industry benchmarks against which to test Marcelo's numbers. For them, BomFarm was just one more revenue-producing client. I tried to think that way, too; Thursday's phone call with Sam dealt with project issues. Life was getting back to normal.

Familiar patterns returned at home, too. George worked late at the hospital while I worked late at GCC. We drove to Marblehead on the weekend to see Sue. In Red Sox baseball caps, David and Mark were playing catch in the yard. George joined in. Inside, Sue and Melody were wrapping a birthday present.

"Welcome back, sis." Sue interrupted to welcome me. "Melody, give Aunt Beth a hug; she's been far, far away."

Reluctantly, Melody left the half-wrapped package to give me a halfhearted shrug. "Ashley is already six," she explained seriously. "Mom says I can have a party when I'm six in February."

"I hope I'm invited."

"You will be." Nonchalant, Melody went back to her wrapping.

"Honey, let me help you tie the ribbon." Sue curled a bow with a few zips of the scissors. The tranquil mood was shattered as Mark barged through the kitchen door. Rusty reached me first, with his unconditional wagging. Mark was close behind.

"Aunt Beth, will you take us to the dump?"

"Yeah, the trash is taking over," Melody chimed in, abandoning the pretty package.

"Yeah, you have to rescue us." Mark pulled me toward the garage. Going to the dump with the children was a tradition. The dump was officially "The Transfer Station" where suburbanites brought recyclables to be hauled away to a community that didn't boast BMWs or Audis.

With Mark and Melody pulling me outside, I cried in mock panic, "I'm a hostage." The children giggled. "These kidnappers look serious. Get the ransom money ready," I begged Sue.

"If you're not back in an hour, we'll come rescue you," Sue promised, as she loaded empty bottles and boxes into the minivan. "Here's some junk I hauled out of the basement to make your trip worthwhile." A broken beach chair and a crumpled umbrella were tossed onto the pile. Trying to claim his usurped space, Rusty attempted to jump into the back of the van, but Sue grabbed his collar. "Stay, Rusty. Dogs aren't allowed at the dump," she explained to his perked-up ears. In a jolly mood, we drove off; in the rearview mirror, Sue was waving with one hand and holding Rusty with the other.

The Transfer Station had a paved entrance and neatly painted signs: "Residents Only. Permit Required." Inside, dumpsters appeased the environmentally conscious. "Green and Brown Glass." "Crush Cans." "Newsprint Only. No Mags."

The glass bin was Mark's favorite—a place where he could be destructive without getting into trouble. Gleefully, he smashed each bottle with all his might. I wondered, *Should I tell Mark about a boy named Paulinho who saves empty coffee jars to use in his humble kitchen?*

Melody loved the box compactor. She dropped a sturdy L.L.Bean box into the bin. Then, she pushed a big button that flattened it with a satisfying, mechanical crunch. *Should I tell Melody about the mule-drawn carts that collect cardboard like this for recycling in São Paulo?*

Next, we stopped at "the pit." I held my niece and nephew by their shirttails as they heaved in the beach chair and umbrella. *Should I tell them that these would have been treasures on a Guarujá beach?*

With the recycling done, we stopped at the Swap Shed. This volunteer service proved that "one man's trash is another man's treasure." Town residents deposited unwanted items and claimed the rejects of their neighbors. A smartly dressed lady unloaded a birdcage; another resident snatched it up. A shiny pick-up arrived with a boat anchor and a three-speed bicycle. A pregnant woman eyed a rocking chair in perfect condition.

Mark and Melody pawed through the toys. Melody found a Hula-Hoop. Mark found a skateboard. Their booty would be enjoyed until something else caught their attention.

A big glass jar sat on a table at the entrance to the Swap Shed. Rumpled dollar bills covered the bottom. Its dog-eared label read, "To benefit the homeless." I had never seen a home-less person in Marblehead, but I had seen plenty in Brazil. I pulled a ten from my wallet and stuffed it through the slotted lid.

Back at the house, Sue and I fixed lunch. "Here, you stuff the celery. The peanut butter's in the cupboard." Sue was in her "big sister groove."

"I may have been to Brazil, but I haven't forgotten where to find the peanut butter," I mocked indignation. I knew Sue's kitchen better than my own.

Sue was loading the bread slices spread out on the counter. No crust for Melody. No mustard for Mark. Extra tomato for David. No tomato for George. "So tell me about Brazil," she said, opening the mayo.

I described the Beetle taxis, the beach vendors, and the *favelas*; I wanted Sue to see what I had seen. I described the *caipirinhas*, the hearts of palm, and the cheese bread; I wanted Sue to taste what I had tasted.

"And the people? What are they like?" she asked, capping the mayo.

"Brazilians are warm and easygoing. Their world flows from work to play with fewer boundaries and constraints. Imagine this big, bearded guy doing financial analysis in a yel-low Walkman. You won't see that at the Boston office."

Sue started cutting the sandwiches—in quarters for the children, halves for the adults. "What about that guy Sam, the one who resisted you as Project Manager?"

"Surprisingly, Sam and I have a great partnership. I'm succeeding because of his support, coaching, and companionship."

Sue paused her cutting. "Companionship?"

"We've spent so much time working together, I should be sick of him. But, I'm not. He's grown on me," I admitted fondly.

Sue looked askance. "That sounds like you like him," she said in a hushed voice as we worked side by side, putting a sandwich, celery, and chips on each plate.

"Come on, Sue. Don't be suspicious. Remember, this is the guy who looks like Woody Allen. I'm just saying that a threatening adversary has turned into an indispensable ally."

"Things are going better than expected, that's good," she conceded. "In fact, you sound pretty elated with the whole adventure. I haven't seen you this happy in a long time." Instead of celebrating with me, Sue remained guarded. "Just watch your step. Being the center of attention and far away from home could be a dangerous mix. You're married to a great guy; don't forget it." She carried two plates to the table and banged them down as if driving stakes into the ground.

"You're making something out of nothing, sis." Her attitude perturbed me. "I'm not down there to have an affair; I'm down there to earn a promotion. Don't worry about George and me. I'm so busy; I might as well be locked away in a tower." I didn't tell her that Jaco had been lurking around the castle walls.

Sue stopped bustling to put her hands on her hips and hold me with her penetrating stare. "You can talk all you like, Beth, but I know you. You are glowing; something good is going on."

Sue was right about my happiness, but wrong about its cause. It was not a new man in my life; it was a new woman...an adventurous, more confident me. Saying so would be egocentric, so I just said, "If I'm oozing enthusiasm, it's because I'm having a great time and you don't get defensive or angry at my stories."

"You mean, not like George?" She was concerned. "Is he still bitter?"

"We're trying to get back on track. It's getting better, but things get rocky every time Brazil comes up."

"Let's patch things up over lunch," Sue proposed. "David and the kids will love hearing about your adventures and George will get caught up in their enthusiasm." Before I could object, she'd summoned the family. The right dose of sandwiches, celery, and anecdotes would remedy the friction that plagued my marriage; of that Sue seemed convinced.

Sunday Night—September 28
En Route to Brazil for Round Two

Dear Diary,

Three weeks at home have grounded me. Disoriented at first, I felt normal again within a week. Sue's prescription for marital harmony seems to have worked. When I told my travel stories, the silly questions of Mark and Melody made everyone laugh, even George. Brazil may not be his favorite topic of conversation, but at least it's not taboo anymore.

At the office, Northern Airways got the attention it deserves and, according to Sam, BomFarm is under control. Now I am heading for Brazil again; the second time around isn't so scary. Last time, I was swept up in the professional and personal thrill. This time, it will be easier to keep Brazil in balance with my real life.

And a good life it is. Yesterday, we went sailing on Sea Spirit. It was a glorious September day. Perched on the foredeck, I relished the swish of the bow wave and the surge of the hull. George steadied the helm while David tinkered with the sails. In her battered hat, Sue rubbed sunscreen on the children's faces. The scene and scenery filled my heart with tranquility.

Why, then, is Brazil drawing me like a magnet?

"If You Want to Make an Omelet..."

"They'll be bankrupt in six months." **Marcelo** passed the graphs to me, jetlagged in the backseat of Vicente's taxi.

Once again, the three men had met me at the airport, but this time Sam and Marcelo were gaining time. "We're obliged to share these conclusions with BomFarm immediately. If they don't act fast, we won't have a client," Sam insisted.

"Are we sure this data is right?" I didn't want to cry wolf. "If the trend is so certain, why have they missed it?"

"They never put the pieces together this way," Sam explained. "Marcelo combined financials with data from marketing and operations. No one has run these correlations and projections before."

"Let me study this. We can't afford to be wrong." Outside the car window were the sights that had shaken me up a month ago. This time the shock was the threatening analysis in my hands. I quizzed Marcelo on his sources and assumptions. I checked his formulas in my head. I found no errors.

"Even if reality is off by twenty-five percent, it won't change the conclusion, just the urgency." Sam was right.

"Why didn't you send this to me last week?" My voice was harsh. "I could have reviewed it with Bob White." *I would have even welcomed help from Roger Doyle*, I admitted to myself.

"Simple. We didn't have it then, but we have it now." Sam was unapologetic. "We got the latest financials on Friday. Marcelo worked all weekend to finish the projections; he printed these pages while you were in the air." Sam's defense of his colleague neutralized any further objections from me.

"Getting the data has been...how do you say in English... pull teeth?" Marcelo struggled to explain. "People are afraid of Mueller; no one wants to tell bad news."

BomFarm's CEO had a commanding posture, even when all was well. Confronting him with these findings would not be fun, but it was our job. "I don't blame them," I told Marcelo, "but we're being paid to be honest messengers... good news or bad."

Vicente was already navigating the city streets near the office. No rest at the hotel this time; straight to the office. My carefully crafted schedule called for several more weeks of diagnosis, followed by Bob White's presenting our findings. However, BomFarm could not afford to follow the GCC time-table; I would need to make a case for changing it.

"Start preparing a presentation for Mueller while I call Boston," I directed as we entered the office.

"*Bem-vinda, Senhora,*" Paulinho hurried to take my bags. Not even BomFarm's precarious condition could keep me from smiling as he brought me *café puro*. I needed a jolt before calling Bob.

"He's at the two-day offsite for Parker Medical," his secretary Mary said curtly.

"Can you reach him? It's urgent that he call me in Brazil."

"He didn't give me a number. He might call in tomorrow morning."

"Could you call his hotel and track him down?"

"I never interrupt him when he's with his clients." Mary was a good gatekeeper and Bob liked it that way.

"Where are they running the meeting?" I would call Bob myself and take the consequences.

"I'm not sure." I didn't believe her. Bob's wife was about to go into labor. Mary knew how to reach him, but had decided that my plight did not merit bothering her boss.

Frustrated, I hung up. I looked again at Marcelo's charts. "Can we wait until tomorrow?" I asked rhetorically.

"You're the Project Manager, but this is my client. BomFarm is hemorrhaging. I won't waste a day waiting for Bob White. I'm going to schedule a session with BomFarm now. If Boston complains, they can go to hell." Sam's refusal to compromise was admirable, but it put me in a tough spot.

"Wait. Wait. Cool down. Let me call Harvey. I hate to end-run Bob again, but this grim news demands senior attention." Taking a deep breath, I dialed and found my mentor in his office.

Having heard my breathless account of the situation, Harvey said calmly, "Put Marcelo on." Without a speakerphone, Marcelo would be on his own; he was sweating as he took the receiver. Silence, then replies in English mixed with Portuguese. More silence, then replies again with more English. By the third query, Marcelo was more relaxed. A bit more give-and-take, and then a big grin as Marcelo handed me the phone.

"It sounds solid." Harvey's exam had been even tougher than mine and Marcelo had passed. Then he conceded, "Your case is strong and the client's welfare is at stake. I would be happier if a Senior Partner could deliver this news, but time is of the essence. Go ahead, but emphasize that these findings are *preliminary*."

"I understand," I assured Harvey, "thanks for the green light." I signaled thumbs up to my colleagues and then threw a bone to protocol. "I'll keep trying to reach Bob."

"Don't waste your time. He's got his own problems with Parker Medical. I'll talk to him when he gets back later this week. Meanwhile, you've got to do what you've got to do."

"Good job, Bartlett." Sam swaggered over when I hung up.

"We'll see. Bob will be furious."

"If you want to make an omelet, you have to break some eggs." Sam reached for the still-warm receiver. Within minutes, he'd set up a meeting with BomFarm for the next morning.

"Speaking of eggs, we'd better scramble." My play on words was lost on Marcelo, already inside his Walkman, preparing a defense of his projections.

Relishing a challenge, Sam said, "We can't just deliver bad news. We must suggest ways to slow this trend immediately." The worse things got, the better he performed. Sam picked up his magician's wand and we started to brainstorm options to keep our client afloat.

The next morning, our trio sat across from Mueller and Isaac; the air was thick with tension. We wasted no time. I expressed a few caveats; then Marcelo presented the dismal trends.

Already stern, Dr. Mueller pulled his shoulders back ever so slightly. "Let me see those numbers." Mueller was silent, intent on the page before him. "What do you think?" he asked Isaac.

Unable to read Mueller, Isaac was cautious. "Like you, I am seeing this for the first time. These guys have combined information in an unconventional way. Given the grave implications, we must check it more carefully."

Mueller lifted the phone. "I need Alvaro to come here immediately." Marcelo shot a worried glance at Sam as we waited for the Chief Financial Officer. Marcelo had built some credibility with the CFO, but would it be enough?

"Only part of the data comes from Alvaro's area," Sam hastened to point out. "Historical financial data doesn't reveal the threat. The danger lies in the trends in sales, pricing, and operating costs."

Alvaro entered the charged room and shifted from foot to foot, ready to dodge whatever was coming. "Alvaro, take a look at these projections," Mueller commanded. The muscles around Alvaro's mouth tightened as he picked up Marcelo's graphs.

"This is not my data; I can't vouch for it," Alvaro protested.

Mueller ignored his subordinate's defensiveness and continued, "Alvaro, go work with Marcelo; review the assumptions and confirm the results. Come back within the hour." Marcelo followed Alvaro out the door. If Marcelo's work held up under the CFO's scrutiny, we would be heroes. If not, our credibility was shot.

Once they were gone, Mueller turned to Sam and me. "If the projection is right, what do you suggest?" It was a hint that he believed our grim findings. "I could cut costs quickly by closing down some operations," Mueller proposed.

"Reducing expenses must be part of the solution, but cost-cutting must be done with great care," Sam warned. "Highly visible plant closings and layoffs will be read by the market as trouble. Fearing future shortages of drugs, customers may abandon BomFarm for competitors; that could lead to lower revenues and a downward spiral."

I buttressed Sam's position. "Edicts can shrink a company, but they won't energize transformation and growth."

In a delicate discussion, we tried to convince him that BomFarm needed a critical mass of executives to work to reverse the situation. Finally, Mueller bought the idea of using teams to recommend ways to save the company in the short term and reshape it for the long term. GCC would guide the teams and integrate their proposals into a cohesive plan.

When Isaac saw that his boss was accepting a participative approach, he asked, "Specifically, what will the teams work on?"

"For the short term, revenues and costs," Sam replied quickly. "For the long term, we're still debating."

Isaac turned to me, expectantly. "Bete, how would you organize them?"

Isaac was testing me and I wanted to sound smart. "Revenues and costs for the short term," I echoed Sam, and then introduced a new idea, "customer groups for the long term, such as pharmacists or doctors."

The idea was not original. In Boston, Bob had insisted that BomFarm needed economies of scale. "They've got to replace those regional divisions with customer-oriented business units," Bob had said confidently. I trusted his experience and hoped that following his advice would compensate for his absence.

I forged ahead, "For other GCC clients, organizing around customers has improved market share and profits dramatically." Isaac nodded. Mueller was silent. Sam stiffened. "Let me show you," I hastened, digging into my briefcase for some of Bob's data. Before I could find it, a knock announced the return of Alvaro and Marcelo.

Four tense faces watched them join the table. Alvaro spoke with guarded confidence. "The numbers look accurate, at least the ones from my area," he hedged. "I can't vouch for the other departments, but the methodology looks solid and the assumptions are transparent, so it is easy to test them." Self-importance had replaced defensiveness. "In fact, here are some different scenarios and they all point in the same direction." Alvaro proudly handed Mueller a sheaf of papers. Marcelo was giving the credit for his hard work to Alvaro. For now, the CFO was an ally.

After studying the numbers in silence, Mueller said to no one in particular, "I knew the government's plan was hurting BomFarm, but I thought we had more time." He paused, and then looked sternly across the table. "This situation is very serious and could disrupt the whole company. Today's discussion must remain absolutely confidential." Every head nodded in agreement. "Isaac, set up a conference call with the shareholders this afternoon. Bomfortes don't like surprises."

"Yes, sir." Isaac shifted in his chair, as if shifting the burden that was now on his shoulders.

"Shall we meet again tomorrow, after you talk to the shareholders?" Sam asked Mueller.

"Yes," Mueller said, checking his agenda. "At 11:00. We'll finalize the plan to move ahead. Meanwhile, keep this quiet," he warned again as he stood up. Stiff as a board, he marched from the room.

Silence until the door latched behind him, then an unintelligible buzz as the men broke into animated Portuguese. Hunched over the printouts, Isaac asked questions. Alvaro listened intently to Marcelo's answers while Sam added occasional remarks. Isaac said something commanding to Alvaro, who nodded agreement and left. After a few more minutes, they remembered I was there and switched back to English.

With Mueller gone, Isaac turned complimentary. "Marcelo's analysis was innovative and very revealing. *Parabéns*! Congratulations to all of you. You delivered very tough news and survived."

"Mueller accepted the blows better than I expected," I confessed tentatively, basking in Isaac's praise.

"And your idea to use executive teams is brilliant. Organizing by customers sounds great and obviously works for other companies." Isaac was enthused. "It's high time to break the silence around here and debate BomFarm's future."

"Let's not get carried away." Sam was less optimistic. "Mueller keeps his cards close to his chest. He won't give the green light until he talks to Bomforte."

"True," Isaac agreed, "but he has seen the threat and doesn't have many options. He can't fix this problem without giving up some control. You can assume this will fly and start designing the team assignments now. In fact, let's go to my office, where you can work and bounce your ideas off me."

Sam fidgeted like a man who wants to leave a party. "Thanks, but I'm expecting an important call at the office." He gathered the papers and closed his briefcase.

"Wait. Wait a moment," Isaac insisted. "At least let me tell you which guys should be on the teams. You already know most of them." Isaac scribbled a list on his legal pad. Marcelo huddled beside him confirming the names. Still impatient, Sam paced near the door. Knowing none of the players, I was useless but grateful that Isaac was being so helpful.

With a flourish, Isaac ripped the page from his legal pad. "I'll let you know if I think of anyone else," he said cheerfully as he handed the list to me. I tucked the page into my portfolio.

Isaac accompanied us to the elevator. "Good work. Keep me informed."

Hurrying to the "important call" that Sam had fabricated, we scurried to Marcelo's car in pouring rain. I clambered into the backseat. Up front, the two men spoke in rapid Portuguese, blocking me out. I had assumed we would debrief en route to the office. Instead, Marcelo popped a cassette into the tape deck; music was incongruous after the intense business meeting. I felt stymied until Marcelo grinned back at me. "Here's one for you...in English...Caetano singing 'London, London.'" Marcelo upped the volume. The refrain about looking for flying saucers captured the unworldly quality of consulting in Brazil. I just listened and wondered what was coming next.

At the office, Sam remained aloof. I didn't get it. Why was he so sour? "Sam, what's bugging you?" When he didn't respond instantly, I kept going. "We should be celebrating. The meeting went well. Marcelo's analysis held up under scrutiny. Mueller didn't throw us out. Isaac is enthused. What's wrong?"

"Who are you talking to?" Anger had replaced his usual good humor. "You ask a question and then answer it. Obviously, you don't need me! If you want to know what I think, shut up and let me answer."

"I'm sorry. I'll keep quiet." My mouth went dry at his rudeness.

"Who do you think you are? The Lone Ranger? Recommending customer-oriented teams—something we haven't even discussed, something with huge implications."

"I wasn't being a Lone Ranger," I insisted. "I was being responsive." In fact, I felt proud because I had used *jogo de cintura*. But, apparently, it had backfired.

"Just yesterday we agreed to wait to define the strategic topics. Remember?" It was true; we had run out of time and tabled a decision. Sam paced on the far side of the conference table. "But today, out of the blue, you say 'customer groups' like a fait accompli."

"It wasn't out of the blue," I shot back. "Bob and I discussed it in Boston. I didn't think of it yesterday, but today it came to me as the obvious answer."

"Well, you took the project into your own hands."

"Isaac was pressing me. What was I supposed to do? Keep my mouth shut?"

"Yes," he fumed. "You should have told Isaac that we'll get back to him with some alternatives."

"What!...and sound weak?" I protested. My blouse was stuck to my armpits. "Clients pay us to use GCC's expertise and I did. It's a good strategic solution and it will make Bob happy."

"Since when does Bob count? He's been totally absent. What worked for other clients may not work for BomFarm," Sam continued his attack.

"After the bombshell we dropped today, we don't have the luxury of time." I was shouting. "We need to draw on industry experience. Besides, Isaac loves the customer approach."

"Of course he does," Sam scoffed. "You're so naïf." Sam paused for effect. "Organizing by customer groups will give him the chance to run a major part of BomFarm. Sure, Isaac was thrilled, but Mueller closed down. Just when Mueller was buying in, you scared him off."

Sam had a point. The CEO had gone cold when Isaac had warmed up. Had I made a mistake or was Sam jealous because he hadn't posed this solution? I defended my actions. "Mueller doesn't like to rock the boat, but this boat is sinking," I barked back. "We don't have a lot of time; customer teams are the way to go and we have Isaac's support."

"Watch it. There is a thin line between support and manipulation. Isaac likes where we're headed. He even wants to hand-pick the team members. But if Mueller thinks he's controlling us, we'll be out in a flash." Sam knew what made people tick. He understood political risks that I had ignored. My nose got red and tears welled into my eyes. I had acted on impulse, without consulting him. But what bothered me most was this outburst; I was dismayed at my uncontrolled frustration. I brushed a tear from my cheek and steadied the quaver in my throat.

"You're right. I got swept up. Jumping to a solution was a mistake."

Sam came around the table and put his hand on my arm. "What's wrong? Why the tears?"

I swiped another tear away, ashamed that stress was taking its toll. "I blew it with our client. I let you down."

"You didn't blow it. Customer groups are probably the right approach…but the implications are big…for BomFarm and for us." Sam reached for his wand. He was cooling down and so was I. "Next time, let's thrash it out first, not after the fact. Don't head down any paths alone; remember, we're a team."

"You're right. I'm sorry and I'm sorry I got into a fight," I said with a weak smile. "I shouldn't have yelled at you."

"There's nothing wrong with a good quarrel. Better to voice our differences than let them fester. Now the air is clear and we can move on." Sam stepped away. "Paulinho, *café*. Marcelo, bring the flip chart. It's time to rip up the work plan and start over."

Sam might have been comfortable with conflict, but I wasn't. I promised myself to keep my cool next time…and I was sure there would be a next time.

Meanwhile, another storm was brewing in Boston. Back from Parker Medical, Bob found a stack of phone messages.

"What the hell is going on in Brazil?" he demanded to know as he barged into Harvey's office.

"Unexpected developments. Beth tried to reach you. BomFarm is in critical condition."

"So, they're going to cancel the project?" Bob sounded hopeful.

"To the contrary. Marcelo made some compelling projections they'd never seen. BomFarm needs more help, not less."

"When I met with Beth last week, she didn't mention any of this. I won't tolerate her concealing this serious situation," Bob huffed.

"She didn't know; they met her at the airport with the data. You were locked up with Parker Medical, so after grilling Marcelo, I gave the go-ahead to show the trends to the client."

"Jesus. If BomFarm is going down the tubes, let's collect our fees and run. Why develop a strategy they'll never use?"

"Bob, you may be right, but it's hard to make that call from so far away. I say, let GCC-Brazil work until you can go assess the situation personally. If we have to pull out, you'll do it as the Partner-in-Charge."

The phone rang. Harvey picked up. "For you." Bob grabbed the phone and turned pale. "I'm on my way." He handed the receiver back to Harvey. "Her water broke." Bob tipped a chair over as he rushed out the door.

Shaking his head, Harvey rounded his desk and righted the chair. Beth would have to steer BomFarm through the choppy waters for a few more weeks.

Feijoada

Absorbed in the client's crisis, I lost track of time, but Marcelo knew it was Wednesday. As we left BomFarm with a new game plan approved by Mueller, Marcelo said, "Let's go for *feijoada*."

"Good idea. We deserve a break," Sam concurred.

"*Fei-what?*" I inquired, wondering what joke they were pulling this time.

"*Feijoada*, a little light food," Marcelo said with relish.

"You guys go for lunch; I have too much work to do." I was upset by the interruption and moody because I dreaded the pending phone call to update Bob. But, Marcelo insisted, "You won't understand Brazil until you eat *feijoada*." In the driver's seat, literally, Marcelo drove to his favorite restaurant.

Groups waiting for friends spilled onto the sidewalk in front of The Place. We jostled at the restaurant entrance, then elbowed through the bustling bar toward the maître d'. The room was a sea of white shirts…men with jackets off. There were no other women in the packed restaurant.

Joviality and cigarette smoke engulfed us as we squeezed among the chairs. Our progress was slow. Marcelo paused several times to meet acquaintances with *abraços* and cordial greetings. On Wednesdays, cutthroat competitors exchanged business rivalry for repartee about soccer and Formula One racing.

We passed a massive table, laden with black pots, perfect for witch's brew. Steamy haze hung over the table and the smell of animal fat fended off any stray vegetarians.

Once seated, we ordered beer and *caipirinhas* before heading to the buffet. I was relieved to see that the pots were labeled with small brass tags...but, oops, they were in Portuguese.

Paio
Linguiça
Carne Seca
Bisteca de porco
Orelha de porco

Marcelo dipped into the caldrons, heaping his plate with mysterious pig parts. Suppressing the slaughterhouse image that bubbled before me, I ladled a tiny taste from each pot.

Next came *arroz e feijão*. Rice and black beans, essentials that still sustain many Brazilians and give this traditional feast its name. A little of each went onto my plate. Next, wilted greens and deep-fried rinds, accompanied by a powdery garnish, *farinha de mandioca*. At the end of the table, I loaded up on bright orange slices, the only thing that appealed to my palette.

The happy mound on Marcelo's plate made mine an anemic sampler. Although I had little taste for the food, I savored the unabashed gusto that surrounded me. Men from every table served themselves a second round.

The rhythm of drums and the squeak of the barrel-shaped *cuíca* added to the happy hubbub. The African beat was a very distant relative of the cool jazz heard at Sunday brunch in Cambridge. When Portuguese slave ships had brought their human cargo to the eastern bulge of Brazil, they'd also carried music and dance in the hold. Now, a century after the abolition of slavery, white-collar workers shed their ties on Wednesdays to become one with the basics...*arroz, feijão, e amizade* (rice, beans, and friendship).

Wednesday Night—October 1
Maksoud Plaza

Dear Diary,

I seem to be breaking all the rules:

1. Fighting. Yesterday, I had a shouting match with Sam. Instead of swallowing my anger, I fought back, abandoning my self-control. I don't know whether to applaud myself or feel ashamed.

2. Unabashed Eating. Today I ate feijoada—friendship, the joy of eating, and the belief that work can wait until tomorrow. Could this custom cure the rat race? No one can run in circles with a stomach full of pork and beans!

3. Ignoring the Partner-in-Charge. Bob's baby arrived today. I was all charged up to brief him and then found out he'll be out for the rest of the week. By the time we talk, the strategy teams will be off and running. The horse will be out of the barn and I'll have a lot of explaining to do.

4. Thinking about Cheating. A message from Jaco is on my bedside table. Should I return his call? I would love to hear his voice. Instead, I called George but he wasn't home.

Tomorrow, I will try to behave.

Quicksand

Morning came. I dragged myself from bed. I tried to bring my husband's face into focus, but George was a faraway blur. My glasses didn't help.

A quick shower and room service breakfast. Papaya with lime was perking me up when the phone rang.

"Bethania?" said a sexy bass voice.

"Hello, Jaco. I got your message, but it was too late to call last night."

"Working late?" he sounded doubtful and disapproving.

"Unexpected events have kept me running."

"Bethania, you didn't call me before going home to Boston and you didn't call me upon coming back. I hope you're not avoiding me, because I want to take you to my favorite restaurant." Even when scolding, Jaco was seductive. "Let me pick you up at 8:30 this evening?"

A tinge of guilt was not enough to stop me from accepting. "Dinner sounds lovely, but I have a big day tomorrow. I wouldn't want to be out too late."

"You'll be in bed before midnight." I fantasized about whose bed he had in mind. "I'll see you this evening." Before my better judgment woke up, the line was dead.

I finished my papaya, tied up my hair, and tucked Jaco's number in my purse. I would cancel the dinner once I got to the office.

Luciana greeted me at the door of GCC-Brazil. "Do you want to review this?" Her page was divided into the teams approved by Mueller: three crosscutting issues: Costs, Revenues, and Infrastructure; plus three customer groups: Pharmacy/Doctor, Hospital, and Veterinary. Each team had members with different functions, expertise, and personal characteristics. The Pharmacy team read as follows:

Correia	Z. Osteiro
João	Chester
Marcos Eduardo	Josinei
Jorge Neto de Souza	

As Human Resources Director, Hélio had helped finalize the lists, making sure to complement BomFarm's experienced middle managers with the rising stars. Correia and Z. Osteiro were strong with numbers. João and Chester brought experience from the field. Marcos Eduardo was a good leader. Josinei was creative and had good intuition. Jorge Neto de Souza was a new MBA who was full of energy. Four of the seven came from Isaac's list.

"This looks fine; just put their full names in alphabetical order to reduce speculation about who is most important." Luciana looked puzzled. "Alphabetical, with last names first," I clarified. She was still hesitant, so I explained further. "This list has full names like 'Jorge Neto de Souza' mixed up with last names like 'Correia' and first names like 'João.' 'Z' is an initial; 'Josinei' is a nickname. It's not professional."

By now, our exchange had caught Marcelo's attention. "Let me take a look." After glancing at the paper, "*Não faz mal*; never mind, it's OK." He defended Luciana as he handed the paper back. "Don't make a storm from a cup of water."

The idiom was cute, but I stood firm. "The official list of the project teams should have real names," I insisted.

Marcelo scratched his beard. "These *are* real names. If we write something else, no one will know who we're talking about." Luciana nodded agreement.

"You're pulling my leg." I was sure that Marcelo was testing my gullibility again.

"No, I'm not kidding. People use the name that works."

It hit me...the diversity, authenticity, and relaxed self-expression that is Brazil. I remembered Jaco. "So, these are noms de guerre."

"*Exatamente*, Babs!" Marcelo gave me a congratulatory pat on the back. No one had called me "Babs" since my Abbot days. I caved in with a warm sense of belonging.

Agreeing upon the teams was one thing, being ready to guide their work was quite another. To ensure the control that Mueller demanded and the quality that GCC expected, we needed to work all weekend, something common in the States but not in Brazil.

A reluctant ogre, I announced, "No beach this weekend. We'll need all hands on deck today, Friday, and Saturday."

"No problem," said Luciana. "Sometimes I study all night for exams. This is more fun...it's a real case."

"We can set up shifts to use the computer around the clock," Ed proposed seriously to overcome the bottleneck posed by our single desktop.

"Sandra will fix Saturday lunch," Marcelo volunteered. We wouldn't go hungry.

"*Traz o flippy*," Sam instructed Paulinho, who set the flip-chart easel in the middle of the work area. Quickly, we planned the what, who, and when to meet our deadlines. The energy was palpable. Marcelo's foot tapped an impatient beat. Ed scratched Japanese characters on a yellow pad. Luciana taped note-filled flipcharts on the wall. Sam twirled his magician's wand, a sign that he was thinking full speed ahead. Soon we dispersed to start our respective tasks.

In Boston, consultants would have disappeared to the quiet isolation of their offices. Could we be productive in these cramped quarters? I spread out at one end of the conference table, Luciana at the other. Within minutes, she asked me a question while Ed was huddling with Marcelo. Before long, Sam dragged his chair next to Luciana so she could correct his *Portuñol* (a blend of Portuguese and Spanish). In constant motion...conferring, debating, and helping each other...one room made one team.

In Boston, tight deadlines provoked solemnity. In Brazil, the crunch stimulated bursts of laughter, jokes, digressions, and the occasional "*Opa*" from Marcelo as he celebrated a breakthrough. Thank goodness Bob White could not see us now!

At lunchtime, Ed called the sushi bar two blocks away. "Very fresh," he assured me, as the team dipped raw fish into soy sauce spiced with wasabi. Praying that food poisoning would not derail the project, I stuck to the California roll.

Late afternoon, we paused for a status report. Out of the jovial chaos had come creative ideas and a pretty solid first draft. "We're in good shape," I pronounced. "Thank you all. Let's call it a day; no one needs to work late tonight." As we dispersed, Ed insisted on replacing Marcelo at the computer.

"What do you feel like eating?" Sam assumed we would dine together, just as we had each night since my arrival.

"Thanks, I think I'll head back to the hotel." I tried to sound nonchalant. I had not called Jaco to break our date.

"Are you feeling OK?" Sam was concerned.

"Oh, I'm fine." The hectic day was the perfect excuse, but Sam deserved the truth. I looked down, like a confessing child. "In fact, I have some dinner plans."

"Who with?" Sam was suspicious. Maybe he thought I was getting between him and his client.

"Don't worry. No one from BomFarm."

But he wasn't satisfied. "Who then?" he insisted.

I turned away to hide my uneasiness. "Just someone I met on the plane."

"Man or woman?"

"Does it matter?" It really was none of his business.

"Of course it matters," he said, as if any fool would agree.

"He's a lawyer. Knowing someone who can provide legal counsel might come in handy." Who was I trying to kid?

"Watch it." Sam's jaw tightened. "If he's a lawyer, the bastard knows how to get what he wants."

Sam's rough language took me aback. Sanctimonious, I defended Jaco. "Swearing isn't called for. Don't generalize about lawyers or anybody else; he's a nice guy." In a huff, I gathered my briefcase to signal my departure. "Just enjoy a night off. Let someone else bear the burden of hosting for a change." Words that should have conveyed appreciation were defensive and rude.

"OK. You're the boss," he countered with cool indifference, before adding, "Just be careful."

"Don't worry," I cajoled. "Relax." But Sam just looked glum. As I exited the office, I called out, "See you all tomorrow." But my cheery pretense was blown when I tripped on the threshold and the door slammed shut behind me.

Walking to the Maksoud failed to calm me. Anticipation, guilt, excitement, and doubt swirled inside. While I was showering, the phone rang. Shampoo and cold water dripped down my towel-wrapped body as I grabbed the phone. Maybe Jaco was backing out. "Hello?" I didn't know what I hoped for.

"Hello." It was just Sam. My clenched fist relaxed; the towel slid loosely to my hips.

"Oh. Hi, Sam. What's up?" Had my hasty departure left a loose end at the office?

"Nothing's up...I just called to urge you to be careful."

"As Marcelo would say, 'You're making a storm from a cup of water.'" I hoped Sam would lighten up, but my jesting produced unnerving silence. Shivering, I pulled the towel back up over my breasts. "Really, there is no need for worry. I'm just having dinner with a nice guy."

"For a lady who went to Harvard, you're not so smart. Call me when you get back to the hotel."

"Sam, thanks for your concern, but it will be too late to bother you."

"Bother me. No matter what time it is. Call me, you silly woman."

"Bye, Sam." I hung up and hopped back in the shower. "Call me, you silly woman." A touching insult...sexist...condescending...and tender. I dried off and switched on the hairdryer. Through its roar, I heard the phone again. That would be Jaco and I was still in my underwear.

"Good evening," I answered formally.

"Good evening," came from the other end, equally formal.

"I'm not quite ready."

"Ready for what?" It was Sam again.

Aggravated, I chastised him. "Sam, I'm trying to get dressed. It's getting late. Stop calling or I'll have to go naked."

Unimpressed by my attempt at humor, Sam said flatly, "I forgot to give you my number. Got a pencil? It's 555-2139." I already had his number and Sam knew it, but, in compliance, I jotted it down on the scratch pad with the Maksoud logo. "Remember, call me. I won't be able to sleep until you do. If I don't hear from you, I'll go out and find you."

"OK. OK. I'll call," I promised. Hopefully that would get him off my back.

Hanging up again, I shook my head. Did Sam think I was a teenager? Despite being annoyed, I felt a little sheepish. A Project Manager missing in Brazil would be problematic. No doubt that was the root of his pestering.

I hurried to don a black silk skirt, sequined shell, and wide belt that would show off my narrow waist. Eye shadow and blush were pending when the phone rang once more; this time it was Jaco, waiting downstairs.

The marble atrium felt like a catwalk. Jaco seemed to relish my crossing under the envious gaze of men clustered in the lobby bar for happy hour. As I reached him, possessive arms pulled me close against his firm body. His spicy cologne recalled our airline encounter. In no hurry, his strong hand held my soft cheek against his rugged one. With choreographed grace, he released his hold, switched hands and held my other cheek against warm lips that were tantalizingly close to mine.

"*Bem-vinda*. Welcome back. You look lovely," he said simply. With dance-floor smoothness, his warm hand on the small of my back guided me toward his waiting Mercedes. Despite the attendant holding the car door, Jaco stayed near as I gathered my flowing skirt. Once I was settled to his satisfaction, he raised his eyes from my ankles and signaled to the valet. My car door closed with a luxurious sigh. Leather, smoke, and male scent infused the cocoon.

Tan hand on the gearshift, he navigated São Paulo's streets with ease and reestablished the comfortable mood of our Maksoud brunch—unhurried remarks delivered with a disarming smile. At an elegant canopy, another valet took the keys. Helping me from the car, Jaco took my hand and ushered me past the doorman into the cozy foyer. The maître d' escorted us past hushed duos in intimate booths to a secluded corner where *"Reservada"* marked a half-moon banquette bathed in candlelight.

As we passed other couples, I realized Jaco's hand still held mine and that anyone watching would assume this was a tryst. I had no intention of being unfaithful to George and pulled my hand away. Blatantly romantic, the restaurant was glamorous but troublesome. Sam had read the situation better than I had.

The folds of my skirt clung to the curved red velvet, exposing a lot of leg as I slid into my seat. A bottle of Cuvée Dom Pérignon appeared in a silver bucket. As bubbles rose in two flutes, I wondered how to offset the amorous ambiance. Jaco raised his glass, "To a most lovely and unusual lady."

Raising my own glass, I beseeched my wits to help me out. "Thank you, but I'm really not so unusual. There are many women consultants; they just haven't found their way to Brazil."

"I'm glad this one did," he replied. Touching my glass to his, I knew my allusion to business was a weak defense against his unnerving hazel eyes.

A tuxedoed waiter set down a silver tray. "Caviar?" George always shunned the expensive black goo, so I had never tried it. As Jaco deftly loaded a toast point with the salty roe, egg, and onion, I grew intrigued. He slid closer, but before his offering reached my mouth I took it delicately in my fingers. As I savored the unusual taste, the waiter poured two small glasses of chilled vodka. Another clink, then the cold sips that made the caviar even more delicious.

"Your trip home, how was it?" Jaco posed the question with another loaded toast point.

"It was great to reunite with my husband, my sister, and her family; they loved hearing about Brazil." I crafted the glowing report to remind Jaco that I was married. "But, it was strange. I kept seeing my familiar world in a new light."

Eyeing me with amusement, he distracted me with more caviar, which I relished in silence. As I swallowed the last bit, he asked, "Was that good or bad?"

"Very good," I replied, licking my lips to savor the last salty taste.

"Not the caviar." He laughed. "Seeing your familiar world in a new light. Was that good or bad?"

"Oh." I giggled, embarrassed by my gluttony. "Mostly uncomfortable," I admitted more thoughtfully. "I kept comparing and judging." A sympathetic arm reached around my shoulder. I hungered to be close, but pulled away and said matter-of-factly, "Well, they say, 'You can never go home again,' so I shouldn't be surprised if there's a price for going abroad."

The intimacy was further dispelled by the arrival of stuffed mushrooms. Jaco shifted subtly toward his place; I overtly did the same. As wine was poured, I wondered when Jaco had ordered and what else was in store. As Sam had predicted, my companion knew what he wanted and how to get it.

"Those look delicious." To retreat to safer ground, I tried boarding school small talk. "Do you have any brothers and sisters?"

"Two brothers and a sister. We all grew up in a small town in the interior of Brazil. My mother still lives there with fourteen cats," he said fondly. The rural setting didn't jibe with his urban ease until I learned that his family owned large tracts of land. His brothers managed the ranches, while Jaco's law firm represented wealthy Brazilian families with major agricultural interests.

He paced his story to unfold with the meal, featuring perfectly cooked steak au poivre. "I like French cuisine," he said almost apologetically, as the crème brulée was served. "It's my sister's fault. She married a Frenchman; they convinced me to go with them to St. Barts for gourmet food and celebrity watching. On our first night, I met Genevieve; we spent two weeks together; I proposed; she said yes." He chuckled. "We've been married for twelve years, two of them happy. *Café?*" he asked.

Stunned, I nodded "yes" and scrambled to process his last remarks. Jaco was married, but behaved like an unattached Don Juan. He had none of the qualms that kept me in check. When the coffee and petits fours were served, Jaco beckoned the violinist to our table. With the opening notes of the romantic melody, he placed his arm around my shoulders. Goosebumps pricked my neck. Before his revelation, I would have been tempted to snuggle, but now I was suspicious. The evening had been flawless, too flawless, too rehearsed. How many other women had been seduced in this booth?

The serenade ended; a tableside cart with liqueurs and cigars replaced the violinist. I straightened my back and pulled away from Jaco's embrace. My hand trembled as I accepted the warm snifter.

As the cart rolled out of earshot, awkward words gave voice to my conscience. "Jaco, this has been lovely, but I was foolish to accept your invitation."

"Foolish?" One quizzical word and a nonchalant sip of brandy.

"You know why," I swirled the globe, trying to collect my thoughts. "I am married. You're married. If I've led you on, I'm sorry. Forgive me, but this evening must end with a handshake." "Handshake" sounded silly in a country of *abraços*, but I was too flustered to care.

Jaco lit a cigarette, leaned back against the red velvet, and fixed his eyes on mine. "Bethania…you surprise me." I sipped in silence. "I was sure you felt something for me." He exhaled smoke in a way that was sexy, even to a non-smoker.

"My feelings for you are irrelevant," I struggled to resist his allure. "Jaco, we shouldn't be here tonight." Another beguiling smoke ring drifted up.

Leaning forward, he whispered softly, "Feelings are always relevant. Bethania, you are a beautiful woman who should enjoy life." The Dom Pérignon was on Jaco's side. His hand encircled mine under the brandy. Warmth flowed from all sides. "On the airplane, I found a woman on the verge of a great adventure. You have embraced Brazil, and Brazil wants to embrace you. A world of sensuous delights awaits you. I want to guide you to them." His provocations made me feel desire and desirable. The scent of tobacco and brandy were a prelude to the kiss that hung in the air between us.

Somehow I managed to pull my hand from his, set the snifter down, and pick up my purse. "Excuse me while I use the Ladies Room." A waiter stepped from the shadows and edged the table out. As I stumbled out of the banquette, I asked, "*Onde é o banheiro?*" just as Jaco had taught me. The server gestured toward the entrance foyer. With deliberate steps, I touched empty chair backs to steady myself as I sought privacy.

Alone, surrounded by polished marble, I slumped on the toilet. It was a long pee, and my head was swimming when I looked in the gilded mirrors with glassy eyes. The classy lady who had left the Maksoud looked cheap. I twirled my wedding band and tried to get my bearings. So far, I had fended off Jaco's advances. Now I just had to keep my resolve and get back to the hotel.

With fresh lipstick and renewed determination, I emerged to find Jaco at the door with a long-stemmed red rose. Full of promise, the bud had opened just enough to reveal petals of velvet. With a chivalrous bow, Jaco offered it without malice.

"Thank you." I accepted the stem gingerly, wanting to avoid thorns and temptation. "If the hotel is out of your way, I could take a taxi." It was a ridiculous suggestion and a feeble attempt to sidestep the quicksand still to come.

"After dark in São Paulo, a lady never travels alone." Jaco's hand on the small of my back was possessive as we waited for the valet to bring his car. The slightest turn would land me in his embrace. I stared at the night traffic, blurred by champagne, vodka, wine, and brandy. Unsteady, I leaned against him and felt his breath on my neck. The Mercedes pulled up just in time.

Fortunately, the drive back to the Maksoud was short. His hand on the gearshift was within easy reach, but I sat motionless and quiet until we arrived at the hotel. Jaco accompanied me into the deserted lobby; I paused a discreet distance from the elevators. "Jaco, you were the first to welcome me to Brazil. Knowing you has been fun, but tonight was beyond casual friendship. I must bid you farewell." It sounded so stilted; I tried Portuguese instead. *"Obrigada e boa noite."*

"Your Portuguese is improving, but you must say, *'Até logo*, until later,'" he chided gently. Without comment, I lifted my chin to put my cheek next to his, but met the taste of smoke and brandy as his lips found mine with insistent warmth. I pulled back, but he held me at arm's length. "Not bad for a gringa," he said softly. "If you ever change your mind, I'm ready for more. Just call me, Bethania."

"Please...don't tempt me." Our eyes met before he released me. *"Boa noite*, Jaco." I walked unevenly toward the elevators. Alone in the empty bubble, I faced inward, but felt him watching my ascent. When I reached my floor, I went to the glass and raised the rose in farewell. He waved back from the lobby bar.

Jaco sipped Chivas as a saxophone crooned. *I was sure she was mine,* he thought. *I must be losing my touch.* The elevators moved little this time of night, but enough to keep him hopeful. She had seen him in the bar and might change her mind.

A businessman with an escort slow-danced past his barrel chair. Swirling the whiskey, Jaco imagined holding Bethania. *She's smart but suppressed,* he thought. *Obviously, she has never had a real lover, never had a lover like me. The woman deep inside is struggling to be free. I could release her.*

He watched the suspended car on twelve start down slowly; it paused at seven, and then descended. A silhouette with bouffant hair and tight pants belonged to a solitary woman, but not Bethania.

The sax played the first notes of a tango—a melancholy song of betrayal and loneliness. The elevator came to rest at the lobby level. Bethania had not changed her mind. High heels were headed his way with a proposition. In a different mood, Jaco might have been interested. Tonight, he downed his whiskey and headed home to his wife.

I plunked down on the bed in Room 1202. How had I resisted the most seductive man I had ever encountered? He had aroused an unknown lust that left me greedy and ashamed. Bittersweet pride flowed beneath the alcoholic haze as I called Sam.

He was waiting. "Hello. Bartlett?"

A heavy tongue betrayed me. "Yes, it's Beth. You made me promise. I'm...I'm in the hotel."

"Alone?"

"Very alone," I echoed with silly pride.

"Are you OK? You sound drunk."

"Just a little tipsy." In fact, a bad hangover was in the making. "If I arrive late tomorrow, could you...*hic*...keep the team on track...*hic*...'til I get there?" I didn't bother to stifle the telltale spasms. "I won't be much use first thing in the morning."

"The question is, 'How are you now?'" A pause. "You *are* at the hotel, right?"

His query should have offended me, but didn't. "Sam, don't worry. I'm going to bed to sleep this off. Your Project Manager will be back in gear tomorrow."

"To hell with the Project Manager. I just want *you* to be safe. Sleep well, Bartlett."

"Goodnight...*hic*...Sam."

"Goodnight, you silly woman." Voiced with affection, his simple scolding made me glad that I wasn't with Jaco.

Who's in the Driver's Seat?

On Friday, Marcelo marked my late arrival with raised eyebrows and a smirk, but everyone else was wrapped up in meeting deadlines. After Thursday's energetic high, the office was subdued; analytical scrutiny and editorial precision tamed our collective burst of creativity.

Taped to the wall was a task list; much remained to be done. If I didn't buckle down I would slow the team's progress. I started drafting questions to help BomFarm's executives develop recommendations. An hour later, "Sam, could you take a look at this?" I moved on to my next task.

Ten minutes passed. "Too academic," Sam said without sugarcoating. He sat down next to me; my pages were covered with scribbled notes and X marks.

"How so?" I asked defensively.

"For instance, you wrote, 'Which customer segment is your target? What is the size of the target market?' These guys never heard of segments or market size. Let's ask them, 'Who are you going to sell to?'"

"But that's so vague," I protested. Then I quoted the GCC training manual: "Precise language makes for precise analysis."

"Are you sure?" Sam countered. "Remember, BomFarm is in trouble. We're demanding a lot from these guys in a short time. Textbook terms will turn them off. Besides, many words don't translate well into Portuguese; using English won't help them grasp new concepts." I tipped my head in thought, but wasn't convinced. Sam kept pushing his case. "Keeping it colloquial will put them at ease."

"Let me see." I studied his notes. I preferred the academic style that was GCC's hallmark. Nonetheless, Sam had a valid point. "Let's go one by one," I compromised.

We fought for two hours and Sam won most of the battles. I started to appreciate the power of simplicity. Yet, something haunted me. Bob had charged me with bringing rigor to this office. Was there rigor in "Who are you going to sell to?" And if so, would Bob perceive it? "Do you really think these questions will work?" I asked Sam.

"Don't worry," he assured me. "Marcelo and I will get results from these guys. Just trust me. If we can engage them, we'll get lots of good ideas. If they feel lectured, we'll get nothing."

My three-page document shrank to one page. I rather liked the concise strategic checklist. It was structured without being intimidating. The important ideas were distilled to their essence. What had been cut out? Self-important consulting buzzwords.

While Luciana started to translate the final draft, I compiled a package for Bob. Protocol required sending him all client working papers, whether he would look at them or not. We had to ship a courier package to headquarters anyway; it was time to submit monthly timesheets.

Like lawyers, GCC consultants recorded hours dedicated to each client. A budget established the "billable" hours expected for each team member. Project Managers looked good by "making" budget. An overrun meant renegotiating fees (always uncomfortable) or a black mark against the Manager (even worse). Consultants looked good by being billable; high "utilization" meant a bigger bonus. These conflicting interests provided checks and balances.

The BomFarm budget allocated sixteen days per month for Marcelo, Sam, and me; nothing for Luciana and Ed. The budget was laughable. From day one, everyone had spent countless hours to execute the revised work plan. Completing the timesheets would force us to confront reality and threatened to derail our precious team spirit.

Nonetheless, it had to be done, so I interrupted everyone. "Can you guys come over here for a minute?" Work stopped; everyone pulled their chairs around the conference table for an instant meeting. The blank forms sat accusingly on the table. "Unfortunately, we need to send timesheets to Boston…but, we have a problem." Everyone was solemn. "I never dreamed BomFarm would require so much time. Thank you all for working so hard. You've all exceeded my expectations, but we've also exceeded the budget. The new work plan is making it worse, not better."

"Yes, we're working full-life, not full-time," Sam concurred seriously.

Marcelo scratched his beard before joining in, "That includes weekends. It's against my religion."

I wanted to motivate them without looking bad myself. "What if we split the difference between budget and reality?" There would still be a huge overrun, but I wanted them to get credit at headquarters.

Marcelo pulled out his calculator, punched a few buttons, and showed the result to Sam. Sam nodded seriously, huddled with Ed and Luciana. Four hands reached for the blank forms.

They filled in the uncompromising grids, scrawled signatures, and shoved them toward me. Lines labeled *"Formação"* and *"Fantasma"* complemented "BomFarm."

"What's *Formação?*" Ed and Luciana had filled in that line.

"Development. Training," Sam clarified. "Our trainees aren't billed to customers." In Boston, clients paid for hours spent by trainees. Sam's violation of firm policy was good for me, but I felt like I was shortchanging these capable students whose skills surpassed Boston's billable Research Associates.

"And *Fantasma?*" I asked suspiciously.

Knowing looks crossed the table; even Ed suppressed a smile. "Fantasma is a 'ghost' that haunts this office," Sam claimed. "The phantom was our biggest client until BomFarm came along." The Boston office used "promo" as a catch-all for non-billable time; consultants avoided recording promotional hours, lest they look bad at bonus time. In this start-up office, Sam had reinforced the need to invest time in future clients by creating a fun, fictitious name without a negative stigma. So far, no one from headquarters had picked up the fact that invoices were never issued to Fantasma.

I studied the sheets. The BomFarm hours matched my budget. "Wait a minute. You didn't understand." Scolding lines creased my forehead. "You should report more BomFarm hours." Sam and Marcelo didn't accept the forms I pushed back. "I don't want to hide the true commitment to BomFarm," I paraphrased GCC's Project Manager training.

Sam returned his sheet with a deprecating flip. "This is nothing but GCC bureaucracy." Marcelo mimicked his boss and sent his sheet scooting off the table.

"Not really." In a huff, I retrieved Marcelo's timesheet. "These records provide an accurate measure of customers' demands and help GCC evaluate consultants' performance," I lectured.

"Bartlett, lighten up. Timesheets don't measure what goes on here. They don't tell me that Ed revived the computer at midnight or that Luciana coaxed critical information from BomFarm's competitor or that Marcelo's projections were a breakthrough." His employees beamed.

"I know, but Boston should know how hard you're all working," I protested.

"Boston doesn't care about us," Sam said, gesturing to the team. "They care about profits from Brazil and they'll get them if we invest time and energy in BomFarm. Sorry, Bartlett, your budget is irrelevant."

With loyalties torn between Brazil and Boston, I gathered the sheets and separated the white originals from the yellow carbons. "You win this one," I conceded. "It's not so easy to get rid of ghosts," I rationalized as I gave each consultant their yellow copy. "These are for your files."

As I slid the originals into the DHL envelope, Sam asked the group, "Shall we put these in the circular file?" They playfully wadded the papers and aimed for the wastebasket. Marcelo and Ed scored. Sam and Luciana missed. The crumpled papers lay on the floor, belligerently. Mine lay alone on the table; it would join fading pages in a battered manila folder—every timesheet I had filed in my decade at GCC. If Sam's stance made my meticulous accounting ludicrous, I wasn't ready to admit it.

An ant crawled across the table, burdened by a grain of rice, a big load for a small ant. Struggling alone, far from the colony, he approached my solitary timesheet. I raised my hand to brush him to the floor, but hesitated. A creature of social order, he had sought new territory. I wondered whether the maverick would return to the nest as a hero or an outcast. I let him go on his way.

Our hard work over the weekend paid off. Monday's orientation of the BomFarm teams was flawless. After the introductory session, the six teams dispersed to the separate conference rooms where they would work for several weeks.

Compelled to control the process, I visited each room. At my first stop, I asked the Revenues team, *"Algumas perguntas?* Any questions?"* With self-importance, one man switched to English, leaving his teammates in the dark. That taught me to just watch and listen. In the next room, a wiry man was drawing a diagram on a blackboard; the others proposed changes; the Hospital team seemed to be on track. The Pharmacy team was discussing soccer, not strategy. The Veterinary team was having a raucous debate—about what, I had no idea. In the Costs room, smoke and silence prevailed; figures with sleeves rolled up were bent over spreadsheets. At my final stop, two men argued fiercely in one corner; the rest of the Infrastructure team doodled.

Making the rounds was humbling. I failed to help the struggling groups and may have hindered the effective ones. "Do you think these teams are going to work?" I asked Sam anxiously. "The Revenues and Hospital teams have some leadership, but the others are adrift. Either everyone talks at once or no one talks at all."

Sam was unperturbed. "Remember, teams go through stages—forming, norming, storming, and performing."

"That's the theory." We had read the same textbook. "But these guys are storming or stalling," I whined.

"Give them time."

"We don't have much time, just a few weeks. A false start could be fatal and I'm useless." I was dejected.

"True, true. Right now, you'll intimidate the teams and frustrate yourself," he asserted. Then he gloated, "At last. Something the superwoman can't do! Cheer up, Bartlett. Marcelo and I will keep them on track."

"But this shouldn't rest on your shoulders. We designed this approach together; I'm responsible, too."

"You've got plenty to do," Sam assured me. "Go back to Boston and convince Bob White that all is well. That will save us a lot of trouble down the road."

"But this is a critical moment. I should be helping." It was wishful thinking given all the rapid-fire Portuguese.

"Marcelo and I will keep things going here. No problem." Although forced to depend upon them, I was reluctant to relinquish oversight. Sam read my mind. "You won't be able to control every step, no matter how hard you try. This process will take on a life of its own."

I rocked from foot to foot, weighing the pros and cons of being in the north or south. "By Friday, we should have some sense of the teams' progress. Armed with that, I can go back to Boston and interact with Bob."

"Speaking of Mr. White, don't you need to update him?" Sam was pushing me to make the overdue call.

"I'll phone him while you and Marcelo shepherd the teams," I agreed reluctantly. "Could you check the Infrastructure team? They were going nowhere a few minutes ago."

"Yes, ma'am," he said, clicking his heels. "Meanwhile, good luck with the Partner-in-Charge."

I prepared for Bob's wrath. Since our last interaction, I had shared threatening projections with BomFarm and launched untested strategic methods with unprecedented client participation. Given his absence, I had usurped the Partner's role.

After congratulating the arrival of his newborn, I summarized why and how I had redirected the project. "Sounds like you've run into trouble down there. Strategic transformation turned rescue operation." Bob was curt.

"We hope to do both by enlisting BomFarm's executives and accelerating the timeframe."

"You're down there to train GCC consultants, not BomFarm's executives." I heard him snap his suspenders to punctuate his tirade. "People inside a company can't produce strong, unbiased recommendations. You'll just get a hodge-podge of self-interested opinions. There's no way this will be up to GCC standards."

Having just seen the floundering teams, I feared Bob might be right. Still, I defended our unorthodox approach. "Traditional methods will produce a beautifully bound report, while BomFarm goes down the drain." Emboldened, I continued and drew on Sam's coaching. "I admit that bias is a risk. Therefore, we'll need a strong Devil's Advocate; your senior review will be more critical than ever." Fingers crossed, I hoped I'd touched his ego.

"So, you still need the Partner-in-Charge?" Bob's retort was sarcastic.

"Absolutely, Bob. Circumstances forced me to act, but I drew heavily on your experience to structure the customer teams. Your suggestions..."

"Just a minute, Beth." His secretary had interrupted my attempts to appease Bob. He returned to the line. "Sorry, I have to take another call. Keep me posted. In a few weeks, I'll go to São Paulo to see where we stand."

"Bob, please, don't hang up," I pleaded. "To gain time, let's review everything in Boston next week. Can you block a day for an in-depth work session?"

"Fine."

His attention was elsewhere, but I still made a final appeal. "As for the Brazilians, trust them. Their jobs are at stake; they will find a way to save BomFarm." My conviction was earnest, but with no substantiation. Sam's influence was rubbing off.

155

Blame It on Rio

"Rio is on the way to Boston. We could sightsee before you fly out Sunday night." It was one of Sam's outrageous ideas at which I scoffed, but later embraced.

So, Friday afternoon, we jostled among smog-infused businessmen, anxious to board the *ponte aérea* or air bridge between São Paulo and Rio de Janeiro. Several airlines co-operated the popular forty-five-minute shuttle; I wondered exactly who was getting me from point A to point B.

In one line, we waited for a priority number. In a second line, we waited to pay for our tickets. We endured a third line to check my baggage. Then, the drama began. As each arriving plane spewed out arrivals, an agent shouted numbers to a crush of hopefuls. Finally, climbing up the rickety boarding ladder of the fourth outbound plane, I doubted whether having a seat was better than waiting.

Noisy props thrust us into the sky; we leveled off at a low cruising altitude. With São Paulo in a haze behind us, lush hills and an expanse of tropical waters beckoned. I stopped fretting. Here was the famed beauty of Brazil. In contrast to

São Paulo's monochromatic expanse of gray concrete, Rio boasted undulating green hills, sparkling blue water, and curving white beaches.

"Caesar's Park," Sam told the taxi driver. Black bodies hung precariously off a passing train; exotic plants hung from elegant apartments; a sprawling *favela* spilled down a steep hillside behind luxury hotels.

After checking in to two "junior suites" facing Ipanema Beach, we strolled along the mosaic sidewalks with tiny black and white tiles laid in distinctive curves. A setting sun spot lit lean young men who spiked volleyballs in skimpy suits. A bit farther down the beach, others showed off with *jogo de cintura*—fancy footwork—and head shots in a pickup soccer game.

At the sidewalk bar where Jobim wrote "The Girl from Ipanema," I sipped a drink as hips swayed past with comfortable sexuality. After a feast of grilled shellfish, we entered a smoky nightclub where Fátima Regina sang Brazilian melodies. The barrel chairs, the J&B, the smoke rising from Sam's cigarette, the throaty lyrics, and the dim light…together made me feel deliciously decadent. Between songs, Sam approached the earthy alto; they huddled with her accompanist, who played a few opening bars. Sam nodded and slipped a bill into the tip jar.

As Fátima sang, the only words I understood were "*coração*" (heart) and "*feliz*" (happy). Sam leaned over and whispered, "I'll translate later. It's mushy but I like it." That was enough to put a smile on my face.

We clapped as Fátima bowed. Sam nodded appreciation and then spoke softly to me. "It's called '*Carinhoso*'; that means 'sentimental' or 'tender.' The lyrics say, 'I don't know why my heart beats happily when I see you.'" Even in the dim light, I saw the sincerity in his deep blue eyes. "It ends with 'but just the same, you escape me.'" To avoid reading too much into his gaze, I took a sip of whiskey. "I warned it was mushy," he apologized. Fátima began an upbeat samba that dispelled the intimacy.

After the last set, we ambled back to Caesar's Park under moonlit skies. With Sam beside me, Rio's shadowy streets didn't feel too ominous. Nonetheless, I was nervous and sought refuge in business talk. "I hope things go well in Boston; we need Bob on our side."

"Well, you're going to have some help pulling him over." Sam paused for dramatic effect.

I stopped mid-step. "You?"

"I wish. I would love to go to Boston, but I need to be here." He was right and it was as we discussed. Uneasy on the dark sidewalk, I resumed walking. Sam continued, "I told Isaac about your project review. He's going to join you in Boston."

"He's what?!"

"Isaac wants to know what the firm's seniors think about BomFarm's prospects. Besides, he'll use any excuse to go to the States."

"Was this your idea?" I queried suspiciously.

"I planted the seed," Sam confessed, "but Isaac jumped at the idea. If he shows up in Boston, BomFarm will get the attention of the top brass." The two men had hatched a clever plot, but I was uncomfortable and grasped for an excuse to stop Isaac. "It's just a one-day work session; can that be worth the time and expense of his travelling all the way from Brazil?"

"Definitely. BomFarm is in the balance." Sam left no room for doubt.

I dreaded springing another surprise on Bob, but this would give him a firsthand impression of BomFarm. Once we were safely in the hotel lobby, I confronted Sam. "I'm not sure how to view this. Isaac's crashing an internal work session could be interpreted as a sign of support, a vote of no confidence, or an act of desperation. Regardless, it is most unorthodox."

"Unorthodox." Sam chuckled. "Everything about this project has been unorthodox." He retrieved our keys from the concierge. "I'll escort you to your room."

"Why didn't you tell me sooner?" I demanded, as we stepped off the elevator.

"Because I'm selfish," he said sheepishly. "I wanted you to enjoy Rio without worrying." He unlocked the door; the room was lit, curtains drawn, a breakfast menu and mints waited on the turned-down bed. It looked most inviting. "Good. Housekeeping has been here. Do you need anything else?" Sam asked from the doorway.

Touched by his protectiveness, I couldn't stay mad at him. "Sam, you really should have consulted me about Isaac. Don't forget who's managing this project." My consternation didn't last. "I'll forgive you this time…and Rio is a very special place. Thank you for bringing me here. Forgetting work for a few hours has been a treat."

"The best is yet to come," Sam promised. "Tomorrow, I'm taking you to the Sugar Loaf." He handed me my key. "Be sure to chain the door behind me. See you for breakfast. *Boa noite,*" he mimicked a Brazilian accent as he stepped into the corridor.

"*Buenas noches,*" I stage-whispered from my open door. My Spanish surprised and pleased him.

The elevator opened. "*Buenas noches, querida.*" He waved and disappeared, leaving me wondering what *querida* meant.

Sunday morning, the rooftop breakfast room offered a delicious buffet and unbroken views of Rio's beaches. We joined the beachgoers for some hours on the sand. Pineapple *caipirinhas* successfully quelled my worries about Isaac as an uninvited guest, Bob as a displaced Partner, and George as a disgruntled husband.

After a leisurely lunch, we bought tickets to ride the cable car to the top of the famous *Pão de Açúcar*. At the base of the Sugar Loaf, we squeezed into a tiny cabin with other sweaty tourists. When it started to sway, I gripped the overhead handhold and hoped that the engineer had some German ancestors despite his very Brazilian name, Augusto Ferreira Ramos.

As we disembarked, a mulatto boy coaxed us to a well-worn spot for a photo with "no obligation." Before us, a cameraman made us smile; behind us, on Corcovado Hill, Christ blessed the city with open arms. After a few clicks, we wandered away to explore the peak.

To me, "exploring" had meant a heavy backpack and sturdy hiking boots. Here, my only gear was a disposable camera; my garb was a summer skirt and open sandals. To me, the word "peak" evoked the isolated wilderness of the White Mountains or the Adirondacks, not soft, curvaceous hills hugging a bustling city where high-rise dwellings circled sunlit lakes.

A bronze plaque marked the vista's edge. I approached, expecting to find an informative map highlighting distant points of interest. Instead, a poem was etched in the metal. As I searched for familiar words, Sam offered to interpret.

> *The tresses, the forests;*
> *The breasts, the mountains;*
> *The waist, the beaches;*
> *The skirt, the waves of the sea;*
> *The silhouette, the grace of the woman from Rio;*
> *At the statue's feet, the Ibis.*

Already sensuous, the city became sexual. Sam's sensitive reading awakened a longing I had denied. I wanted to embody the womanly grace of the verse. More surprising still, I wanted to know this complex man who I had kept at arm's length. The man who had challenged me, coached me, cajoled me. The man who was *carinhoso* and had used a song to tell me how much he cared.

He repeated the verse, this time in musical Portuguese.

A cabeleira, as florestas;
Os seios, as montanhas;
A cintura, as praias;
A saia, as ondas do mar;
A silhueta, a graça da mulher carioca;
Aos pés da estátua, a bis.

Melody and rhythm poured in; emotion and tears poured out. "What's wrong?" Sam was alarmed.

"Nothing's wrong," I sniffed. "Too much is right." Gently, he placed one arm around my shoulders and held me firmly by his side. Quietly, we looked out at the beauty, each with our private thoughts. A bubble rose up inside me, magical but fragile. I felt no need to suppress it; it lingered for a few moments and then drifted away. I shifted my weight; he dropped his arm and we headed back to the tram, not quite hand in hand.

At the cable car station, we were routed past a wall of snapshots, enhanced by souvenir frames and china plates. Our smiles beamed from one of the ceramics. We bought two dishes with no obligation.

During the jerky descent, I clung to a pole and let other passengers come between Sam and me. His heart had rendered a poem dangerous. Touching me only with words, he had unleashed hidden feelings. The beauty of the Sugar Loaf had caught me off guard. At the ground station, we were just two more tourists, two consultants taking a break in Rio. I felt the ceramic plate through the Toucan tote slung over my shoulder. Not meant to last, the cheap photo would fade. Cracks would fragment the image of togetherness. But at that moment, I cherished the five-inch round that made us one.

Sam gripped the armrests on his creaky seat aboard the prop plane to São Paulo. Bouncing in the thunderstorm, he resented the turbulence outside and the turbulence inside.

"What will you do while I'm gone?" Beth had asked at the airport. "You'll have lots of free time. Maybe you should go out with one of Sandra's friends." It was like ice water, and it hurt.

"If I want company, I can find it," he had barked. "Don't try to manage my life." The curtain that fell between them had stayed down while the border guard had checked her passport. Then, she had crossed a line where he could not follow.

Still fuming, he brusquely refused the nuts offered by the flight attendant. He wasn't hungry. *Jesus, she makes me mad. She may be the Project Manager, but she isn't going to control me.* The wound was especially raw after the weekend in Rio. So much for any illusions he might have had on the Sugar Loaf. *"Is she blind to my feelings or is she afraid of them?"*

He wanted to be with Beth every minute of every day. He admired her as a professional—her intelligence, her insights. But it was her vulnerability that made him love and want to protect her.

In Rio, he had been content to watch her soak up the sensuous city, laugh in the waves, and shed tears on the Sugar Loaf. For a moment they had been a man and a woman, not an Office Head and a Project Manager.

Sam glanced at his watch. By now she would be airborne, talking to the "interesting man" sitting next to her. Despite his jealousy, Sam couldn't help smiling. *She's munching nuts with a gin and tonic*, he mused. *She's the only woman I know who loves to eat and isn't afraid to show it. I bet it costs more to feed her than to dress her in those dull business suits.* He longed to take her to the fashionable shops in Buenos Aires and buy stylish clothes to show off her long legs and small waist.

An air pocket jolted him out of his reverie. *Nah, stop imagining things. She went to Harvard; she's a doctor's wife. I'm divorced, broke, and without a degree to my name. There's no contest.* Another bounce strengthened his resolve. *Snap out of it. Cool off. For Beth, Brazil is a rung on the career ladder and an exotic adventure. If she's looking for something, it's a fling. That was the most he could hope for* and the last thing he wanted.

The frantic whirl of the propellers announced descent. The lights of São Paulo stretched endlessly in every direction. *Good. Soon I'll be back in this fucking city where I don't care about anyone and they don't care about me.*

Sunday Night—October 12
En route from Rio to Boston

Dear Diary,

Something clicked on the Sugar Loaf. I felt like a beautiful woman and it wasn't just the poetry. Afraid of feelings, his and mine, I panicked at the airport. I pushed him away; suggesting that he go out with other women was stupid!

OK, maybe our relationship isn't "just professional." Sam has taught me to laugh at myself and to accept being imperfect. He's taught me to believe in myself and voice my convictions. He's a wonderful friend who is taking me to places I've never been, some of which are inside myself.

I promised to keep Brazil in balance with my real life. But what is real? Boston evaporates when I'm in Brazil. George recedes into the background. I should feel guilty, but I want to bask in this afterglow before touchdown snuffs it out.

Stone Walls and
Stonewalls

I returned to married life without drama. I listened politely while George told me about using radiation to treat cancer patients. To show interest, I asked questions; it felt like a client interview.

In return, George tolerated my abridged account of work challenges and a touristy weekend in Rio. "Would you consider going down to Brazil with me? I have one more trip before the project ends; it's an interesting country and the people are friendly and fun." It was a weekday morning and we were dressing for work. Inviting George to join me was a sham and I knew it. Committed full throttle at the hospital, he couldn't have gone if he wanted to. George shrugged and I told myself, *At least I gave him a chance.*

One evening, we had tickets to the Boston Ballet. Autumn's crisp air was an excuse to wear wool, a little black dress with pearls. George donned a suede blazer over a navy shirt and well-cut pants. A successful doctor and his wife, we joined the sedate audience in balcony seats for a program that featured modern dance, tutus, and Tchaikovsky. The highly trained dancers evoked dispassionate admiration, an intellectual reaction worlds away from my emotional response to Jobim.

After the ballet, George pulled chilled champagne from the refrigerator. As he popped the cork, I tried to silence Jaco's bass voice toasting "to a most lovely and unusual lady." When we sat on the sofa, George draped a relaxed arm over my shoulder; I tried to block the memory of Sam's touch on the Sugar Loaf. We sipped the sparkling wine on a couch chosen with painstaking care. Bang & Olufsen speakers played acoustically balanced smooth jazz. Congenially, we critiqued the ballet and planned a drive to see the fall colors.

Without finishing the champagne, George announced, "I have a new sex video. Women with women."

"That sounds fun," I fibbed, but appreciated the gesture. For the past year, our sex had been enhanced by watching others. Soft porn provided an erotic kick to intercourse that had grown monotonous. George put the VCR on fast forward to bypass the early frames. Apparently, he had watched this flick before. He paused at a scene in which two women were undressing and caressing each other to the beat of unimaginative music. We followed their lead and climaxed to the groans of strangers.

The next morning, the stale champagne symbolized a life with sparkling moments that often went flat. As I poured the expensive liquid down the drain, an unexpected tightness filled my chest. George and I shared the fruits of two successful careers; we lived in picture-perfect luxury. Any strife between us was muffled in good behavior. Determined to make our marriage work, I had kept my vows and made love with a clear conscience; I had never missed passion...until Brazil.

Work, the dependable broom, swept marital dissatisfaction under the rug.

As the week progressed, I felt like a puppeteer trying to get marionettes to behave. I was powerless to prevent Isaac's attending GCC's project review. "Given the new pace of this project, we need the input of GCC's Partners sooner rather than later" was his irrefutable argument. Isaac expected opinions from Bob *and* Harvey.

Isaac's coming to Boston got Bob's attention. After initial outrage, Bob took a liking to the idea. "Under the circumstances, maybe it does make sense," he conceded. "If this project has derailed, we'll have the right players to cut the client loose. As a matter of fact, I want Harvey there to help make that call."

Bob's reasoning worried me. Thinking that the project should be cancelled could be a self-fulfilling prophecy. I wanted to open Bob's mind. "Far from derailed, this project proves how much consultants can help. Isaac is counting on an exchange with a real industry expert."

"If he wants to pick my brain, it's OK with me. After all, he's still a paying client." Bob spun around in his chair, a sure sign he was ready to move on to something else.

"Bob, this project has not gone as planned, we can agree on that. But, I'm asking you to reserve judgment until you have more information. BomFarm is complex. I'd like to brief you on the company before Isaac arrives."

"A drug company is a drug company," was Bob's comeback. GCC training drummed in that every client was unique. Had Bob skipped that class?

I tried once more to engage him. "Isaac will ask you about building economies of scale. We should discuss BomFarm's profit dynamics and ways to improve them before he gets here."

"Go over the numbers with Roger. He's done the modeling for two of my pharmaceutical clients."

"I'll talk to Roger, but Roger's not the pro you are. Let's mark a time to meet on Friday, including Roger, if you like." Bob picked up a pencil. "In addition to the numbers, we can discuss what is coming out of the teams in Brazil."

"OK, bulldog Bartlett," Bob smiled as he gave in. "What time on Friday?"

"Ten to twelve." I wanted to capture Bob early before he got diverted by other business. He marked his agenda. "It's a worthwhile investment," I added, as I rose to go. "Isaac is coming all the way from Brazil and he's pretty sharp." Bob enthralled most clients with his charm and *consultantese*, but Isaac would expect substance. Bob better deliver.

"See you Friday at ten," Bob promised. I was pretty sure he meant it.

When I stopped by his office, Roger was expecting me. The protégé mirrored Bob's red suspenders, white collar, and blue shirt. I hid my disgust and got straight to the point. "Look at the numbers for BomFarm. By Friday, we need examples of new profit dynamics, grounded in other GCC clients."

"Should be easy enough." Roger was flippant about the BomFarm preparations. However, involving Roger would keep Bob happy and *might* produce something new to share with Isaac.

Harvey was a ready ally—sympathetic to the twists and turns of the project, delighted to participate in a client case discussion, and intrigued by the presence of Isaac. "Your methods violate GCC protocol, but may work for BomFarm," he said thoughtfully. "Keep a tight rein on those teams. Their work is critical to your success."

Harvey's admonition gave me a good excuse to talk to Sam each morning. We coached each other and reported progress in our respective hemispheres. Sticking to business, we didn't mention Rio; our shared work seemed to dispel the friction I had provoked at the airport. By the end of the week, things had progressed nicely in the north and south.

I readied myself for Isaac's arrival with mixed emotions. I didn't mind crossing the t's and checking the numbers; that was the Project Manager's job. I did mind giving up control. In Brazil, I had been the Partner de facto, but that would change when Isaac met real GCC Partners. Power would shift toward experience and status. Bob would call the shots.

If Bob considered BomFarm a loser, he would terminate the project. If he believed BomFarm could succeed, he would take command and seize the credit. From the start, the "A Team" had been on the sidelines, waiting to finish the game. When I was insecure and intimidated, I had welcomed the thought. Now, yielding my territory made me bristle, even though common sense said that BomFarm deserved the attention of a more senior industry expert.

To unwind, I enjoyed a weekend break with George. We drove through New England's fall colors at their glorious peak. Each bend in the road revealed a maple more brilliant than the last. The spectacular display of sunlit orange, red, and yellow was more precious for its short life. We stopped at farm stands, guzzled apple cider, sucked sweet Concord grapes from their skins, and chose pumpkins for carving.

The quaint tranquility of stone walls, white clapboard houses, and covered bridges was straight out of a postcard. This pacific world would welcome me when Brazil was over.

Isaac's bombshell came at the end of a long day.

The morning had gone well. Harvey and Bob had greeted Isaac courteously, with no indication that his unprecedented visit had caused aggravation. I led the review of BomFarm's challenges and project status. Isaac reinforced my remarks, emphasizing critical points.

Next, Bob started to present his experience. On the third slide, Isaac interrupted. "Let me ask some questions that are relevant to BomFarm." Bob stiffened. "For example, when companies organize around customers, how do they avoid duplication? We certainly can't afford to replicate any activity." Bingo. I had warned Bob about this concern and he was prepared. Bob tried to resume his presentation, but Isaac fired off another question. Harvey had a ready reply. As Bob started his speech for a third time, lunch arrived. Bob turned off the projector, leaving the transparencies ready to embark once more after a sandwich.

"Forgive the informal fare; we thought it would save time," I apologized to Isaac as I set a deli platter in the middle of the conference table.

"So, this is the famous 'working lunch.'" Isaac reached for a sandwich. "It's my first experience with this custom; maybe I'll import it to Brazil."

"Don't do that," I piped up. "You'll spoil the country!"

"Bete is becoming Brazilian," Isaac pointed out with playful pride. Roger snickered; the older men smiled. Isaac reached for another sandwich and began asking about cost dynamics. Between bites, Bob answered the probes with an occasional assist from Roger. I wondered whether Isaac was learning something new or just testing them.

After lunch, we validated the customer focus and debated the emerging recommendations. Things were on track until Bob asked, "What makes you think BomFarm will take the drastic steps necessary to survive?" The question was valid, but Bob's tone was disparaging. To offset Bob's aggression, Harvey itemized why BomFarm had the potential to overcome its crisis. A healthy give-and-take followed, leaving Bob and his sidekick on the sidelines.

Finally, it was time to wrap up. "Here is the work plan for the rest of the project." I handed out copies to all. "As you can see, I'll be back in Brazil next week; Bob will join me the week after that for the final report. It's ambitious, but doable with an all-out effort. Reactions?"

Bob raised the first objection. "We need to push that schedule back at least two weeks. I need to see preliminary recommendations; after that, Roger here will run some numbers. We need at least a month to develop the final report." The projector hummed with my work plan still up on the screen. I picked up a marker to make notes on the flip chart.

"Now there's a reversal." Isaac scoffed as I uncapped the marker. "Everyone says South Americans are laid back and North Americans are go-getters. What I just heard is the opposite. Bete, sit down," he barked and then added "please" as an afterthought. I sat. No one snickered this time. "A month isn't acceptable," he stated flatly.

"It will have to be," Bob countered. "That's what we need for a quality product."

"Maybe that's what your firm needs, but it's not what my company needs." Isaac pressed his bulky frame against the table toward Bob. The table shook, and I leaned over to switch off the projector. "Mr. White, you live in an ivory tower where things are neat and tidy, but I live in a vortex of messy change. Our best executives have been pulled off the line to save BomFarm. They've been working their a—," Isaac looked over at me and rephrased, "They've been working overtime to find solutions. There's no way I'm going to slow down just so new players can get up the learning curve." His disgust was targeted at Bob and Roger.

A thin line of perspiration highlighted Bob's receding hairline. Harvey turned to me for clarification. "Is this plan realistic? It's mighty ambitious. Where did it come from?"

We had negotiated the chronogram with Mueller in Brazil. "It's extremely ambitious, but so far we are on schedule thanks to the commitment of BomFarm and our local consultants," I explained.

Isaac pressed, "We've got to maintain the project pace." He turned to address Harvey. "This crisis calls for speed; we can't afford to divert energy or slow things down. Just consider the language barrier. Translation alone will drain time," Isaac pushed his case. "We'll lose at least three or four days if we have to work in English."

"Are you asking GCC to back out?" Bob was belligerent. "If so, we'll do so gladly." Intentional or not, the Partner-in-Charge had placed his lack of commitment squarely on the table.

Isaac's bald head turned pink as he reined in his temper. When he spoke, he was deliberate and calm. "I'm not asking GCC to back out; I'm asking *you*, *sir*, to back out."

"Fine." Bob rose abruptly. "Suits me." He started toward the door. "Consider me gone. We should have rejected this project to begin with." He stomped out, with Roger in his wake.

An awkward silence fell. Harvey seemed torn between appeasing Isaac and corralling Bob. "You have strong views, Isaac. What do you expect from GCC?"

"Foremost, I expect the advisors I hire to respect their client." I prepared for another negative outburst, but instead Isaac continued, "We have had utmost respect and outstanding work from GCC's São Paulo team," he looked straight at me, "led by Ms. Bartlett. They are committed to this schedule and I am confident they will meet it."

"Your confidence is gratifying," Harvey acknowledged, "but BomFarm hired GCC and that includes direction by a Partner." Isaac nodded agreement. "Clearly, the chemistry does not work between you and Bob White." Isaac nodded again. "Would you accept me as the Partner-in-Charge? I can provide guidance by phone from Boston and engage Bob behind the scenes to take advantage of his industry experience."

It was an elegant solution and I suspected it had been Isaac's goal all along. "Done." Isaac shook Harvey's hand. "Your firm is guiding us in the right direction. My coming to Boston gained critical time. The day was most instructive. However, I will say," he paused for effect, "the food for thought was better than the food for the body." Isaac was happy with the way things were ending.

"Speaking of food, would you join me for dinner at the Faculty Club this evening? To compensate for the working lunch?" Harvey understood egos. Isaac beamed and accepted the invitation.

Rising to go, Harvey turned toward me. "BomFarm has the potential to emerge as a strong competitor. Young lady, we're counting on you. Keep me in the loop and call me when you need me." Harvey picked up his rumpled tweed jacket and left me alone with Isaac.

On one hand, I was relieved. We still had a project. I was still in charge. But, Isaac had been Machiavellian and Bob was really miffed. Knowing I would pay for Isaac's being a deus ex machina, I was agitated rather than appreciative. Criticizing a client was never advisable, but I decided to push back. "You threw a curveball."

"I had to play hardball." Isaac picked up on my baseball jargon. "I had to keep Bob away from BomFarm. He's the wrong man; he doesn't believe in us or respect what we are trying to do."

"What about Mueller? Won't he be upset at your unilateral decision?"

"Not when I tell him Dr. Harvey Osborne is advising us." Isaac donned a Cheshire cat smile.

I still had doubts. "Dr. Mueller doesn't like surprises and this was a big one, at least for me." *And for Bob and GCC*, I thought.

"Don't worry, Bete." Isaac gathered his papers. "Having GCC's founder formally on board will please Mueller; Harvey's ego doesn't get in the way of his intellect." Isaac was visibly pleased with his "negotiations." Bob had been pushed aside. Harvey had been pushed to the foreground. I had been pushed into the hot seat.

"That was a good meeting. Well done. Now, we can move full speed ahead." Isaac picked up his briefcase and moved toward the door. "Point me toward Harvey's office."

"I'll take you there." That's what a Brazilian would do; besides, it was dangerous to leave Isaac roaming the halls alone.

At Harvey's threshold, Isaac confided in a hushed tone, "When you call Sam, tell him my trip to Boston was very beneficial. This was one of his better ideas."

Before I could react, Harvey waved us in. It would be a relief to hand Isaac over to someone else. "Don't be too tough on my mentor," I warned, laughing. Over dinner, Isaac would pump Harvey for ideas, and Harvey would relish the intellectual challenge. "I promise," Isaac assured me. "I've caused enough trouble for one day." Isaac knew he had crossed the line.

I went to call Sam. "So Isaac gave Bob the boot," he gloated. I imagined him—phone cradled between ear and shoulder, feet on the desk, wand in hand.

"Isaac certainly upped the ante. Now the burden is on us."

"The burden was always on us," Sam corrected, "but now we'll get the credit..."

"...Or the blame," I countered. "How does it look down there? Are we going to be able to deliver?"

"The teams are pushing hard to have drafts ready on Monday. If they fail us, we'll invent something." Sam was upbeat. The trickier things got, the better he liked it. "One thing's for sure: life will be a lot simpler without Bob swooping in to upset the applecart." So, he *had* concocted this scheme. He had pushed me onto a tightrope with no safety net. I wasn't sure if I could get to the other side without falling.

The following morning, Bob confronted Harvey. "What the hell is going on? Collapsing a two-month diagnosis into three weeks; relying on the client for recommendations; running a project with no Partner. Where are GCC's standards?"

Harvey was unperturbed. Bob's predictable indignation defended policies that had built GCC's reputation. But, times were changing. "As we grow globally, we'll encounter different cultures. We're going to school on BomFarm." Harvey dumped ashes out of the chamber of his Briar. "This client's crisis calls for expediency. Isaac provoked healthy debate and he certainly made the case for momentum."

"Momentum, my ass!" Bob bristled. "This frantic pace is unprecedented! It gives us no time to question the recommendations. Isaac will lobby for his own interests and Beth doesn't have the clout to oppose him."

"You might be right, but I'm going to back her up."

Bob ran his hand over his bald spot, as if to clear his mind. "I resigned as Partner-in-Charge because I won't oversee a fiasco. I think you're making a mistake. This whole thing could blow up. GCC should ditch this client."

"Take it easy, Bob," Harvey counseled. "Don't take this personally. Let me put things in perspective. You know and I know that we don't have seasoned leadership in Brazil. This episode raises serious doubts about operating in a place we don't understand. The good news is that BomFarm is satisfied and doesn't see those shortcomings. Let this project run its course; it's a trial by fire for Beth and I'll make sure to protect GCC's reputation."

"I guess you know what you're doing, Harvey, but I wouldn't tolerate these shenanigans if I were in your shoes." Being bombastic was Bob's best defense after being fired by a client.

The next day, Isaac left town and I breathed easier. Avoiding Bob and zeroing in on Northern Airways put yesterday's drama behind me. About noon, Harvey stopped by. He plopped down, dropping a manila envelope on the chair beside him. "Decompressing after yesterday?" he asked.

"A little." I chose my words carefully. "BomFarm got its money's worth; we covered a lot of ground." Before Brazil, I would have skirted the conflict, but now I realized that getting things out in the open was healthy. "Isaac was pretty tough on Bob, but he had a valid position. Jumping into the project now is like hopping aboard a speeding train." I believed Bob was at fault, but criticizing him would gain nothing. "Perhaps our roles were flawed from the start."

"There was bad chemistry with Isaac." Harvey, too, avoided placing blame. "Bob's a stickler for standards. If rules have to be bent, it's best if I bend them." In Harvey's mind, all was reconciled.

Abruptly, he changed the subject. "Can you go to New York tomorrow?"

"My day is open," I replied, completely baffled. "What's up?"

"International Foods is exploring Latin American expansion; GCC is bidding on the project. Larry Benson from the New York office is heading the sales effort. Tomorrow he's meeting with I.F.'s executives, including the head honcho from

Brazil." A smile tugged at the corner of his mouth. "Word travels fast; Larry's heard that you know how to handle Brazilians."

"To think that I can 'handle Brazilians' is quite presumptuous, but I'll help if I can." Archrivals, Larry and Bob were in a horserace for sales superiority. Helping Larry would fuel Bob's displeasure with me, but the firm's interest and my own would be served if we could land the I.F. account. "I'll catch the first shuttle in the morning."

"Good. Here's the briefing package." He passed me the thick envelope. Apparently being the firm's new expert on Brazil had made me an asset, instead of a liability.

Masks

Indian corn and bittersweet hung from Sue's door; a scarecrow and pumpkins decorated the front steps. Saturday in Marblehead was my domestic fix before heading back to São Paulo. David and George were at the boatyard winterizing *Sea Spirit,* and the children were at a birthday party. I had Sue to myself.

"Take this." She passed me the natural yarn and said in a hush, "I'm knitting an Irish sweater for David." The ritual of stretching the skein while Sue rolled a big ball created the perfect conditions for a sisterly chat.

"How's work going?" Sue always wanted to know about my job and I was always dying to tell her. As I replayed the drama with Isaac, Sue wound the first skein. With the finished ball in her knitting basket, she looped a second skein around my hands and probed, "Have you seen Bob since?"

"No, but I'm not avoiding him. I had to fly down to the Big Apple for a sales call." Her raised eyebrows demanded more. I explained Larry's special request for my help. With Sue it was safe to brag. I could express the pride that I kept in check at the office. "My rapport with the Latin American executives was great," I gloated. "If we sell the I.F. project, Larry wants me to manage it."

"Maybe your gamble in Brazil will pay dividends. I wish the job were Boston-based, but at least New York is a lot closer than San Pablo." Sue pronounced the city wrong, but at least she was trying.

"Actually," I beamed, "I might have the best of both worlds." Dubious, Sue cocked her head. "I.F. is headquartered in New York, but they want GCC to field a local team. That means Marcelo and Sam."

Sue paused, "Will you keep going to Brazil?" and then resumed winding.

I avoided Sue's stern gaze by watching the rhythmic tip of my hands. "Maybe just a trip or two…and don't forget, we haven't made the sale, yet." Minimizing the likely travel didn't appease Sue.

"What does George think?" I should have seen that coming.

"He's unhappy, of course." I downplayed our marital conflict by imitating George. "'What is it with Brazil?! Why does International Foods need a South American strategy…and why do *you* have to be involved?'"

Sue didn't see any humor in my tone. "You're walking on thin ice," she warned. "Furthermore, landing I.F. won't help your case with Bob."

Brooding about Bob had cost me some sleep. Seeking revenge, he might block my promotion. However, I didn't want to worry Sue. "Bob's a professional; he'll put the firm's interests before his own." My nonchalance didn't fool Sue, but she let it be.

One more ball of yarn done. One last skein to wind. As she draped the yarn around my hands, she asked what she really wanted to know. "How is Sam? Is he still growing on you?"

"We're just professional colleagues and friends." I avoided her eyes.

"Then why are you red?" she probed as she started shaping the ball.

A pause, then, "OK, there *is* something about Sam. Honestly, I don't know what it is, but I do miss him."

In truth, I had a serious case of *saudade*, Brazilian longing for which I had found no translation. I was counting the days between me and São Paulo. Geese flying south for the winter honked, "Come too, come too, come too." Everything seemed bittersweet—autumn leaves swirling in the breeze, the sweep of oars in the pre-class dawn, the stark silhouettes of bare trees against the sky.

I missed the messy office where papers turned yellow from city grime. I missed heated debates that made our results better. I missed Paulinho's instant coffee and Marcelo's practical jokes. Most of all, I missed Sam. The yarn in my hands blurred. I wiped a tear with my upper arm. "I can't bear the thought that Brazil will end," I sniffed.

"You've always wanted to have your cake and eat it, too." Sibling rivalry surfaced as disapproval. "Beth, you've got a successful, loving husband and a great career. You've got the perfect life. Why do you have to want more?"

The slam of car doors announced Mark and Melody. Through the window, Sue waved a thank you to the neighbor who was dropping them off. "I promised the kids we'd buy Halloween costumes this afternoon. Time to set this aside." The last of the yarn slipped off my hands and ball three was done. "Just finish your crazy assignment and come back where you belong," Sue said matter-of-factly as she went to greet her children.

At the party store, we clowned around with the masks. I screeched when Mark put a rubber spider down my back. I acted scared when Melody cried "Boo!" I bought a Dracula outfit for Mark, a princess costume for Melody, and fake fingernails for Sue. Being playful was an act. Sue's scolding attitude made me sad; I wanted to be alone.

"Could you drop me off in Old Town?" I asked as we paid for the costumes. "I need to buy some farewell gifts for my Brazilian friends." Sue didn't press for more. She had shifted from Big Sister to Perfect Mom. She dropped me off on Washington Street.

I rambled past the Lafayette House, where the corner had been lopped off so that the general's carriage could pass. Under the historic overhang, I turned downhill toward the Boston Yacht Club. Late-season boaters were bustling to haul their crafts after a final fall sail. I climbed up into Crocker Park and perched on the hard granite that gave the town its name. Most pleasure boats were out for the winter. Soon, only sturdy lobster boats would ply the chilly waters 'til spring.

The rugged self-reliance that could wrestle a living from the sea was still part of Marblehead. Even professionals who worked in the city, like David, were do-it-yourselfers who preferred productive hobbies to idle leisure. A little hardship added to one's sense of self-worth. Maybe that's why I didn't mind the cold stone pressing into my buttocks...at least for a little while.

When my bottom was sore, I moseyed back to the gift shops. Chrysanthemums brightened window boxes; spiced cider lured me to linger among the antique quilts, wicker chairs, and brass beds. I bought twin cameos, one for Sue and one for me. For the office in Brazil, a ceramic ashtray fresh from the potter's kiln.

At the galleries, oils, watercolors, and sculptures were abundant. Through one glass window, I spotted a wall of life-like faces. "They're leather; the woman artist uses Greek techniques," explained the gallery owner. The masks were haunting and ageless.

All were beautiful, but two touched my emotions. One was a soft blue-gray that seemed to emerge from *The Mists of Avalon*. A windblown headdress framed a serious, pensive gaze. The second was a goddess from a warmer clime, with warm tawny skin and a mysterious smile beneath an alluring veil. There hanging on the wall, I saw Beth and Bethania; I held my breath. An unknown artist had expressed through her craft the duality I felt. I forced back the tears of recognition that welled up.

After a discreet wait, the shopkeeper asked, "Can I help you with anything before I lock up?" Closing time had come and gone.

My choices were simple—buy or leave. I longed to take these spirits with me, but held back. Making such a purchase without George was not the way our marriage worked. He would not welcome artwork that he had not chosen. These pieces were far too mystical for his taste...and far too expensive. But, I was bewitched.

"May I pay with a credit card?" I stalled.

"Of course. MasterCard or Visa."

Then, with a deep breath, I decided, "OK, then I'll take these two." Pleased, the woman lifted my choices gently from the wall and headed for the register.

The voids left behind reinforced my guilt. "I fear you'll have to rearrange the whole wall."

"That's part of the fun...something to look forward to tomorrow."

"Could I make a local call?" She handed me the phone and continued to box the masks. I dialed Sue.

"Hi, Melody. Can I talk to your mom?"

"Sure." The receiver bumped down and I heard her running to fetch her mother. During the pause, the shopkeeper prepared the receipt.

I signed the charge slip, nervous and distracted as I heard, "What's up?" Sue sounded busy.

"Hi. Can someone come get me?"

"Where are you, exactly?"

"I'll be on the bench by the Old Town House. It's past closing time." I threw an apologetic look across the counter. "I want to let this nice lady go home."

"The men are back from the boatyard; I'll send George to pick you up."

"Thanks." Dealing with George was unavoidable. The short trip back to Sue's would not be fun. I handed the phone back to the shopkeeper.

With a sweet smile, she handed me two packages. "Enjoy your art."

"I will," I said, but wondered at what price.

We walked to the door. She turned the sign from "Open – Please Come In" to "Sorry – We're Closed," and then she turned the knob for me. "They will grow on you; I promise."

"They already have," I replied and departed with my treasures.

Across the street, I plunked down on the splintery Town Hall bench. On warm days, old timers swapped stories here, but the crisp October dusk kept people moving. Townsfolk hurried with purpose in puffy coats and blue jeans. A spry old lady walked her black poodle. A car of tourists pulled up, puzzled by the twisting streets, once cow paths. I told the visitors how to get out of town, where to turn, and which dead ends to avoid. I sounded so sure, but as they vanished, I wondered how I would navigate the emotional maze in which I found myself.

Sunday Night—October 25
En route from Boston to São Paulo for Round Three

Dear Diary,

George exploded when he saw the packages and again when he saw the masks and again when he saw the bill. "For me, they're priceless. If you don't like them, I'll just keep them in the box. I bought them for me, not for us!" It was the awkward truth and it upset us both.

Maybe I'm being rash because I don't want Brazil to end. I told George I planned to stay an extra week. "It's my last trip and I want to see more of the country. Remember, I invited you to join me?" He didn't even respond and went back into isolation.

The truth is, sightseeing has nothing to do with my wanting to stay longer. Overcoming challenges, warm friendships, growing self-esteem, and unconditional acceptance from others have made me fall in love with this place.

And there is something else. I've discovered Bethania and hate to say goodbye to her.

Learning to Trust

As my flight took off for São Paulo, my foldout tray was strewn with calendars and To Do lists. My intentions to work were short-lived. After dinner, I slept until the bumpy arrival in a morning rainstorm.

Confident, I handed my passport to the Federal Police for inspection. At customs, I got the green light and strode purposefully toward the exit. I was just one more businessperson arriving at Guarulhos Airport to capitalize on South America's largest economy.

And then, a knocking fist and Sam's crooked grin made me much more than that. He was front and center at the glass wall where greeters jockeyed for position. The schism of our parting in Rio was forgotten. My heart danced as he jostled through the pressing crowd to my trolley.

He pushed my luggage beyond the mob and passed it to Vicente. Arms free, he paused and, without a word, hugged me. We held each other for a couple of silent moments and then followed Vicente toward the door.

Outside it was pouring. "Rain in São Paulo is a nightmare. This downpour could easily flood the Marginal." Once in the car, Sam consulted with Vicente to choose an alternate route to the city. "It will take longer, but should detour the worst conditions," he explained.

Always productive, I dug some papers from my briefcase. "We can make good use of the time. Let's review what must happen before the workshop. Here's my critical path."

Sam scanned my notes. "You left out meetings with Mueller and Bomforte. Mueller doesn't like surprises and Bomforte needs to buy into this before it happens."

Why didn't I think of that? I wished I had Sam's sense of the politics. "You're right. Would you call them when we get to the office?"

"They're already scheduled," he announced with a proud grin. "The rest looks fine." A thirty-minute task had taken five. I stashed the papers back in my briefcase.

Rain pelted the roof and water was halfway up the tires. Vicente crawled through dingy, narrow streets. Ragged figures huddled in doorways or struggled through muddy streams.

"How's it going with the teams?"

"I think you'll be pleased. They've identified some quick hits that don't require any investment. Some costs can be cut by fifty percent or more; BomFarm will get some breathing room."

"You and Marcelo have been busy."

"Busy, but not busy enough. I missed you, Bartlett." Sam's hand touched mine and then encircled it. His palm was soft, without a single callus. The warmth of his flesh on mine filled me up in a sweet crescendo. I leaned against Sam's shoulder and shut my eyes. Rain drummed on the roof and flowed down in curtains that made ours a private world.

Back in Boston, I had resolved to keep my relationship with Sam professional. But now, I felt like a bud yearning to open. I swung around, curled my legs up on the seat and snuggled into Sam's embrace. We held each other close and let the rain do our talking. My heart beating next to his marked time that I wished would stand still. I feared moving would break the spell, but couldn't resist looking into his intense blue eyes. Sam looked back with an exquisite tenderness that drew my lips to his. Our kiss was unhurried and infused with tobacco. It was rich and satisfying. Too special to repeat. Gently, I pulled away. As I sat up, my tongue savored the unfamiliar taste on my lips. Kissing a smoker in a rundown taxi, with poverty outside the window, did not sound romantic. But I would hold this moment forever in my heart. We held hands in silence as our car slogged through the downpour to the office.

Donning a business façade, I greeted Marcelo and asked Paulinho for a coffee. Immediately, I headed for the conference table to review documents, but found its surface empty. "Wasn't this the deadline for team reports?" My impatient query exposed my dread that nothing was ready.

"They need a little more time," Marcelo said serenely.

"Don't worry," Sam assured me. "They're working hard, with lots of positive momentum. We should have their drafts later today."

"Momentum's good, but we need something concrete. There's no commitment until it's down on paper. On top of that, we have to consolidate the recommendations and get input from Harvey. When will I see something in writing?" I insisted.

Sam and Marcelo exchanged looks; they were on the same side in this battle. "Look, we have plans to go to BomFarm after lunch, but if it'll make you feel better, we'll go now and try to wrestle something from the teams."

"Please do. Every minute counts; we need time to convert BomFarm's work into a quality product." Edgy, I struggled to act calm, but kept hearing Bob's warnings: "You'll just get a hodge-podge of self-interested opinions. There's no way this will be up to our standards."

Sam and Marcelo didn't linger. They had the perfect excuse to avoid my disapproval and I was left alone to fret. The reports I hoped to see would be in Portuguese. I pulled out my phrase book but couldn't concentrate. Two hours passed; the delay fed my fears. I peered down from the sixth floor, searching for Marcelo's Parati in the stalled traffic. *A watched pot never boils,* I scolded myself and dropped back down in my chair.

Paulinho set a coffee in front of me with a sympathetic look. With uncommon boldness, he said, *"Fica tranquila, Senhora Bete. Tudo vai dar certo."* Paulinho's assurance that everything would be OK was touching, but it failed to calm me.

At last, the office door opened and my colleagues entered, glum-faced and empty-handed. Marcelo should have been loaded down; his briefcase was limp. Panic poured into my chest. Sam looked despondent. He posed the two questions he always asked upon arrival. "Any news? Any calls?"

"No news. No calls." I rushed ahead to, "What happened? Where are the reports?" Tension raised my pitch.

"Sorry, Bartlett, they aren't ready. One team had a draft, but the others will finish tomorrow." Sam reached for his coffee, laced with sugar.

"Only one draft?! Well, did you bring that one?" I was desperate.

"It wouldn't be fair; we told them *amanhã,* like the others." Marcelo explained. Tomorrow! I wanted to strangle him. Marcelo had said, *"Deixa comigo."* Well, I *had* trusted him, and he had let me down. Bob White's warnings were coming true.

"Did you bring a photocopy, so we could start our review?" They shook their heads no. I grasped for something positive. "Which team delivered?"

"Guess," challenged Sam, lighting a cigarette and relaxing into his chair.

"Probably the Pharmacy team. Isaac has coached them from the start."

"And, if not?"

"The Hospital team," I guessed. "If he put his mind to it, their leader could do the analysis singlehandedly."

"Yes, but Revenues has the best team dynamics," Sam countered.

"But wait," Marcelo pitched in, "the Veterinary team combines *criatividade e pragmatismo.*"

"Yep, that's true," Sam observed. "Sometimes the creative thinkers and the pragmatists can't reach consensus, but when they do, their plans are innovative and viable."

"Oh, stop," I protested. "Those strong points don't count if they can't deliver. Which team came through?"

As Sam and Marcelo huddled in conference, deciding whether to tell me, there was a knock on the door and shuffling in the hall. "Paulinho, *abre a porta por favor,*" Sam requested.

Paulinho unbolted the door and in trooped the six team leaders. "*Uma surpresa para Dona Bete!*" They sang out in unison. Then, each gave me a salute and deposited a big envelope on the table. With a click of heels, they filed out again, leaving me agape. I jumped up, chased after them, and called out, "Wait. *Obrigada.* Stay for a coffee."

"*Não Senhora.*" Pedro spoke for the group, already packed like sardines in the two small elevators. "*À espera de suas ordens.* Awaiting your orders." The six men saluted as the elevators closed and started their halting descent.

Paulinho grinned from his corner. Marcelo and Sam joined me to inspect the booty. "You see, we followed your orders after all," Sam said smugly.

"Why didn't they stay for coffee?" I queried.

"What? And risk the wrath of the drill sergeant?" Marcelo teased.

"Don't ever do that again!" I reprimanded. The knot in my stomach eased.

"It was their idea. We're innocent," Marcelo said with his hands held up like a soccer player accused of a foul.

I shook my head. "No penalty this time." I hoisted the thick envelopes. Here, it was feast or famine. "We're not off the hook yet. How will we review and consolidate all this in time?"

"In fact," Sam winked at Marcelo, "we started the consolidation...in our spare time."

"Another surprise for the Bartlett!" Marcelo bowed as he offered a deck of handwritten pages.

Returning the bow, I accepted their work, a bit skeptical. "How could you do a synthesis without having the reports?" I wasn't going to fall for one of Marcelo's practical jokes.

"We've stayed close to the teams, so we knew the gist of their recommendations. There's room for improvement," Sam hedged, "but at least we're not starting from zero." The smudged pages revealed a diligent application of the outline I had given them several weeks ago.

"Wow, you guys really went overboard," I gushed as they beamed.

I dug into the reports. All six teams had used our frameworks, yet each included something unique. GCC's guidance had helped harness BomFarm's experience. Creativity and collaboration had flourished. Loosening the reins let the teams go farther than anyone expected. We still faced the daunting task of articulating a compelling strategy and making realistic projections, but we were well on our way.

By evening, I was exhausted. I'd gone from passion to panic, from angst to admiration, in a few short hours. I was definitely back in the land of *jogo de cintura*, where surprises were the norm. Today's roller coaster had taught me something important. This morning's anxiety was the result of needing to control and fearing to delegate. Dreading that things would not be done my way, I was sure that they would not be done at all. The Brazilians proved me wrong. Not only did they deliver; they surpassed my expectations. Today's roller coaster had taught me the power of trust.

Jenny was the first to know I was living with Sam.

She caught me, wrapped in a towel, coming out of his bathroom. With a knowing smile, she offered me coffee. With no one around, I had denied my guilt, but now there was Jenny.

Sleeping at the luxurious Maksoud could not compare with sleeping next to Sam in his sparse apartment. Realizing that no one from Boston had ever telephoned the hotel, I checked out. The excuse? Reducing costs to our floundering client. The reality? The delicious prospect of twenty-four hours a day with Sam.

But I had not counted on a maid. In addition to cleaning the office, Jenny was Sam's domestic help. "She needs to feed her family," he stated without elaboration. In my opinion, Sam didn't need her.

There wasn't much furniture to dust. In the living room was a foosball game; on the weekends, Marcelo and Sam played table soccer—a mini-rivalry between Brazil and Argentina. Nearby, another table covered in green felt was ready for a pickup poker game. The bare-walled bedroom housed a double mattress, unadorned by quilts or headboard. The nightstand and wobbly TV table had been assembled with an Allen wrench.

There was no cooking required. Sam didn't eat breakfast. Lunch and dinner were eaten out or supplied by the local pizzeria. One night, I offered to cook dinner. I knew how to make simple, nutritious fare from the *Betty Crocker Cookbook*. Sam laughed and ordered Chinese takeout. When I jumped up to clear the table, Sam chided, "Let Jenny do that."

"Asking her to do something I could do myself seems degrading," I objected.

Sam motioned to my chair. "If she weren't working for me, Jenny would probably be a streetwalker. Let her clear the table."

I sat down and summoned Jenny from the kitchen.

Gradually, I learned to appreciate why Brazilian families have maids. Fresh juice was squeezed from oranges. Mashed potatoes began with a tuber, not flakes in a box. It took time to shop, prepare, and clean up each meal. Although refrigerators, stoves, and sinks were standard, disposals and dishwashers were scarce.

City dirt made daily cleaning a must; clothes were soiled in one wearing. No Maytag washed dirty laundry. No dryer fluffed warm towels at the push of a button. Yet each day, upon returning from work, I found my blouse and underwear washed, pressed, and waiting in the closet. Jenny spoiled me quickly; if only she could attack the overflowing hampers of dirty laundry in Sue's basement.

Laundry was not the only arena where maids helped mothers. One weekend, Sandra's sister Marvi invited us to her country house. She proudly introduced two-year-old Fernanda and four-year-old Clecio. After a few minutes, they went to play under the watchful eye of the maid, leaving us free for adult conversation.

Now and then, the children would run over with a treasure they had found. With a hug or a kiss from a grown-up, they were off again. Little Clecio joined the lunch table; when he became restless, the maid kept him busy while we lingered over coffee. Fernanda nestled on her father's lap until she fell asleep; then the maid carried her off for a nap.

What a life, I thought. Back home, family gatherings brought double duty. The hostess entertained her guests and tended her children simultaneously. No one came to Sue's rescue when the going got tough. Even a babysitter was a treat. Marvi lavished abundant affection on her kids, in contrast to the bedtime kiss rationed to my niece and nephew. *To what extent*, I wondered, *do maids make families happy?*

"Would I be rude to ask you what it's like to have a maid?" I asked Marvi.

"Of course not," she laughed, "but there is not one answer to your question. It depends…on the maid, on the mistress, and on their relationship."

"But, you seem so relaxed. You speak with authority but show respect." Marvi looked pleased. "How do you strike that balance?"

"Trial and error, I guess," Marvi said thoughtfully. "Like any relationship, it takes time. We hired Carmen when Clecio was born. She's not a great cook, but the children love her. In four years, she's learned to do things my way; she knows what to do without my asking."

"Marvi is being too modest," Sandra joined in. "She's a good teacher and keeps her distance while being kind."

"But, here's the catch," Marvi continued. "Carmen is pregnant and will be quitting soon."

"Oh, no," Sandra commiserated. "Just when things are going so well." Sandra continued, "I dread finding a new maid. The young ones don't know anything and the older ones think they know everything."

"Carmen has recommended her cousin; maybe she'll be good, too." Marvi apologized to me, "I didn't mean to burden you with my problems. In fact, losing a maid is part of having a maid." She paused. "Actually, we've been lucky. Our mother's maid has been with her for twenty-five years. It's a blessing in Mama's old age. Jackie knows what Mama wants before Mama does."

"Jackie is so trustworthy," Sandra added. "She is almost family." So, even affection was sometimes part of the formula.

I thought of my grandmother, distressed and confused by the flow of faces in her Massachusetts nursing home. At ninety-nine, she did not have a Jackie or the skills to rely on her. *Maybe being self-reliant has some downsides.* The thought felt blasphemous; independence had forged the Bartletts for generations.

Just then, Carmen arrived with afternoon tea on a big tray. It would be easy to get used to this, but not so easy to find the right balance of control and trust.

Trooping into Mueller's office on Monday morning, I hoped we had enough clout to convince him to accept radical changes for BomFarm. Harvey had validated the need for SBUs (strategic business units), each focused on a different customer group. To us, the new structure seemed obvious. It would not be so evident to Dr. Mueller.

First, we presented the recommendations and their rationale. "This is the work of your executives," I reminded Mueller. "They deserve the credit." Mueller was attentive, but silent. Sam made a small gesture that meant "Wait. Let him react."

We waited. Mueller studied the summary of recommendations. Finally, he queried Sam and Marcelo. "My men are convinced?"

"Yes, sir," Sam assured him. "They are committed to their work." Marcelo nodded agreement. "Of course, each group knows only part of the story. You are the first to see the whole picture."

"And what will all of this mean? In terms of profit and loss?" It was the perfect lead-in to Marcelo's financial projections. Isaac probed the assumptions, testing us in front of his boss. Marcelo's defense was strong.

We closed with the sensitive organizational implications. Restructuring meant a major transformation of BomFarm and its leadership. When we concluded, Mueller looked straight at me. "Senhora Bartlett, what risks will we face if we do as you suggest?"

Now was the time to invoke the senior authority. "Every new direction brings risks, and this is no exception. Working with Harvey Osborne, we've identified two major risks." Mueller and Isaac leaned a bit closer.

"The first is resistance to change. BomFarm's managers will need new skills. Intense coaching and training can accelerate learning, but it is still a big leap."

I paused to let Mueller react. "And the other risk?" he asked.

"Shifting the balance of power. Creating SBUs will disrupt long-established territories—responsibilities, functions, and headcount. There will be winners and losers." Mueller's jaw stiffened. "It will be risky, but not as risky as staying on your current course."

Sam took up the baton. "Sir, change will be easier if people understand what you want to achieve and why it is necessary. A handful of managers have been on the teams, but many important players are still on the sidelines. Sharing the strategy with all the Directors at once will bring everyone on board at the same time."

"All the Directors?" Isaac asked. "More than one hundred people?"

It was my cue to elaborate. "Yes. All the Directors. After the strategy is presented, small groups will discuss the actions needed for implementation. Their participation will identify obstacles and initiate a team spirit." Historically, the Directors met for one-way marathons where monologues kept debate to a minimum. An interactive agenda would be revolutionary for BomFarm.

"What if the Directors disagree with the strategy?" Mueller voiced a legitimate concern.

"We'll set some ground rules," Sam said confidently. "We will be clear. You and the Strategy Steering Group will define *where* BomFarm is going; the Directors will help define *how* to get there."

"Having small groups sounds chaotic. Are they really necessary?" Another valid doubt. I recalled the raucous team meetings. Pandemonium was possible.

"The groups will have narrow mandates, time limits, and pre-assigned leaders," I explained the mechanics. "Even so, noise and movement are signs of engagement; debate will help create buy-in and ownership."

Mueller buzzed his secretary. "Schedule a meeting with the Strategy Steering Group for tomorrow morning." Her respectful *"Tudo bem, Senhor"* crackled through the intercom. Mueller turned to us. "Tomorrow, show the recommendations and the projections, but not the organization chart. It's premature for that." He was firm. "Let's see how the senior group reacts. Then I'll decide about the Directors' meeting."

"Isaac," he added, "secure space for 120 people at a hotel, *tentatively*," he emphasized. "And install some traffic lights for *ordem e disciplina*." Quipping about order and discipline was definitely out of character. A rare smile softened his stony features. Like me, Heinrich Mueller was learning to trust.

Tuesday Night—November 4
São Paulo

Dear Diary,

Discovering passion and potential with Sam, I feel like a blossom opening to the rays of the sun. How did I end up in the arms of a stranger in a strange land?

He loves me as a multifaceted person, including my foibles. It's magical. Our lovemaking takes me to realms I have never been physically or emotionally. Last night, he asked, "What do you want from life?" I was stymied; no one has ever asked me that question! I've spent my whole life trying to make others happy, satisfying their expectations without knowing my own. To his question, I have no reply!

I can't justify my actions. I am cheating George. But something insists, "Seize the day; you can deal with the consequences tomorrow."

Mueller and the Steering Group agreed to everything, even the Directors' meeting! But, Dr. Mueller has invited me for dinner at his home tomorrow. He made it clear that I must come alone for a private conversation! I can't imagine what he wants.

Suddenly, I realize how much I have relied on Sam. The last time I went "solo" was on a Maine island with Outward Bound. I guess if I survived that three-day ordeal, I can survive dinner with Mueller!

I smoothed my hair and skirt before knocking on the impressive mahogany entrance. In lieu of a servant, an elegant lady in a linen dress opened the door. A coiled braid emphasized her cheekbones; a beautiful strand of pearls adorned her long neck. "Welcome. I am Heinrich's wife, Isabel." The gentle voice was refined. "Please come in." Oriental rugs, walls of books, and Mozart created a refuge from the world outside. It took me back to tea with Abbot's headmistress; white gloves were the only thing missing.

"Heinrich will join us shortly. May I offer you something to drink?" As I sipped sparkling water, we conversed about classical music and herbs. Isabel was expert in both. I was relishing the company of this refined woman when Dr. Mueller's arrival snapped me back to the business realm. Even at home he projected formality and respect in a fine cashmere jacket. I rose to greet him, wondering, *Brazilian* abraço *or handshake?* I took my cue from him. It was a handshake; with Mueller, it would always be a handshake.

Without delay, Isabel led the way to a table set with Waterford crystal and monogrammed silver for several courses. A tiny silver bell marked Isabel's place. My mother had had one just like it; when I was sick as a child, she would set it by my bed. Just knowing Mother would respond to its ring made me feel better. Tonight, the familiar shape made the table a bit less forbidding.

Stiffly, Dr. Mueller held my chair. Once seated, my hosts bowed their heads in silent thanks. I prayed that I would make no grievous errors in the evening ahead. Isabel used her Swiss education to pace the conversation and the silver bell to pace the dinner service. My boarding school manners came to the fore; I progressed from the appetizer through the main course without mishap.

At dessert time, Dr. Mueller urged, "You must try *fruta-do-conde*. It's the peak of the season." Wanting to please and being a fruit lover, I accepted his advice. Moments later, the maid placed a knife and spoon to my right and a fork to my left. Next, she set down a plate with a fleshy, white ball, about the size of an acorn squash.

The Muellers had declined the bumpy fruit; with no hostess to copy I was baffled. Isabel explained, "Just carve out one small section. It gets easier after the first cut, like serving pie," she assured me.

Fearing that the slippery ball would shoot off my plate into Mueller's lap, I punctured it with the fork, excised a segment of pulp, and spooned it into my mouth. "Watch out for the pit!" Mueller warned. The white pulp concealed a large stone, which I swirled in my mouth, wondering how to dispose of it gracefully.

"Just spit the seed into your hand," Isabel coached. "It's the only way."

So I spit. The bland sweetness was hardly worth the effort and embarrassment. However, Emily Post would insist on consuming the fruit, lest I offend my hosts (and, in this case, my client). So, I struggled and spit under their watchful eyes until the sweetsop was gone.

"You and Heinrich will have coffee in the library," Isabel announced as I set my utensils next to the pile of pits. "Would you like to use the toilette first?" Was it obvious that I had sticky juice all over my hands? I gratefully accepted her offer.

Lovely imported soaps and embroidered hand towels adorned the lavatory. I had to mar the shining brass basin to wash up, but felt fresher when I emerged. Isabel ushered me to her husband's study, bid me goodnight, closed the door, and left us in privacy.

I was steeled for criticism.

"Thank you for coming this evening." A non-threatening start, then straight to the point. "You have recommended that BomFarm change reporting lines."

"Yes, a different executive will be responsible for building each business. Of course, some functions, such as technology and finance, will serve all the businesses." So far, I was on solid ground.

"Are any of my managers capable of running a business?" Mueller asked bluntly.

The proposed structure required business managers with a cross-functional perspective. Due to his autocratic management, only Mueller had a broad view. The new strategy threatened Mueller, and Mueller threatened the strategy.

I proceeded cautiously. On a yellow pad, I sketched the reporting lines and indicated the strengths needed for each position.

"What are Kipper's strengths?" Mueller asked abruptly. Sam had good intuition about people and could shoot from the hip, but I was more guarded. I skirted the question, but Mueller insisted. With the caveat that I hardly knew Kipper, I related his profile to the strategic requirements. Mueller listened stone-faced. Next, he probed about each of BomFarm's executives, one by one. With careful candor, I indicated the strengths and weaknesses I had observed in each man.

"To summarize," I ventured, "BomFarm has good candidates for these jobs. None is perfect; all need to develop some new skills. Business managers are mini-CEOs." This was the time to tackle the succession issue, a concern Marcos Bomforte had raised weeks ago.

With a deep breath, I took the plunge. "Dr. Mueller, this is your opportunity to groom your replacement." A quick blink confirmed that I had struck a nerve. "I'm sure you plan to serve BomFarm for many years. But the future is unpredictable. With your credentials and reputation, you might be called to serve in the government or in a university post. BomFarm is vulnerable." Hoping flattery would keep his mind open to valid criticism, I brushed my sweaty palms against my skirt.

Mueller seemed lost in thought. I fought the urge to say something, anything, to break the silence. Finally, Mueller's blue eyes met mine. "I value your perspectives. You have a unique blend of intelligence, empathy, and insight. Honesty is of great service." He rose and stretched out his hand.

"The Bomfortes are fortunate that you are running this valuable franchise. You've steered this ship through some rough waters in the past; your steady hand will bring BomFarm to safe harbor again." It would have sounded corny in Boston, but the analogy brought a quiet, pleased nod from the reserved CEO. I added, "Thank you for a lovely dinner. Isabel is a very special lady."

"I'm sure she enjoyed meeting you," he returned the compliment. Mueller escorted me to his chauffeur, who was waiting to drive me home.

The heavy, armored car door closed with a protective thud. Windows of tinted glass were a shield against the unruly world outside. The leather grain of the interior was as unblemished as Mueller's reputation. The backseat unyielding and stiff, like its owner. Before leaving the garage, the driver locked all the doors; then, the secure fortress started to move.

Relieved that the ordeal was over, I leaned back and closed my eyes. I was honored but mystified that this reserved, stern man had invited me into his sanctuary. I hoped I had repaid his trust. I hoped I had helped, not hurt. The business cliché "It's lonely at the top" now had a Germanic face.

I was glad that Dr. Mueller had Isabel.

Crazy Kaleidoscope

Sam was handsome in bed. He always lay down first, waiting for me to come to him. On a mattress, his stooped shoulders and bumpy midriff vanished into a sleeker, younger body. On his back, arm stretched behind his head, he feigned a Greek god.

Sam had an endless lovemaking repertoire. One masterpiece started with a long, still embrace, our naked lengths touching from lips to toes. Then, the slow caresses; each touch asking for a reply. His hand pressed upon a single curve, then paused, committing the moment to memory. My hand answered his, seeking the concave and convex of his back and groin. Hands cupped breasts and balls, offering the globes to welcoming lips and loving nips. Fingertips, first light upon warm skin, and then with tantalizing touch to arouse. Kisses tasted salt, and tongues explored the intimate unknown. Rhythms in counterpoint prolonged the pleasure, until passion made us one. In consuming crescendo, the climax came with a noisy burst of unbearable joy.

And then the best part…pressing my skin against his in happy stillness, listening to life beat in his chest, and letting love flow out in salty tears.

"What's wrong?" he asked at my unexplained weeping. "Was the sex that bad?" Even in bed, he kept his sense of humor.

My sobs turned to laughter. "Of course not; it was wonderful. With you, I'm safe. I'm not afraid." I snuggled deeper into the dark hairs on his chest.

"Afraid of what?" Weaving his hand through my hair, he pressed my head against him.

"Afraid to let go. Afraid to be passionate. Before, I tried to live on a pedestal; I tried to be perfect."

"Well, kid, I hate to burst your bubble, but you ain't perfect. You're a married woman fucking a Jewish spic. Your pedestal has crumbled, for good!" Sam lit a cigarette, inhaled, held it, and then exhaled with satisfaction. Instead of thinking of hazards to his health, I cuddled closer and didn't want to change a thing.

The exhilaration flowed into our work. Happiness and success reinforced each other in a virtuous circle. Everything I touched seemed charmed.

BomFarm's Steering Group praised the recommendations and was encouraged by the prospect of positive earnings in nine months.

Marcos Bomforte was initially cautious. "Can you make this work, Heinrich?" he asked as we concluded his private briefing.

"We have no choice. I've matched our people to the challenges." The CEO pulled a paper from his inside jacket pocket.

Marcos unfolded and studied the notes without comment. An undecipherable glimmer ruffled his mask-like face, and his manicured hand stroked his chin. "I'll give this some thought." He tucked Mueller's notes into his own pocket. "So what happens next? These are good ideas, but how do we bring them to fruition?"

My dry description of the Directors' workshop was spiced up by Sam, who said, "The strategy was conceived in the collective intellectual uterus of your executives, with a little artificial insemination from us." Sam paused for effect. "At the meeting, we'll be midwives and help deliver the baby."

"That mustn't be missed." Marcos chuckled, and even Mueller's steely eyes brightened. "I'll ask my father to open the conference," Marcos added. Mueller permitted himself a small smile. "His presence will silence any doubting Thomases in the crowd." If BomFarm's founder joined us, we would score a homerun.

Good fortune was contagious. Larry Benson called. "We closed the I.F. deal! I want you to manage the team, so block your time."

I grinned into the phone. "Count me in. What about the field work?"

"Line up consultants in Brazil, Argentina, and Mexico. I.F. will be ready to roll in January." Larry was in high spirits. I.F. would push the New York office above its sales target. For him, that meant a bigger bonus and outperforming his Boston rival. Exactly what it meant for me was unclear. Harvey would be pleased at the "inter-office cooperation." Bob White, however, would not reward me for helping his New York competitor; unfortunately, Bob had more weight than Harvey when allocating bonuses to Boston staff.

That evening, Marcelo drove us to Sam's residence. We found the entire neighborhood pitch black. "Electricity kaput," Marcelo declared in his creative English.

Being with Sam in the dark would be no sacrifice, but we had to get to his fourth-floor apartment. "Do you have a light?" I asked.

Marcelo held up his BIC lighter.

"No. No. I mean, do you have a *flashlight*? A lantern?" George always kept an emergency light in our Volvo's glove compartment, along with a tire gauge, first-aid kit, touch-up paint, and the key to the locking gas tank.

"No light. No power. No elevator. No hot water. Why don't you two come home with me?"

"Thanks, Marcelo, but I have a better idea," Sam replied. "We'll go to the Swing." I had seen a huge billboard with a seductive girl dangling a ripe red strawberry above her lips. Concealing her private parts were the words "Motel Swing."

"Have you ever been to a motel?" Marcelo eyed me in the rearview mirror.

"Of course I have," I asserted. "On family vacations we always stayed at motels; I begged to operate the ice maker and the Magic Fingers."

"Magic Fingers!" Marcelo pretended shock.

"Yes, Magic Fingers is a vibrating bed." I had fallen into his trap.

"Magic fingers and vibrations—you're making me blush," he jested. Although Marcelo knew I was sharing Sam's apartment, I tried to be discreet. Because I didn't expect such openness about lovemaking, I figured Marcelo was kidding. He wasn't.

Unabashed, Sam joined the fray. "Here, motels are just for sex. The Swing is São Paulo's best—five stars."

Marcelo pulled in front of his apartment building, where the lights were ablaze. "Last call. Sure you don't want to come in?" he asked rhetorically. "Here, borrow my car," Marcelo said, handing the keys to Sam. "Just remember to pick me up in the morning."

To me he said, "Go do some market research," in his somber economist's tone. "Tomorrow, tell me if there's a lag between supply and demand."

Sam slid into the driver's seat. "Be sure to tell Sandra about this or she'll wonder what your Parati is doing at the Swing."

"She'll be jealous." Both men laughed, comfortable with the subject and each other. Marcelo held the passenger door as I moved up front. "Enjoy the berries!" He slammed my door and mimed "hear no evil, see no evil, speak no evil."

Sam grasped the gearshift. "Shit, it's a manual," he muttered. Sam preferred being driven; he relied on Vicente to cope with São Paulo's unpredictable traffic. Unfamiliar with Marcelo's car, he struggled to distinguish forward from reverse. His awkward movements didn't inspire confidence, but Marcelo looked on without dismay. What a contrast to George, who refused to loan our car to anyone, citing insurance provisions.

Perhaps that is why my mouth went dry as we lurched forward. "I'm thirsty. Do they have water at the Swing?"

Sam guffawed at my naïveté. "They've got just about anything you might imagine and then some." Now I was curious.

After a short drive, the engine stalled in front of a heavy gate with a TV camera. The iron clattered open; we sputtered into the entry; the gate clanked behind us. We idled beside a booth where a young receptionist recorded the license plate and peered into the car. "She's making sure you're not a minor," Sam explained before he made a cash deposit and accepted a key attached to a large wooden plaque.

In first gear, Sam crept around the one-way perimeter, with its high wall on the right and garage doors on the left. Without mishap, he eased Marcelo's Parati out of sight behind door number forty-seven. A private staircase led to a plush room filled with exotic plants, mood music, and a bubbling Jacuzzi. It was no Motel 6.

To quench my thirst, Sam called Room Service. I explored the bathroom's array of soap, shampoo, mouthwash, body lotion...and condoms. On the wall, a cartoon penis smiled and urged in Portuguese, "Wear a shirt. Stop AIDS."

Responding to a buzzer, Sam opened a dumbwaiter in the wall. Strawberries, cream, and bottled water. He signed the bill and shipped it off, all in complete privacy.

My sexual horizons had been defined by fumbling adolescent foreplay, abstinence until I could legally secure an IUD at the age of twenty-one, and honorable fidelity to my husband. My attitudes toward sex had been boxed by prudish morality and ascetic values. Pleasure was rarely, if ever, deserved.

The Swing was designed for carnal gratification. Red lights, erotic photos, and mirrored ceilings. Pay TV offered pornographic options for diverse tastes. Held back by prissy inhibitions, I studied the card of hourly rates and fees for extras. "How many rooms do you think are full right now?" I asked Sam as I calculated occupancy ratios in my head.

"Most of them. Especially with the power outage."

"Come on. You're joking, right?" Despite being here, I couldn't grasp the notion of a building designed exclusively for sex.

"No. I'm not joking. On the weekends, there's a wait to get in. You know that quote from *Shoeless Joe?*" I had no clue; he went on. "If you build it, he will come." Already naked, sprawled on the king-sized sheets, he chuckled at his own pun. "Before you write a case for the Harvard Business School, you need data about the customer experience." He posed provocatively. "Get over here, you silly woman." He dangled a strawberry, just like the one on the billboard.

In Brazil I had discovered new dimensions of myself; now, thanks to Sam, being hedonistic was added to the list.

Isaac phoned the office the next morning. "Bete, *bom dia*. I need to see you alone in my office." My heart fell to my feet. Just when I thought we'd covered every base, something was awry.

"I can get there in about thirty minutes."

"Good. The sooner the better." It was important and urgent.

"Shall I bring anything?" My mind raced through the elements we controlled. The team presentations? The meeting agenda? The list of small groups? My opening remarks?

"No, just come...by yourself," he repeated. It was important, urgent, *and* confidential.

Being excluded, Sam was a little hurt. "Isaac wants to see you alone. Should I be jealous?"

I was too anxious for his humor. "Please, be serious. What could Isaac want?" Then, I was suspicious. "Do you know what this is about?"

"Not this time. Let's go and find out."

"I just told you, Isaac insisted on seeing me alone," I snapped.

"And he will," Sam appeased me. "I'll just ride with you in the taxi. Afterwards, you might need me." Sam knew me. I could hold up under harsh criticism, but would be devastated once I was alone.

Halfheartedly, I protested, "I don't need a chaperone."

"Come on, let's go." In the taxi, we discussed different scenarios and how I might handle them. At the BomFarm lobby, Sam wished me luck. I wanted him beside me, but I entered the elevator alone.

On the top floor, Isaac waved me into his office and closed his door. He was excited but wary. "I am counting on you to keep a secret. No one must know, not even Sam."

"Withholding information from Sam won't be easy, but you can trust me," I promised solemnly as we sat down.

Isaac leaned close and confided in a hushed voice, "I am going to be BomFarm's next CEO. Mueller is moving up to be Chairman of the Board; I am going to take his place." His eyes gleamed.

"*Parabéns*! Congratulations! What an honor!" *And what a surprise!* Nothing in the past few days had foreshadowed Isaac's promotion. "When will it be official?"

"You mean, when can you tell Sam and Marcelo?" Isaac chuckled. Before I could respond, his news poured out. "This morning, Bomforte made the offer. He'll announce the changes at the end of the Directors' Conference. Mueller agrees with the strategy but doesn't want to be the one to reshape the organization. As Chairman, he'll guide BomFarm, but I'll be the hatchet man."

"You'll be much more than a hatchet man," I insisted. "Besides cutting heads, you'll be building up: new roles, new skills, and new revenue streams."

"Precisely. That's why I need help. Having SBUs will require doing things differently. I want a GCC proposal to guide us through unfamiliar territory."

Repeat business was *the* ultimate proof of client satisfaction. This request could cinch my promotion to Partner. It also meant more Brazil...and more Sam. Joy bubbled beneath my professional calm. "Thank you for your confidence, Isaac. It will be a privilege to keep working together." I juggled calendars in my head. Covering New York and São Paulo would be a stretch, but I could do it. Sam would be thrilled. *Oops. I can't tell Sam for three days.*

Isaac read my mind. "Bete, remember, this is top secret until Bomforte's announcement." He tried to sound ominous, despite his enthusiasm. "I would have kept the news from you, but there is no time to lose. The formal hand-off will be January 1st, so I'll need your proposal as soon as possible."

I started to rise, but he motioned me to sit back down. "Let me ask you something. Could the CEO also run an SBU?" From day one, he'd wanted to lead the Pharmacy segment. Anxious to prove himself against his peers, he wanted to captain his own vessel in addition to commanding the whole fleet.

He sought a green light from me but, from Boston discussions, I knew it was not a good idea. *To be a trusted advisor, I must step up to the plate and tell him what he doesn't want to hear.* Gathering courage, I looked straight in his eyes and said forcefully, "Doing both jobs would jeopardize important checks and balances. Business heads should fight for their customers. The CEO must reconcile the interests of all the businesses. So, we would advise against it."

He didn't like it, but listened thoughtfully. After a pause, he confessed, "I was sure I'd get the Pharmacy business. I was looking forward to it." Wistfulness colored his amazement. "I can't believe Mueller is stepping aside. I wonder why."

He was pumping me for information. Perhaps I had helped Isaac's career that evening in Mueller's library. Taking some of the credit would have endeared me to this powerful executive, but would have betrayed Mueller's trust. So I simply said, "Life is full of surprises and this is a nice one." To avoid his further probing, I stood purposefully. "Again, *parabéns* Isaac."

Isaac ushered me to the door. "Thank you, Bete. GCC paved the way; now we have to walk down the road."

Outside, a discreet distance away, Sam was flirting with the secretaries. Had things gone poorly, he was standing by to rescue me. "Remember, not a word to anyone," Isaac said, loud enough for Sam to hear.

"You have my promise," I said, also loud enough for Sam to hear.

With a self-satisfied grin, Isaac retreated to his office. I was left to deal with Sam's curiosity. Waiting for the elevator, he put out a feeler. "Well, you're smiling; we can't be in too much trouble."

"Not too much," I gloated. For once, I had the upper hand.

The elevator door had barely closed when Sam started his interrogation, "So? What did he want?"

Like a local, I nodded to the elevator operator and said, "*Térreo, favor.*" The uniformed attendant in white gloves pushed the button for the ground floor. With a chip on my shoulder, I admonished Sam, affectionately, "No client conversation in elevators—GCC policy."

"Come on, Bartlett. He doesn't understand English," referring to the humble Brazilian.

"Policy is policy," I chided and was tight-lipped as we descended.

Outside, Sam hailed a taxi and I scrunched into the Beetle's backseat. After telling the driver where to go, Sam inquired again. "Bartlett, what's going on? You were in there more than an hour!" he exaggerated.

"Sam, you heard Isaac say, 'Not a word.' And you heard me promise to keep quiet." I was firm, and he was frustrated. "Sorry." Bursting to share, I kissed him lightly on the cheek.

Sam caressed my leg, playfully suggesting sexual favors in exchange for information. "Surely, you can tell me something."

"Don't tempt me." Mischievously, I slapped his hand away. "You're making me mad," I scolded lovingly.

"You're making *me* mad with your secrets. How would you like it if I held out on you?" Arms crossed, he made a show of moving a few inches over in the tiny *Fusca* taxi.

Happy that we were in tight quarters, I mocked dismay, "Don't go so far away!" He eased back beside me.

"Please, please tell me *something*," Sam pleaded like a child.

"I can't and I won't, so let's change the subject," I maneu-vered. "We need to plan where to celebrate the end of the proj-ect. You told me Bahia is beautiful."

Of the *taxista*, Sam asked, "*Você já foi à bahia?*" and the driver laughed and sang something back. After some more Portuguese singing, Sam explained to me. "That's a famous song that insists if you haven't been to Bahia yet, you must go!'"

"So let's." I was enthused.

"A wife can't just disappear for a week; you need to tell George where you're going."

"I already told him that I'm staying for some tourism. I even invited him to come. It's not my fault that he turned me down." My acting pious didn't fool Sam.

"Look, Bartlett. Living together in São Paulo is bad enough. You've gotten away with it because we're working. A romantic escapade would be crazy. No husband would stand for that! Don't risk what you've got. You're married to a suc-cessful doctor; I've got nothing but a lot of debts. I want you to be happy for the rest of your life, not for a few wild and wonderful days."

Casablanca. Rick was giving up Ilsa for a higher cause. The *Fusca* wasn't a foggy tarmac in Morocco, but Sam still sounded heroic. However, unlike *Casablanca's* heroine, I was selfish. I pouted. *Why can't I pretend I'm single for a few more days? Afterwards, I can go back to George as if nothing has happened.*

"*Bem-vindos, senhores...*" The elderly founder of BomFarm paused and eyed me in the front row, "*...e senhora.*" Even the bodyguards craned for a glimpse of the only lady seated with one hundred gentlemen.

After his opening, I took the podium. Knowing the Brazilian fondness for analogies, I used one. "Strategy is not a snowman, here today and gone tomorrow. It is a tree that should be planted with care and shaped as the seasons change." Sam translated with a straight face and then added in Portuguese, "It is fortunate that strategy is not a snowman because it never snows in Brazil!" His humorous side-comment hooked our audience and made my academic remarks palatable.

The happy start was a good omen. The two-day meeting was a huge success. By the end, everyone understood where BomFarm was headed and why. Some new recommendations surfaced that would help accelerate the necessary change.

To close, Marcos Bomforte announced that Dr. Mueller would become Chairman of the Board and Isaac would be the new CEO. Sam and Marcelo were dumbfounded—proof that I had kept my promise.

The next day, there were a few loose ends to tie up at the office. Late morning, I briefed Harvey on the project finale. "The Directors are committed to reversing BomFarm's downhill slide." I was proud and not afraid to show it. "In fact, the shareholders took a dramatic step; Isaac will replace Mueller as CEO."

"So, Goldstein has been pulling more strings." Harvey's tacit criticism pushed me to Isaac's defense.

"I think he's the right man for the job *and...*he wants a follow-up proposal," I bragged. Harvey cleared his throat. "Don't let Isaac pick your brain or tie you down. You're slated for International Foods, remember?"

"Yes, starting in January." Instead of praise, I heard reproach.

"Right. So, don't get committed in Brazil." Something didn't jibe. Follow-on sales always got kudos. The phone line buzzed with an awkward silence. Next, Harvey asked, "When will you be back?"

"I'm going to take some vacation." *Well deserved*, I wanted to add. "I'll be back before Thanksgiving. To miss turkey and pumpkin pie would be sacrilege."

The only reply was Harvey drawing air through his pipe. After deliberation he said, "There's an important Partners' meeting next week. You're up for promotion. Go be a tourist, but call me Wednesday." Evading further explanation, he said goodbye.

Cradling the receiver, I pondered the mixed signals. Finally, I was up for promotion, but Harvey had been subdued. No pat on the back. Putting I.F. over BomFarm. Suggesting I should exit Brazil after sending me here in the first place. Definitely, something didn't jibe!

My quandary was interrupted by bustling as Luciana and Ed arrived. Then the sound of samba filled the office. As I went to investigate, BomFarm's Team Leaders pushed through the door. Everyone started dancing, even Paulinho, who had the best moves of all. Encircled by sexy sway, I knew this could only happen in Brazil.

Marcelo mobilized our troops across the street for a farewell lunch. As we sipped *caipirinhas* and munched *pão de queijo*, Isaac arrived and presented me with a weighty book of Brazilian art. Next, Gilberto, the self-appointed spokesman for the teams, pulled a small package from his jacket pocket. "For you," he said, handing it to me boldly, "so you'll always remember us." I unwrapped a string bikini in orange and black, BomFarm's corporate colors. The men clapped and cheered as I held the "dental floss" against my conservative business suit. A few appreciative whistles turned heads in the restaurant.

As the group quieted, Sam translated for me. "Thank you for a great job reshaping BomFarm," I started solemnly. But then I threw away formality, looked skeptically at the bikini, and added, "It won't be so easy to reshape me!" More cheers and applause. I motioned for silence and said my farewell in Portuguese. "*Vocês vão viver sempre no meu coração. Muito obrigada.*" They *would* live in my heart forever.

On the sidewalk, I got teary. "Hey, Duck Face," Sam cajoled. "This was a celebration; why are you crying?"

"It's just hard when something wonderful comes to an end," I sniffed.

"Don't be sad. The best is yet to come." Full of optimism, Sam squeezed my hand. He hadn't heard Harvey's warning: "Don't get committed in Brazil."

Bahian Memories

Brazil's bulge intrigued me. Jutting toward Africa, tropical Bahia was exotic and romantic, a place to drench the senses before returning to New England.

Despite Sam's noble intentions to protect my marriage, I had coaxed him to abandon his scruples. Knowing I was betraying George, I took cover in the answering machine. "I'm heading to Brazil's northeast with a colleague," I said brightly. "It's a once-in-a-lifetime opportunity I just can't miss." I was telling the truth, but lying by omission. "I don't know what I'll find in the way of phone service up there. It's pretty rustic. I'll try to call in a couple of days." A fabrication to avoid phoning again. There would be hell to pay when I got home, but at least I would have known paradise.

On Salvador's sidewalk, ladies balanced baskets on their heads; layers of white lace made round figures rounder and black skin blacker. Long skirts rustled as they offered their cassava and coconut cakes. Delighting in my awkward Portuguese, one matron posed with me while Sam snapped a photo with our disposable camera. To thank her, we bought treats to savor as we strolled along the highland overlooking the sea.

African influence is ubiquitous in Bahian culture—from cuisine to *capoeira*, Brazilian kick-boxing. A dinner-show for tourists immersed us in both. Pepper proved to be an essential ingredient; the chef's trademark derived from the need to doctor dishes in a climate where ice was scarce. My taste buds, raised on bland Boston scrod, woke up with the spicy shrimp *vatapá*, a soup seasoned with pepper, ginger, coconut milk, and palm oil.

On the show platform, a percussion band assembled with long bows, bells, tambourines, and a ridged gourd that made a ratchet-like sound when scraped with a stick. Discordant tones and off-beat rhythms were musical commands for the muscled young *capoeiristas*. Kicks, leg sweeps, and acrobatics combined sport and ritual. Developed as a survival tool for unarmed escaped slaves, *capoeira* was outlawed for many years. This martial art was becoming an ambassador of Brazilian culture, appreciated for its blend of complexity and speed, game and artistry.

The next morning, we hired a driver to give us a city tour. Our first stop was a large cathedral, built by the Portuguese to promote Catholicism. Reluctantly, we entered the dark cavern, with its gold-leafed ornamentation. The stolen wealth evident in the structure was unsettling after driving through poor neighborhoods nearby.

When we emerged, we discovered that we were not the only skeptics. Mysticism was alive and well on the church steps. A shriveled *baiana* approached. A colorful head wrap framed her deep wrinkles and contorted smile. "*Sorte para a senhora,*" her ancient voice croaked as she held out a talisman. Luck for the lady. How could I refuse? She tied a ribbon around my wrist. A roughly hewn fist, the size of a pea, dangled against my skin.

"This *figa* will bring you good luck," Sam explained her earnest blessing and instructions. "But, there's a catch… You must not take it off or untie it; good luck will come only if you wear it until it falls off." I needed good fortune, but wondered how I would explain my crude bracelet back home.

Our driver offered more cathedrals, but we favored sunshine over gold-leafed gloom. Trading our guide for a rental car, we drove from Salvador to the easternmost point of the Americas. Along the highway, macroeconomics came to life. "Low per capita income" became mud shacks where young, scarcely clad mothers bulged with their next child. "High illiteracy" became young boys with machetes instead of schoolbooks. "Short life expectancy" became barefoot teens shouldering a small unpainted coffin down a dirt road. It was a relief to arrive at João Pessoa.

Playfully translated by Sam as "Johnny Person," this small town was the base from which we would explore the famous sand dunes and deserted beaches. But, first a bite to eat at a rustic café-bar decorated with colorful graffiti. A hand-painted sign announced *vitaminas*; tropical fruit blended into a refreshing juice seemed a safe and healthy choice. We chose a wobbly table beside a waist-high wall that separated us from the sidewalk. A rickety fan spun hypnotically overhead.

As we sipped our drinks, a relic of a *baiano* shuffled toward us. His teeth had deserted him long ago and his calloused feet had never worn shoes. Breathing heavily, he grabbed the wall and halted. After a short respite, his gaze locked onto Sam and his music began. His quavering voice was scratchy, like an old LP that had played the same tune over and over. Crooning for tourists kept his scarecrow figure alive.

When he finished the samba, Sam asked him to sing "our song." The face of the tattered troubadour lit up with a toothless grin and a knowing look. He croaked the lyrics about unrequited love.

Vocalists in the nightclubs of São Paulo and Rio had sung "*Carinhoso*," but none could compete with this sidewalk songster. Each verse brought more life to the wrinkled face as memories took over. Gone was the old man, barely able to stand. In his place was a young lover, happy at the sight of his beloved.

The barman silenced the blender. Pedestrians clustered on the sidewalk. The man collecting cardboard stopped his horse-drawn cart long enough to hum along. When the song ended, applause pulled the *baiano* from his reverie. With an unsteady bow, he took Sam's generous tip. Then, bobbing like a marionette with a broken string, he scuffed precariously to the next sidewalk café. His body was frail and his days numbered, but his song would live with us forever.

At sunset, a fisherman hauled his boat onto the beach. A few trees lashed together were the hull. He tipped it up, sticking the edge in the sand; the sapling mast was its resting post. Soon, others like it were lined up like dominos of faded blue, yellow, and red. The fleet would wait for the morning tide, when the men would load their nets and follow the wind and currents to find another day's catch.

I thought I knew about sailboats. Marblehead Harbor was "The Yacht Racing Capital of the World." In the summer, kids learned to sail on Widgeons in the shadow of America's Cup contenders. My father had taught me to distinguish a ketch from a yawl and a schooner from a sloop. My hands were at ease with a tiller and mainsheet. But for all that, I felt reverence for these simple Bahian craft. No roller-furling jibs or two-speed winches. No spinnaker poles or running backstays. Not even topsides or keels. Just the spirit to coax a living from some trees, the breeze, and the salty sea.

Paradise Lost

Having met our sightseeing quota, we sought the pleasure of each other. In a private hammock, we drank in hibiscus perfume and slow kisses. Beneath the hotel's sluggish fan, I wore only the good luck *figa*. So far, its charm was working.

"You need to call Harvey," Sam reminded me on Wednesday morning. "Meet me for breakfast by the beach when you're done." Knowing I preferred private phone conversations, he slipped out of our hotel room.

After three attempts to dial the long string of numbers on the rotary phone, I reached Harvey. "Good morning, Beth. Where are you?"

"As close to Africa as I can be without getting wet."

"Sounds exotic; I'm sorry to interrupt your vacation, but I have some big news." I was sure his next words would be "Congratulations, you've been promoted." Instead, I heard, "The Partners have just endorsed a new strategy for the firm. GCC is stretched too thin. We tell our clients to focus; we're going to take our own medicine." On pins and needles, being patient with the professor was difficult, yet I kept myself from barging in.

"We're going to focus in Europe—London, Paris, Frankfurt, and Madrid. We'll be closing five offices—three in the U.S. and the two in South America." I was dumbstruck. I had had no clue that GCC might abandon the office I had been struggling to grow. Feeling used, I said nothing, lest I lash out. "Beth, are you still there?" Harvey queried.

"Yes...yes, I'm here. Just caught off-guard... I didn't see this coming." At the risk of sounding stupid, I ratified my understanding. "So, you are going to close São Paulo?"

"I'm afraid so, along with Buenos Aires."

"Why close down now? It's a huge market; management consulting is a young industry. We're building GCC's reputation." I echoed Sam's business case. "BomFarm is one of the country's leading brands...and they have already asked for a new phase of work. Isaac wants a proposal next week." Months of effort were swirling down the drain. Our credibility with Mueller and Isaac and Kipper would vanish. Marcos Bomforte would sneer at the shortsightedness of American companies. "We have a springboard for growth." I prayed that Harvey heard my conviction, not my chagrin.

"The essence of strategy is saying no." The professor again. "GCC has to say no to some markets and some clients." A bit of regret tinged his next remark. "It was a tough business decision, but it's been made and now it's time to execute."

Although Harvey was citing the strategy textbooks, the case seemed weak. I was suspicious. "Did the conflict between Bob and Isaac lead to this decision?" I wouldn't have dared to ask such a question six months ago. However, the subservient wallflower had grown a few thorns.

Harvey's chair creaked. I heard him draw on his pipe as he crafted his response. "Bob argued that GCC should exit markets where we lack adequate controls. There is no doubt that you have stretched GCC protocol. And Brazil is not unique.

We're closing Dallas, Denver, and Detroit because they too lack the seniority to ensure GCC quality." The criticism stung. BomFarm had embraced the new methods; my client was on the road to recovery. Yet GCC saw our achievement as a liability. My hopes of partnership were dashed.

Trying to set my ego aside, I made another plea. "What about the impact this will have on our clients? Not just BomFarm; we won the I.F. contract due to GCC's presence in the region. How will this sit with them?"

"A valid point. One the Partners debated at length. We'll use resources from the Mexico City office; Sam and Marcelo can cover Argentina and Brazil from their new locations."

"New locations?"

"They are both on the transfer list. They've proven themselves as strong players. They can choose between Madrid and Mexico City." My heart raced. Sam might uproot, but what about Marcelo? He spoke Portuguese, not Spanish. Could a Brazilian economist add value in Spain or Mexico? And what about the rest of the staff? Familiar images filled my mind: Marcelo bobbing inside his yellow Walkman, Paulinho preparing coffee in chipped mugs, Luciana editing Portuguese in her low-cut tops, Ed eating sushi and peering into the computer. What would happen to them?

"Is this official? Can I tell my colleagues in the Brazil office?" I steadied my voice to conceal my desperation.

"It's official. We'll break the news to the Boston staff this afternoon. If you can do the same down there, I'll appreciate it." I was stuck with Harvey's dirty work. Dropping this bomb would be painful, but at least the Brazilians would hear it from a friend instead of a cold voice from the north. "Have Sam call me to discuss a timetable for closing the office." He was so callous; he'd never met Sam, Marcelo, Luciana, Ed, or Paulinho.

"When will you be back?" Harvey pressed. "We need to have a face-to-face chat as soon as possible." I had planned to stay a few more days to work on the BomFarm proposal, but now that was moot. It behooved me to get to Boston as soon as possible. Being out of sight when big changes were afoot was dangerous.

"I'm in the boondocks, but I'll try to get a reservation for tomorrow night. That will put me in the office about noon on Friday. Can we meet then?"

"You've got it. Friday at noon," he confirmed. "Now, go soak up the tropical sun; it's freezing in Boston." Harvey sounded too cheerful for someone who had just axed an office. He was killing a fledgling that was just taking flight; Sam's dream was crashing down. The firm was pulling the plug on my first big client; Isaac would be disgusted.

Betrayed, I hung up the phone and wanted to rip the *figa* from my wrist. Where was my good luck now? My bathing suit and sandals seemed incongruous. Outside, an ocean breeze wafted in the palms; azure ripples lapped the sand. But for me, paradise was lost.

Alone in the coffee shop, Sam saw my distress before I reached him. "What happened? You look like the world caved in." My lower lip quivered and the news stuck in my throat. An attentive waiter arrived to pull out my chair and take my order. Sam waved him away with a request that he come back later. "*Depois, por favor...*Beth, tell me. What can be so terrible?

"Let me guess," he filled my choked-up silence. "You didn't make Partner." I nodded confirmation. "Don't let that upset you." He put his hand on my arm and kissed my cheek. "I told you I'd love you, with or without the title of Partner." I forced a weak smile. "Actually, I was wrong. I love you more than ever now."

"You're so sweet," I said between sobs. "I wish this were just about me, but it's much bigger. They're closing the São Paulo office," I blurted out.

"Closing? GCC is closing us down?!" Sam placed a new cigarette in a hardened jaw. "That's crazy. Doesn't make any sense."

"Harvey claims it does, says it's a new strategy, says GCC will focus in Europe and a couple of big U.S. cities. Mexico City will be the only Latin American office. They're pulling out of Buenos Aires and São Paulo."

"Bob is getting his revenge," Sam scoffed. "He couldn't tolerate Isaac, someone smarter than he is, calling the shots. But Harvey, why would Harvey abandon such a big market, especially when someone he trusts is here to grow the business?" He patted my forearm.

"Obviously, Harvey doesn't hold me in such high regard; instead of promoting me, the firm is punishing me for BomFarm," I bemoaned.

"Did you tell him about the new proposal?"

"I did, but he didn't seem to care." Straightening my back, I set aside my own disappointment and focused on his fate. "There is some good news; GCC will transfer you and Marcelo—to Mexico City or Madrid. They see you both as valuable resources."

"Well, Mexico City is closer to Boston than São Paulo. Maybe GCC is smart after all." Sam took both of my hands in his. I was still teary.

"Bartlett. Look at the bright side. *A rió revuelto, ganancia de pescador.* It's a Spanish saying: a raging river is good for the fisherman. Of course, you have to be willing to get wet." I could almost hear Sam's mind whirring. He waved the waiter over and ordered my breakfast. "Has GCC set a closing date?"

"Harvey wants you to call him to discuss that," I spit out, bitterly.

"That's OK. Let's not prolong the agony." The waiter brought fresh coffee, warm milk, a bread basket, and a plate of juicy papaya. "While you eat your breakfast, I'll call Marcelo." I would have procrastinated. Marcelo had passed up excellent jobs to join GCC; now GCC was pulling the rug out from under him. Yet, as he hurried off to make the dreaded call, Sam was upbeat.

"Those guys in Boston are crazy," Sam told Marcelo. "They claim to be global and yet abandon an entire continent." After a silence on the other end of the line, he added, "Marcelo, you have options. You can transfer with GCC—to Madrid or Mexico City. But your value is highest right here in Brazil. Why don't we start Cohen and Pereira?"

Sam made it sound solid. "Cohen and Pereira?" Marcelo echoed the names, but without Sam's confidence.

"Yes, we'll call the firm COPE...get it? We help companies 'cope' with change."

"Or how about COPA because we can make them winners?" Marcelo extended the word play. "Copa" would appeal to soccer-crazy executives who live for the World Cup. Marcelo turned cautious. "Joking aside, it sounds pretty risky. Who will hire two guys they never heard of?"

"We already have two important customers," Sam pointed out. "One. BomFarm. They will come through this crisis and could be really big. Two. International Foods. GCC has a contract that commits them to work from the field. Someone needs to deliver and it ain't going to be Roger Doyle."

"You make it sound simple, but I have a family to support." Sandra was pregnant and Marcelo already felt the responsibility of fatherhood.

"Listen," Sam countered. "We don't need start-up capital, just talent. Today, we collect fees for GCC. Brazil keeps about twenty-five percent. Our price can be much lower, and we'll still make a bundle, even if we sell a lot less." Marcelo did his own calculations; just one big job with BomFarm would pay their salaries for a year. "Think about your options, Marcelo. I'll respect whatever choice you make...but, I really want you as my business partner."

"Thanks." Marcelo was flattered. "I'll talk to Sandra. She'll want to stay near family, especially with our first son on the way. Mexico and Spain are out of the question." Marcelo hesitated, then asked, "What does Beth think?"

"I haven't sprung this on her yet. She's worried about hurting the staff in our office, including you. And she's very upset about deserting BomFarm. But, she'll get over it. Her going back to Boston is inevitable; this will make a clean cut. Maybe that's good for everyone."

Marcelo could tell that Sam was using the professional subterfuge to accept losing Beth. He said simply, "You're probably right." After a pause, he added, "COPE has a nice ring; I'm honored that you want me as your partner. Thanks."

Sam had been gone for an hour; breakfast had been cleared away. Anxious, I went back to our room. As I entered, I heard formal business-like Portuguese. By paying close attention, I understood, "Yes, sir. Thank you for your confidence." With Marcelo he wouldn't use such deference. Feeling like a snoop, I backed away, but Sam motioned for me to stay. "Let me talk to Ms. Bartlett and get back to you." He paused for the reply and then smiled into the phone. *Brasil é uma grande oportunidade. BomFarm é uma grande oportunidade.*

Dying of curiosity, I plopped down in the wicker chair. Seeing my puzzlement, he just looked devilish. After more Portuguese, he hung up and did a little jig. With a flourish, he pantomimed pulling something from the sleeve of his beach jacket. "Brazil is a great opportunity. BomFarm is a great opportunity," he sang the refrain in English, for my benefit. "Brazil is a great opportunity. GCC won't seize it, but I will...with my own consulting firm." He held his arm aloft in triumph. "Cohen and Pereira, to be known affectionately as COPE." Next, he posed a childish invitation. "Want to join us?" Even Sam knew that idea was far-fetched!

"You're kidding, right? About starting your own firm? Transfers with GCC are a sure thing. Why would you pass them up?"

"Aha," he gloated, as if he had pulled a fast one. "Without working for GCC, we can work with their clients." A pause for effect. "First, BomFarm...second, International Foods." He moved close for a conspiratorial whisper, "GCC needs us; we're named in the proposal."

He backed away. "Watch closely, my dear." Another magician's sleight of hand. "We'll help GCC save face and start COPE with a backlog!"

I hated to be the ogre, but Sam needed to be realistic. "Starting a business is risky. What makes you think you can sell enough to pay your salaries?"

He came close again. "Because, I've already got my first client." I waited. "I just talked to Isaac." So that explained the Portuguese. "I asked him if he'll hire us without the GCC name...and he said yes."

"So you already told him about GCC's plans?" I didn't know whether to be peeved or relieved. I dreaded facing Isaac and Mueller.

"I did. He's counting on us, so I told him."

Still unsure whether to scold or thank Sam, I asked, "How did he react?"

"His exact words were, 'I don't care about the letterhead, as long as I have the same team...including Beth Bartlett.'" Sam let this sink in. "So, we need your help," he confessed, "for just a little while." I wanted to scream, "Stop. Slow down," but he was on a roll. "If I sub-contract your time from GCC, Isaac will be happy and GCC won't desert a valued client."

Sam amazed me. In one hour, he had founded his own firm and made his first sale. Where I saw bad news, Sam saw a gold-mine and was already digging.

I admired his optimism, but needed to sort out my own life. João Pessoa was not the right place to do it. Reading my mind, Sam shifted gears. "You need to get back to Boston and talk to Harvey. Take the pulse at GCC. Figure out what's going on and where you stand." Businesslike, Sam picked up the phone and changed our itineraries. "We'll travel to Rio tomorrow," he confirmed. "From there, you'll go to Boston and I'll go to São Paulo." He made it sound so easy.

"But what about BomFarm? I promised Isaac a proposal," I whined.

"Isaac can wait." Sam put his arm around me. "This time, put Beth Bartlett first." We hugged tenderly. "I love you," he said softly. "I've loved you since that morning in August when you arrived, looking lost and confused. Sort of like you look now," he kissed me gently. "Think hard about what is best for you, for your life." He paused and tried to lighten up. "Don't worry, Duck Face. I'll *cope*."

We couldn't recapture our romantic mood, but needed to kill time. So, we hired a speedboat to take us to the "disappearing island" shown on a tourist poster. The captain left us on a sandbar with nothing but a few rocks, seaweed, and each other. Soon, numerous small craft anchored nearby and disgorged jovial tourists. A rising tide fostered togetherness that dispelled our glumness.

With a tiny patch of sand still exposed, a launch rescued us. Our youthful driver revved the engine and we zoomed back toward the hotel. I stared beyond the churning wake until the island was gone. My eyes stung with salt spray and raw emotion.

That night we didn't sleep. Spent from making love, we lay awake and talked. "The hardest part for me," I said, "will be keeping you a secret. How can I hide away something as beautiful as this?" I asked rhetorically. "Being with you is sinful, but concealing this joy feels even more blasphemous."

"What if you don't hide it? What's the worst thing that can happen?" Sam's question took me aback.

"Well, it would really hurt George. He would file for a divorce."

"What else?" He lit a cigarette. Sam thought best when he was smoking.

"It would really upset Sue. She thinks I have the perfect marriage; after all, she set it up. Furthermore, Bartletts don't get divorced. We make things work." Sue's disapproval would be devastating.

"We're so different, you and I," Sam mused. "I have no history, no roots, and you have so much. If only someone could shake us up in a blender." He was thoughtful as he inhaled. "I wouldn't call you 'Bartlett' if I didn't love your *Bartlettness*. But, I think you tend to hold up the mirror and see nothing but your parents or your sister. And there is so much more to you. Forget the mirror; craft your own mosaic. Use lots of family tiles; don't throw them away. But add bits and pieces of your own choosing—new expectations, hopes, and perspectives. You have already begun; I see the artist at work. Keep crafting something extraordinary." He snuffed out his cigarette and pulled me close.

After a long silence, Sam's melodic voice was barely audible in the dark. "You *must* do what is best for you."

"If only I knew what that might be. I don't know what I want." I whispered my confession into the hair on his chest. He kissed the top of my head tenderly. "I just know that I've never felt like this with anyone before."

"You feel something now, but those feelings may fade. Let's face facts. You needed me to stay afloat in rough waters, sort of like a life ring. Now you can swim on your own." Sam was trying to make it easy for me. He squeezed me tighter before adding, "Swim away from me, if you can."

Thursday—November 20
En route Home to Boston

Dear Diary,

I've abandoned you. The past 2½ weeks have been hectic, but that's no excuse.

The truth is: I've had someone else to talk to, someone else who cares about my deepest emotions. Sam cares about me—all of me.

Don't be jealous. I'm going to need you once more when I am alone again.

On second thought, I'd better burn these pages. I'll mark the end of this fabulous journey with a fitting tribute; I'll cremate these memories. Thank you for keeping me company.

Tchau.

Strategic Choice

Connecting at JFK, I phoned George. "Hi. I'll be in Boston in two hours."

"What happened?" he asked coldly. "I thought you were being a tourist in Brazil." I sensed the tight pulse in his jaw.

"I came home early because a lot's happening at GCC. I need to meet with Harvey."

"Harvey gets your attention better than I do."

I ignored his caustic tone. "What's your schedule? Will you be home tonight or are you on call? We have a lot to talk about."

"I'm on call but I'll switch. The sooner we talk the better." Perhaps it was my imagination, but it felt like a veiled threat.

I focused on mechanics. "I'll pick up some carry-out." A shrill voice over the airport's public address system announced the boarding of the commuter jet. "Got to go or I'll miss my flight. See you tonight." Grateful for an excuse to keep it short, I signed off.

Two hours later, feeling like Phileas Fogg entering the Reform Club in *Around the World in Eighty Days*, I arrived in the Boston office at precisely the appointed hour. Changing in the Ladies Room from my travelling garb to my consultant's costume was the first step back into GCC's world. A deferential knock on Harvey's office door was the second.

"There you are! Come in." Harvey shook my hand before taking up a pipe cleaner. "Your Brazilian fans have been calling. It seems they can't survive without you." He blew into the stem to ensure no obstruction.

"Oh? Who called?" I tried to sound nonchalant as my heart skipped a beat.

"Sam Cohen thinks we're making a big mistake leaving Brazil. No doubt you already know his plans to start his own firm."

"He's convinced about Brazil's potential." *Stay neutral and professional*, I reminded myself.

"And he's right." Harvey tamped his pipe. "Can't fault him. If I were a younger man, without a big company to think about, I might do the same."

"So, you worked out the details for closing São Paulo?"

"For the most part, yes. Among other things, I've signed a letter addressed to our South American clients. Sam insisted that we neutralize their negative reaction to GCC's departure." Harvey passed a copy across his desk. Adopting the perspective of Mueller or Bomforte, I scanned the text. After announcing GCC's withdrawal, the letter endorsed Cohen and Pereira as a firm that would retain ties to GCC for global support." I recognized Sam's language and suppressed a smile. This document gave COPE prestige and international back-up from the get-go.

"This will certainly make things less awkward with respect to BomFarm."

"BomFarm's a special case." Harvey examined me over his glasses. "After I hung up with Sam, Isaac Goldstein called. He claims it's imperative that you guide his new organization. This puts you in an awkward position." Circling a match over the bowl and taking a few shallow puffs, he kept me in suspense. "Sam's willing to pay your full billing rate, so time in Brazil will count toward your utilization. I'm willing to approve it, but that wouldn't be in your best interest." Unwittingly, I tipped my head and raised my eyebrows. Reading my puzzlement, Harvey rounded his desk and eased himself slowly into the chair next to me.

"A lot has been going on while you were away; there are things you should know." He tamped again lightly and achieved the true light with a second match. "Given our new strategy, the firm's org chart is changing. As of January, I'm going to London to oversee GCC's European growth; Bob White will head up the Boston office." I clasped my hands a little tighter in my lap. Bob saw Isaac as a manipulative maverick; working for BomFarm would be a liability and earn me black marks.

"What did you tell Isaac?" I asked, hesitantly.

A puff on the pipe. "That the decision is up to you. BomFarm's your client, so you call the shots, but I advise you to disengage sooner, rather than later. GCC is getting out of Brazil and would rather use your talents elsewhere."

"Before deciding, there's more you should know." Harvey set the pipe bowl on a worn ashtray and pressed back in his chair. "At the recent Partners' meeting, I put your promotion on the table." Harvey avoided my eyes. "It didn't fly. Bob opposed your nomination, arguing that Boston doesn't need more Partners. He's right. We've got too many in a small market." Tight dryness filled my throat. "In fact, we're going to downsize the office and lay-off excess staff. Your name is on the list." I was being fired! This was Bob's revenge!

Instead of the success and accolades I expected, I was being canned. The firm that had been my home for a decade was putting me on the street. Emotionally drained after leaving Sam, exhausted after the overnight flight, and apprehensive about facing George, I had no reserves to absorb this blow. The tightness in my throat invaded my cheeks and nose. Unstoppable tears spilled down my face. Like a drenched windshield, my glasses obstructed my view. I removed them with one hand and covered my eyes with the other.

As my sobbing subsided, Harvey quieted my shaking shoulders with his large hand. "I know this is hard; I'm sorry that you're the fall guy in Bob's power play. Life isn't always fair." I met his eyes as he lifted his hand. Red-nosed and rattled, I wasn't Partner material. The firm had seen that all along. Harvey handed me his handkerchief. I dried my tears and blew my nose.

"Take a deep breath," Harvey consoled. "There's more." *Impossible*, I thought. *Nothing can be worse than this.*

"It's not so bleak." He relit the extinguished tobacco, while I composed myself. "The Boston office is shrinking, but New York and London are growing. Larry Benson wants you in New York and I want you in London. So, Ms. Bartlett, you are in demand; the question is: Are you willing to move?" He fell silent. I sat stunned. A few months ago, I would have said anything to break the silence, but I had learned the power of listening.

"I hope you'll join me in Europe. Like São Paulo, London is a young office. You've just managed a team of new consultants and a client in another culture." His praise was lost in my confusion. "If you come to London, it will be easy to make you a Partner." He was smiling now. "Of course, Larry feels the same way; he wants you full-time on International Foods. So, my dear, you have options."

Harvey was playing mentor and sponsor, but this time I felt manipulated. Promotion was contingent on my moving to New York or London. Feeling like a pawn in the men's chess game, I quelled the resentment that was pushing gratitude aside. Carefully, I voiced guarded appreciation. "Harvey, thanks for your support, and Larry's. Obviously, I have a lot to think about and need to talk this over with my husband."

"Of course you will want to do that," Harvey affirmed. George would not welcome this twist in GCC's corporate plans. My being fired would reflect badly on him and he would never leave Boston. "In fact, I was exploring posts for radiologists at leading British hospitals…until I got this."

Harvey leaned over the desk and retrieved something from his top drawer. On a letter-size envelope was George's scrawl. "Arrived yesterday," Harvey seemed uneasy. Heat seeped into my cheeks. "Take it. I don't plan to respond." I steadied my hand on the polished surface of the desk, but was trembling as I deposited the envelope in my purse. With a fleeting glance toward my bag, Harvey said, "Let me know if I can help."

"Thank you." Lest I sound curt, I fell back on formality, "Thank you for your confidence in me. I need to digest everything. Regardless of what comes next, I appreciate your support."

"You've earned it, my dear." Harvey pushed up and escorted me to the door. "Take time to sort things out." His hand weighed on my shoulder. "You're a good professional, Beth, and I would like you on my team in London, with or without your husband. Let's talk again next week." His paternal gaze held me a moment longer. "Strategic choice is never easy."

Somehow I mustered the semblance of dignity to walk through GCC's corridors to my office. With the door closed, I unfolded the single sheet of masculine stationery.

Dear Mister Osborne:

I am obliged to bring your attention to the following.

You have been the mentor to my wife, Beth Bartlett. Recently, you asked her to manage a project in Brazil. I disapproved and resented this assignment, but I did not prevent Beth from accepting a job that would advance her career.

Now I have every reason to believe that she is having an affair with another GCC consultant. Her adultery damages my marriage and harms your firm's reputation. I ask you to prevent further assignments with Mr. Cohen, who shares the blame for this most illicit behavior.

George Pickering, M.D.

As I feared he might, George had heard what I had left unsaid in my superficial phone message. But I had expected him to fester in silence until my return. Instead, he had fought back by divulging his suspicions to the man who had championed my professional life. Self-righteous indignation had swept aside his pride in appearances. Had his rash revelation played a role in derailing my career?

I felt vulnerable and guilty for my wrongdoing, but was desperate to hear Sam's voice. My shaky "Hello" was enough to trigger, "What's wrong, Bartlett? I know you. You're really down."

Between sobs, I told him everything. That Bob had blocked my promotion and fired me. That Isaac wanted my help, but Harvey warned against it. That New York or London might make me Partner, if I moved there. That George had written an exposé that I could not deny.

Without judging, Sam let me vent. "Everything is messed up!" My voice quavered. "No promotion. No job. Probably no husband. I'm a disgrace." Without control, I sobbed into the phone. "What will my family think?"

"Take it easy, Bartlett," Sam soothed. "Take it easy. It doesn't matter what your family thinks. What matters is what *you* think."

"But, I don't know what to think!" I wanted to scream.

"Maybe not right now, but only *you* can figure out what is best for *you*," he insisted. "Take the time you need. I promise I won't call you." He tried to cheer me with humor. "Of course, I'll have to cancel the phone service to stay away, but I'll keep my promise." He paused while I took deep shivery breaths. "Just do me a favor. Be honest with George and be honest with yourself."

"That's easier said than done." I was discovering that honesty wasn't my strong suit. Denial was my specialty.

"No one said it was easy." There was a long pause while we postponed the goodbye. "I love you, Bartlett, but that's not what counts. What counts is *you* loving yourself...loving yourself enough to break the mirror so that you can look within to see who you really are and what you want."

A tender martyr, he added, "I'll call you in a week...to resolve how we handle BomFarm." A week would be an eternity. "Take care of yourself."

"You, too." To suppress a new torrent of tears, I simply said, "Bye, Sam."

"Bye, Bartlett." Trembling, I sat alone for a long time with my hand on the receiver, trying to hang on to Brazil.

Be honest with George. Be honest with yourself. My heart pounded with the mantra as I transferred sweet-and-sour pork from a carry-out box into Pyrex. *Be honest. Be honest.* The beat quickened as I set the table and uncorked the wine.

At 7:30, keys rattled in the lock. George brushed past me without a hello kiss. Shedding his overcoat, he uncovered the crisp white jacket, blue shirt, and impeccable necktie that distinguished him from more lowly staff who wore nurses' uniforms or scrubs. Abruptly, he pointed to the nametag on his jacket. *"Dr. George Pickering, Radiology,* just in case you forgot." He snapped the badge with his index finger and stepped toward the kitchen counter. "Any important mail?"

"I haven't looked yet. I was busy fixing dinner."

As if verifying my claim, he glanced at the set table. Next, he ripped open the American Express bill and scrutinized the entries. He thrust the page at me. "You have the receipts for all these purchases?"

"Of course." He would cross-check my receipts to the penny, before allocating the expenses to the appropriate accounts. "I'll clip them to the bill as soon as I unpack my briefcase."

"File for reimbursements from GCC...while you still have a job." Bitterly, George threw the bill back on the granite top. "While you still have a job," set off an alarm bell in my head. *Does he think his letter is cause for dismissal?* He strode to the bedroom to shower and trade his hospital uniform for a button-down shirt and jeans. "It reeks in here," he shouted. "Have you taken up smoking, too?"

Oblivious to the cigarette smell that angered George, I had dumped my dirty clothes on the bed while hurrying to unpack. "Of course not," I shouted back as I grabbed a thirty-gallon garbage bag. When the bathroom door banged shut, I raced to stuff my garments into the plastic…everything, including my nightgown and underwear. "I'll go to the cleaners tomorrow," I yelled at the closed door as I heaved the sack into my closet.

The shower helped George regain his composure. He poured a glass of wine from the open bottle. "Want some?" he asked.

"That would be nice." Alcohol was not a wise choice, but would dull some of the pain. "To being home," I raised my glass. His plunking onto the sofa was the only reply. "We can talk while dinner is warming," I suggested. A nod. I settled gingerly into a facing armchair.

"So, talk." George's wine glass was already half empty.

"Harvey Osborne showed me your letter." Gone was the Beth Bartlett who avoided confrontation. I wanted to get the worst over as fast as possible.

"Do you deny my accusations?" George asked with controlled calm, but a marked pulse in his cheek betrayed his fury.

"No."

"I knew it." His anger came out as a whisper, not a scream. "I never should have let you go to that damned place. How could you do this to me? How could you have an affair when I trusted you?"

"George, all I wanted was a successful project that would advance my career. Please believe me."

"Right," he growled cynically. "Why should I believe you? I didn't stop you from going to Brazil. In return, you betrayed me! If you want to get promoted, why don't you sleep with Harvey?

Why don't you sleep with Bob? Oh! Maybe you already have!"
Anger distorted his usually handsome face.

"George, that's a low blow. I've been faithful to our marriage. Believe me, I've turned down plenty of offers. And, for
your information, I'm not having an 'affair' with Sam. It is not
about sex; it is much deeper." With a sudden decrescendo,
my voice had become a whisper. "He makes me happy...very
happy. I think I might love him."

"Love him! You love him?" George was incredulous.

Although his fists were clenched, I delivered the hardest
blow. "I don't know whether I love Sam, but I do know that our
life, yours and mine, is not what I want."

"What?! I thought we were happy."

"Maybe we were, but my life has changed. I was living in
black and white; now I know color." His shoulders shook. "I'm
sorry, George. It's not your fault, but I want more." I'd just low-
ered a sledgehammer on the fragile shell that had been holding us together. Watching him slump into the sofa, I knew I had
inflicted irreparable damage. A wall of painful silence rose
between us. Finally, I asked, "Do you want me to sleep at Sue's?"

He looked at me with sad, dead eyes. "No, just sleep on the
couch. Maybe we can coexist while we figure out what to do
next. Tomorrow, I'll stay at the hospital."

Somehow we went through the motions of eating and washing up that eerie, surreal night. Decorum was the linchpin of
our marriage and, even though trust was gone, somehow civility
remained. For that, George deserved the credit.

Sisters hear trouble without being told. Sue arranged family schedules so that we could be alone the next day. Leaves
crackled underfoot as I skirted the plastic toys on her front

walk. Soon, the Indian corn would come down and a Christmas wreath would go up. I envied the predictability of Sue's life.

Behind the front window, Rusty barked a welcome. Before I could lift the brass knocker, Sue pulled me in out of the cold. She hung my coat on a peg and dragged me into the kitchen for a cup of coffee. "You've been crying. What's up?" Sue demanded as we settled on ladder-back chairs at the pine table. "No promotion?"

It was the logical assumption and a good place to start. "Right. At least not for now; at least not in Boston." I explained the turmoil at GCC, Bob's control of the Boston office, Harvey's move to London, the closing of São Paulo.

"What?! They're closing Brazil? I don't get it. Why did they send you so far away if they were pulling out? Why did they complicate your life?" She was miffed.

"What's done is done. I don't have all the answers; I just know that things have gotten very messy. With Bob in charge, I'll never make Partner in Boston; in fact, I've been sacked."

"You've been fired?" Her eyes got wide before narrowing to angry slits. "Those sons of…" Sue muted the profanity.

"Wait. Wait," I gestured calm. "Don't bash the whole firm. Bob's my only enemy. I can stay with GCC and even make Partner, if I move to New York or London."

Sue processed this. "Do they think you're a puppet on a string? Don't they realize that your husband is a sought-after doctor at Mass General?" She would feel better if she knew Harvey wanted to find a post for George in London, but it was a moot point. I hadn't come all the way to Marblehead to talk about GCC.

"I'm going to ask George for a divorce."

"You're what?!"

"I'm going to ask George for a divorce," I repeated slowly. Then, I hastened to add, "He hasn't done anything wrong, I have."

She scraped back her chair and went to the coffee pot. An awkward silence filled the kitchen before Sue came back, empty-handed. "Tell me what happened," she said in the same tone she used with Mark and Melody when they came in crying. The kids' drawings on the refrigerator and herbs drying over the sink made me wonder if Sue could understand.

"Going to Brazil, I got much more than I bargained for. I discovered a new culture, new ways of thinking, new ways of feeling." It was too academic. "Sue, I discovered *myself*." Tears welled into my eyes. "I love New England, my family, my roots, but I feel like blinders have been stripped away. I've found a wide world out there." My throat tightened and I could barely voice my next thought. "I don't want to give it up." My nose prickled and a big tear rolled down one cheek. Always prepared, Sue grabbed the Kleenex box from the counter. I tugged a tissue from the slot.

"Don't want to give *what* up?" Sue leaned over and touched my arm.

"Everything. The exhilaration. The fun. Being appreciated. Being loved."

"Loved, by whom?" she was catching on.

"By Sam." At last it was out.

"I knew it," she said with teeth clenched. "I saw it coming; last time you were home, I warned you." Sue rose brusquely and seized the back of her chair. "Beth, listen to me. I am very uneasy with this Sam situation. You might think you love him, but you love all that has happened to you during the past three months. Sam was just part of the package."

"Maybe you're right." I gripped the mug, as if it could steady my thoughts and calm the tumult in my chest.

Her tirade went on. "Think about everything you have with George." Our high-rise apartment with its sleek furniture came to mind. "George is David's best friend, my

242

brother-in-law. I can't imagine weekends and holidays without him. I don't want to have to choose between you and George." Sue's angry outburst was understandable; she did not know how empty my marriage had become. I had perfected the act of the happy couple.

"Sue, I'm not asking you to choose. George and I can visit at different times. Besides, I never said I was going to marry Sam. I just said that I don't want to give him up, not yet."

"You're suffering post-partum depression, the career woman's version." Sue was matter-of-fact. "After these intense weeks, it's natural to feel a letdown. It's OK to feel emotional. You just need some distance to put things back in perspective. Time is a great remedy," she reached over and stroked my hair. "Just give it time."

She went to retrieve the coffee pot. As she refilled our cups, she appealed to the career woman. "Beth, you have the perfect career. Bob White is just a bump in the road." She set the carafe back on the hotplate. "Think of International Foods. You can live in New York and come home on weekends. Let things cool off. Work things out with George. Most women would kill for him."

I grabbed another Kleenex and blew before responding. "You might be right, but my heart is fighting with my head."

"Don't tell me you have doubts about this," she scolded.

"Sue, just hear me out." I clasped my mug with both hands and took a deep breath. "My motive for going to Brazil was professional growth, a chance to prove myself." Under my long sleeve, the *figa* dangled against my arm.

"Right," Sue affirmed, "and you succeeded. You did a great job and you *will* get promoted. What's the problem?" Sue's eyes held more rancor than understanding. But she was my sister. I had to make her understand.

"Sam plans to create his own firm. A contract with BomFarm would guarantee a running start, and Isaac is ready to buy."

"Isaac. He's the one who pushed Bob off the project, right?"

"Good memory. Yes, he's been appointed CEO, so Sam would be starting out right at the top."

"Well," Sue huffed, "I'm happy for Sam. More power to him. What's this got to do with you?"

"Isaac wants the same team...and that means me," I confessed.

"Give me a break," Sue exploded. "GCC is leaving Brazil; you'd be crazy to keep working there." Her voice was sharp with disapproval. "Don't throw your career away because you're lovesick! Don't waste your time. Wake up, little sister." Wound up, she kept arguing. "GCC wants you elsewhere. Harvey made that clear. Don't put everything at risk...including your marriage!"

"Please don't yell at me." I started to weep.

"I'm sorry, sis. I don't mean to be harsh." She came over and put her arms around my shoulders. "I just don't want you to get hurt."

"I know," was muffled by her fleece vest. I pulled away and raised my mug. "To being sisters."

"To being sisters," Sue echoed. Our blue eyes locked. Passed down from our mother, they bound us as siblings. But mine had seen a world to which Sue was blind.

"I'd better go." We went to retrieve my coat. "Thanks for listening."

"Any time, sis." Sue hoisted the collar as I struggled to stuff my arms into the sleeves. "Better get into practice for winter," Sue chided gently.

We hugged goodbye and I walked through the brittle leaves to my car. Out of sight, the Bahian charm pressed against my skin.

Before leaving Marblehead, I drove to Lighthouse Point. The cold gray-green of the north Atlantic crashed white against the bold granite. Sometimes rough, sometimes tranquil, the relentless ebb and flow was shaping the land, just as time was shaping me. Despite the wan autumn light and a blustery wind, I lingered. Surf pounding on the rocks was the soundstage for chaotic thought.

Being truthful with George had been painful but liberating. Being truthful with myself was the next step in coming clean. I wasn't sure who I was or what I wanted.

While driving from Boston to Marblehead, I had listened to Simon and Garfunkel sing "Patterns"; its lyrics were about patterns that shape our lives and hold us captive. I reflected on the constellation of my family, the rituals and rhythms that were satisfying to Sue and David, the happiness of their marriage.

Sam was right. I had held Sue's life up as the model for my own. Unlike many younger siblings who fight for their own identity, I had adored Sue. I had lived for her approval and assumed that what was good for Sue was good for me.

That worldview had been shattered. A kaleidoscope, my life now held strange and familiar fragments of self that were tumbling into new designs. Even if I wanted to, I could not put the pieces back where they had been before.

Fragments. Pieces. Sam had spoken of a mosaic, of creating something extraordinary. Remembering Sam carried me back to Brazil. I was far from those tropical beaches, yet one sea touched both worlds. The Atlantic bashing this headland had also carved a bluff in Bahia where a tiny chapel stands, its door open to worshipers and curious tourists alike. Just a few days ago, I had bent down to pass through the low stucco portal. Musty air had enveloped me. My bare arm had brushed a gritty wall and my sandals had nudged objects at my feet. Slowly, dilated pupils and votive candles had converted darkness to dimness in the refuge, no bigger than an elevator.

A crude altar had been covered with wilting bouquets and rosary beads. Children's faces had looked out from worn photos; carved driftwood and other small offerings had crowded the floor. Jesus had hung on a simple wooden cross, his feet worn smooth from worshipers' touch. A few feet away had been another figure, hewn from a single driftwood block; her robe, once painted a brilliant blue, had also been worn from worshipers' touch.

Iemanjá, goddess of the sea, displayed none of Christ's anguish. With outstretched arms and understanding eyes, she offered solace to those close to home or far out on the ocean. Gently, I had touched her robe in tribute to all the unexpected gifts that had come to me in Brazil.

Inhaling an earthy mix of smoke, incense, and rotten stems, I had thought, *In this tiny chapel, a pagan goddess lives in harmony with Christ. If they can share this sacred space, maybe I can harbor the old and new facets of my life.*

My reverie came to an abrupt halt as the cold northeast wind slapped my face. *Forget the mystical, Beth,* I chided myself. *You've got decisions to make. Think rationally.*

"Strategic choice is never easy," Harvey had warned. From my coat pocket, I pulled the yellow sheet on which I had scratched a matrix. Four boxes organized the pros and cons of GCC versus COPE.

Clear benefits filled the box in favor of staying with GCC: *Prestige. Money. Partnership. New York (near home, I.F. opportunity). London (global leadership, work with Harvey).* Although it might be a little uncomfortable for now, the rift with Bob would heal with time.

Nebulous hopes were scribbled in the box for COPE: *Help start-up company. Preserve and create jobs for Brazil team. Build BomFarm relationship. Be with Sam.* Brazil was no longer a rung on the ladder to success; it was no longer a project with start and end dates. Yet, the tug from São Paulo grew stronger the more I tried to resist it.

But, there were obvious cons for COPE in the third quadrant: *Sacrifice secure career for high-risk venture. Live far from family.* Sue was right; it was crazy to abandon GCC for COPE.

I had written nothing about cons for GCC. I dug out my pen. As I scrawled *Lose Bethania*, a gust of wind snatched the sheet and blew it out to sea. Iemanjá had spoken. If Bethania was to live, she would have to leave her safe haven and take a few more risks.

As the speck of yellow paper sank from sight, it carried with it the *shoulds* and *oughts* that threatened to entrap me in the good life I had known until Brazil. An exuberant tingling seeped in to replace them. I think it was the same tingling that tells a rosebud that it is time to open its petals.

Epilogue

I chose well.

Sam is my partner in work and life. He stopped smoking, but still waves his magic wand when he's hatching an idea.

GCC disappeared...swallowed by a large consulting conglomerate. Harvey is a professor emeritus and still smokes a Briar pipe.

COPE is flourishing. On the unpretentious office walls hang my academic diplomas, two leather masks, and a faded ceramic plate.

George is curing cancer with radiation; on weekends, he still crews on *Sea Spirit*.

Each summer I visit Marblehead, where Sue and her family welcome me with cherished rituals.

Swaying between continents and cultures, I keep composing my mosaic, forever a work in progress. When Beth and Bethania struggle to be one, I seek solace in the sea that unifies my worlds. And there, thanks to Iemanjá, I feel whole.

Acknowledgements

This story has been shaped by countless people who broadened my global horizons and by an intimate few who have helped me discover within. My thanks reach out to all of you, with special mention and acknowledgement...

To the Brazilians who embraced me with *abraços* and hearts, unmatched anywhere in the world.

To the clients whose challenges and companionship give me something to write about.

To family and friends who read early drafts and kept sending me back to tell the real story.

To Ian Shimkoviak, whose artistry captured the soul of the story and transformed it into a book cover.

To Brookes Nohlgren, my editor and book producer, who as a gentle midwife delivered the manuscript into the published world and gave the book its name.

To Mother, who saw her little girl writing in a library carrel and gave the author life.

Above all, to my husband, Oscar, for the gift of time alone and the joy of time together.

*Until **Brazil***

Bethe Lee Moulton

Reader's Discussion Guide

1. As *Until Brazil* opens, Beth faces resistance to her going to Brazil. Who is resisting and why? Why does she go anyway?

2. Beth is surrounded and influenced by numerous men. Sometimes, the reader hears the men's point of view of which Beth is unaware. In what ways does this literary device contribute to the novel? In what ways does Beth's relationship to men change in the course of the novel? In what ways does it stay the same?

3. How would you characterize the relationship between Beth and her sister, Sue? How does this compare or contrast to the sibling relationships with which you are familiar?

4. How does the author use the sights and sounds of Brazil to reveal Beth's changing perspectives? Did the descriptions of the places or people affect your own views? If so, how?

5. The plot of *Until Brazil* centers on a consulting project that requires Beth to travel between two continents and cultures. How does that structure contribute to the dramatic tension and character evolution in the novel?

6. There are several scenes in which Beth buys things without George's approval—the purple separates, the Brazilian beachwear, the two masks. What is the significance of these purchases?

7. What role does the diary play for Beth? For the reader?

8. Portuguese words appear throughout the novel. How did you respond to these words? Why do you think the writer chose to use them?

9. Toward the end of the novel, several mystical elements enter the story—the *figa* from Bahia, the masks, the goddess Iemanjá. What do these references suggest about Beth?

10. What themes from the story do you see in the cover of *Until Brazil*?

11. *Until Brazil* is a story of personal transformation. What forces allow Beth to change and make the choices she makes? What price does she pay for doing so?

12. What aspects of the book speak to you and your own life experiences? How, if at all, has reading the novel changed your insight into yourself or someone you care about?

About the Author

With a combination of deep family roots and global experience, Bethe Lee Moulton brings unique perspectives to her writing.

Bethe grew up in Ohio and Massachusetts in a post–World War II "family of four." Her parents shared their love of books and boats, and from them she learned the values of exploration, self-reliance, and self-expression. Today, she divides her time between Boston (MA), Buenos Aires (Argentina), and Boca Raton (FL) to be with her far-flung friends and family, spanning four generations, multiple cultures, and diverse worldviews.

She emerged from college as a biologist and medical librarian, but with other women of her generation she questioned old assumptions and gender barriers. Next, Bethe earned her Harvard MBA at a time when women were a marked minority. As a business consultant, Bethe advanced with a prestigious firm until an assignment in Brazil opened the door to become an international entrepreneur. She co-founded a strategic planning company to focus in Latin America. Soon the company was serving corporations around the globe.

Bethe is dynamic and seemingly tireless. On her desk, the flags of 30 nations pay tribute to the places and people that have shaped her life and her writing. In her stories, vibrant characters face the personal dramas that emerge when globalization affects life choices and bonds with family and friends.

www.UntilBrazil.com